About Island Press

Since 1984, the nonprofit Island Press has been stimulating, shaping, and communicating the ideas that are essential for solving environmental problems worldwide. With more than 800 titles in print and some 40 new releases each year, we are the nation's leading publisher on environmental issues. We identify innovative thinkers and emerging trends in the environmental field. We work with world-renowned experts and authors to develop cross-disciplinary solutions to environmental challenges.

Island Press designs and implements coordinated book publication campaigns in order to communicate our critical messages in print, in person, and online using the latest technologies, programs, and the media. Our goal: to reach targeted audiences—scientists, policymakers, environmental advocates, the media, and concerned citizens—who can and will take action to protect the plants and animals that enrich our world, the ecosystems we need to survive, the water we drink, and the air we breathe.

Island Press gratefully acknowledges the support of its work by the Agua Fund, Inc., Annenberg Foundation, The Christensen Fund, The Nathan Cummings Foundation, The Geraldine R. Dodge Foundation, Doris Duke Charitable Foundation, The Educational Foundation of America, Betsy and Jesse Fink Foundation, The William and Flora Hewlett Foundation, The Kendeda Fund, The Forrest and Frances Lattner Foundation, The Andrew W. Mellon Foundation, The Curtis and Edith Munson Foundation, Oak Foundation, The Overbrook Foundation, the David and Lucile Packard Foundation, The Summit Fund of Washington, Trust for Architectural Easements, Wallace Global Fund, The Winslow Foundation, and other generous donors.

The opinions expressed in this book are those of the author(s) and do not necessarily reflect the views of our donors.

Green
Urbanism
Down Under

Green Urbanism Down Under

Learning from Sustainable Communities in Australia

Timothy Beatley
with
Peter Newman

⬤ ISLANDPRESS

WASHINGTON | COVELO | LONDON

Library of Congress Cataloging-in-Publication data.
Beatley, Timothy, 1957-
    Green urbanism down under / by Timothy Beatley with Peter Newman.
        p.   cm.
    Includes bibliographical references and index.
    ISBN-13: 978-1-59726-411-2 (cloth : alk. paper)
    ISBN-10: 1-59726-411-3 (cloth : alk. paper)
    ISBN-13: 978-1-59726-412-9 (pbk. : alk. paper)
    ISBN-10: 1-59726-412-1 (pbk. : alk. paper)
    1. Urban planning—Australia.   2. City planning—Environmental aspects.   3. Sustainable
development.   4. Cities and towns—Australia.   I. Newman, Peter, Dr.   II. Title.
    HT243.A8B43 2008
    307.1'2160994—dc22
                          2008013296

British Cataloguing-in-Publication data available.

Printed on recycled, acid-free paper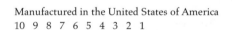

Manufactured in the United States of America
10 9 8 7 6 5 4 3 2 1

Contents

Acknowledgments   *ix*

Chapter 1
Introduction: A Different Land, Similar Challenges   *1*

Chapter 2
Greening and Sustaining Cities   *9*

Chapter 3
New and Hopeful Perspectives on Ecological Assets   *67*

Chapter 4
Strengthening Place, Building Community   *100*

Chapter 5
Bush Cities: Australia's Urban Ecological Capitals   *150*

Chapter 6
The Importance of Regional and State Planning   *188*

Chapter 7
Learning from Australia: Some Final Thoughts   *233*
on the Value of Comparative Green Urbanism

Afterword, by Peter Newman   *239*

                    Notes   *246*
                    References   *248*
                    Index   *257*

Acknowledgments

This book grows out of six months of intensive travel and research in Australia, during which I interviewed many people and met with many agencies and organizations. I can't begin to recognize or thank them all. In Sydney, I am especially grateful to my university host, professor Linda Corkery, and her amazing colleagues at the University of New South Wales. Nicole Gurran, of the University of Sydney, was also especially helpful and supportive during my time in Sydney, and I enjoyed our conversations very much. Alison Dwyer helped set up visits and appointments in Adelaide and spent much of her own time with me. Helen Favelle, in Brisbane, and Rob Adams, in Melbourne, did the same.

Many other individuals should be recognized, including Raoul Abrutat, Maria Atkison, Penny Barker, Nina Baurheim, Garry Baverstock, Kieron Beardmore, Denis Beros, Ed Blakely, Heidi Bonnaffon, Neal Bougher, Keith Bradby, Ian Burney, Robert Close, Robert De Poloni, Paul Downton, Paul Edwards, Anne Elliot, Catherine Evans, Suellen Fitzgerald, Rebecca Fogg, Tony Freeman, Steve Frost, Dave Galloway, Daniella Gambotto, Jan Gehl, Herbert Girardet, Peter Graham, Mary Gray, Julie Hassall, Paul Heath, Nicole Hodgson, Bob Humphries, Rosh Ireland, Murray Johnson, Jeff Kenworthy, Daniel Kuebler, Robert Lambeck, Deb Lavis, Steve MacDonald, Peter Maganov, John Maitland, Ian McBurney, Ione McLean, Robert Moore, Mike Moritz, Deirdre Murray, Henry O'Clery, Mary O'Neill, Jan Orton, Barbara Pedersen, Brad Pettitt, Natalie Reilly, Ben Roberts, Peter Robinson, Balinda Rollason, Craig Salt, Rosanne Scott, Sid Shea, Paula Sherry, Deborah Tabart, Ilka Tampke, Bruce Taper, Ryan Taylor, John Tunney, Alexandra Vandine, Garry Whisson, Simon Whitehouse, and Steve Wilson. Many, many others not mentioned here also helped along the way.

Special deep thanks go to Peter Newman, who is now professor of sustainability at Curtin University, in Western Australia, and was formerly professor and director of the Institute for Sustainability and Technology Studies at Murdoch University. Peter was my academic host during my time in Western Australia and has been my personal and professional guide and wise sage in understanding all matters sustainable in Australia. It was at his encouragement that I turned my academic attention to this unique and special continent. Peter's immense help and encouragement have contributed to this project writing and recording the stories and good practice in Australian cities and states. A Fulbright award allowed Peter to spend four months at the University of Virginia, allowing us to continue our collaboration. Although the style and tone of what follows are mostly my own—Australian sustainability viewed through the eyes of this American—Peter has added his own extensive insights and elaborations in many parts throughout the text. Peter's inserts, and overall editing guidance, have added much to this book. He has also kindly written an insightful afterword, which points out some of the important things that I missed in my traveling or have paid only passing attention to and which provides especially insightful commentary about what is to be learned from Australian sustainability experience.

As always, this book would not be possible without the love and help of my family: my wife, Anneke, and my daughters, Carolena and Jadie. They were enthusiastic, behind-the-scenes travelers on this grand adventure, which would have had little meaning or enjoyment without their presence. It was an especially formative time for the kids: Carolena made good friends and experienced what it was like to attend a primary Australian school; Jadie spoke her first words (beyond "Mama") by identifying that endearing Western Australian marsupial, the "Quakka," It was the trip of a lifetime to a magical land.

Thanks also to my friends and colleagues at Island Press, especially to my editor Heather Boyer, who, as usual, provided good counsel and expert editing. What follows is in no small part thanks to her good suggestions, careful review, and enthusiastic support for this project.

1

Introduction

A Different Land, Similar Challenges

My first real appreciation of the value of living, working, and researching in another country came in 1996–97 when I lived in the Netherlands.
It was a tremendously productive time learning about and understanding
in great detail the innovative green and sustainability practices there. That
experience resulted in a book called *Green Urbanism*, which documents the
urban ecology and green urban planning work in thirty European cities.
Yet, the more essential outcome of my time there was an understanding of
the possibilities of a profoundly more sustainable existence, one without
dependence on a car, where one's own foot power means gleeful inde-
pendence and a healthier life. I also learned what a sustainable *home* could
look and feel and sound like.

As unlikely as it seems, *Green Urbanism Down Under* in many ways
builds directly on my time in the Netherlands, and while the lessons are
not the same, they are of the same kind. Australia is a nation confronting
many serious sustainability and environmental pressures and challenges,
but like the European cities I explored, there are many positive stories of
hope, of innovative practice, and of concerted positive and passionate work
toward sustainability.

Also like my European experience, I've learned more from my time
living in a different country than I have from researching the technical details and bureaucratic vagaries of programs and policies. I return to my
home country with lots of good ideas, with creative new ways of addressing problems, of building communities, of looking at people and places—
many things that I would not otherwise have imagined or seen as possible.

The history and development of Australia and the United States have
much in common that makes Australia's parallel sustainable lessons and

partial urban and landscape solutions relevant in the United States. Australia is also a large country, though with a much smaller population (Australia has about 21 million residents versus more than 300 million in the United States). Common roots in the legal system and social and cultural legacies of Great Britain also suggest parallels, and an arrival in a new world with a similarly exploitative ethic makes the two countries quite alike in some not so commendable ways.

Many of these historical parallels apply equally today. Ironically, both nations have until recently been governed at the national level by conservative governments that have been antagonistic to international environmental accords and agreements—for example, the United States and Australia were for a long period the only two industrialized nations that chose not to sign the Kyoto Climate Change Treaty. (In 2007, when the new prime minister took office in Australia, one of the first things he did was sign the Kyoto Treaty—encouraged considerably by Al Gore's movie *An Inconvenient Truth* and by the growing political importance of and popular concern about global warming.)

Both countries remain highly resource consumptive and have similar types of population and development pressures. Whereas the ecological footprint of an average Australian is smaller than that of an American (a bit less than 8 hectares per person compared with about 10 hectares for an American), both countries qualify as mega resource consumers, holding the dubious distinction of second and fourth place, respectively, among the footprints of nations. Although the cars and homes may not be quite as large in Australia, and the energy consumption not as great, excessive patterns of consumption found in the industrialized world are present in both nations. Both nations are heavy consumers with huge per capita footprints (with the Australian mark on the world much lower, of course, because of its relative small aggregate population size). When it comes to global warming, the story is quite similar. Australia's per capita greenhouse gas emissions are immense, just slightly behind those of the United States and second among larger industrialized nations (World Bank, 2007).

Australia, like the United States, is highly urbanized, leading again to useful policy and planning parallels. In fact, an even higher percentage of Australian residents live in cities—nearly 90 percent (compared with about 81 percent in the United States) (United Nations, 2007). This is perhaps not surprising given the hostility of the inland landscapes and rural climate and environment in Australia as well as the country's settling occurring in a more urban period of history. Also like the United States, Australia's population is heavily oriented toward and clustered around the coast (figure 1.1).

Figure 1.1 The distinctive skyline of Sydney harbor. Australian cities suffer from many of the same ills as American cities, but also provide hopeful stories and compelling examples of the shift toward urban sustainability. *Photo credit:* Tim Beatley

The basic governmental structure in place in Australia will look very familiar to Americans. Australia is a constitutional democracy, with a parliamentary governance structure. Debate still rages about replacing the queen as the symbolic head of the nation, but the governmental contours are understandable to Americans: six states and two territories, with many local government authorities (councils and shires) within and beneath them. States are unusually large compared to those of the United States, which helps explain the government's success promoting regional- or metropolitan-scale planning. Nevertheless, the importance of state governments in both nations suggests that much can be learned that would apply in the United States. The impressive efforts at promoting sustainability at the state level in Australia, in particular, have promise for application in American states.

So there are many positive and creative efforts at managing resources, guiding urban growth, and stimulating innovative thinking and action to reduce ecological impact that Australian cities offer to us in the United States. We need not make huge cultural, economic, or political leaps to imagine their application. All of the ideas described in this book are feasible and possible in the United States.

At the same time, of course, certain unique conditions and qualities of Australia, beginning with its special natural environment, make the environmental policy, planning, and sustainability responses different. Australia is an ancient land mass where aboriginal culture has continuously existed for thirty thousand years. Although Australia has a large land mass, and a relatively small population (again, only about 21 million), it faces extreme environmental problems and challenges.

It is the driest continent, with much of its interior a dry desert (though high in biodiversity) and relatively inhospitable for human habitation. Some 80 percent of its population lives in zones that receive less than 600 millimeters of rain per year, mostly along its coastlines. Water, then, has been from the beginning a special concern and limiting factor, and as urban populations have become more water consumptive and faced with a period of long-term drought, the issue has risen to special importance in places like Western Australia, New South Wales (NSW), and Queensland in recent years. Many parts of the United States face drought and water shortages in the future, and Australia has much to tell us about what to expect here.

Australia's energy circumstance is similar to that of the United States, with a heavy dependence on fossil fuels. And while there are exemplary projects and impressive steps in the direction of renewable energy, there seems little possibility that fossil fuel dependence will be broken anytime soon. On a per capita basis, Australia's greenhouse gas emissions are high, mostly due to its heavy emphasis on energy-consuming mining and mineral processing. Australian homes use about a third of the energy of U.S. homes and about half as much for household transport. Many good stories exist about how Australian cities have begun to change in their energy consumption; however, as nations and as a people, we are in a similar place—perhaps accurately described as a kind of denial—about the declining supply of oil, the perils of climate change, and the need to move quickly toward a sustainable postcarbon future.

Both nations have immense resources and capabilities to move away from fossil fuels. In Australia, it is estimated that fifteen thousand times the energy the country needs falls from the sun each year—an absolutely tremendous resource that is barely being tapped. In this sense, the two countries' circumstances are remarkably similar.

Australia's spectacular biological diversity, which many people think of first when picturing Australia, has been hard-hit, especially since settlement by Europeans. It is one of the world's so-called mega-diverse nations.

About one third of the world's mammals that have become extinct in recent history have been in Australia. A combination of massive vegetation and land clearance, overgrazing, increased salinity, and the introduction of nonnative species has threatened this immense patrimony. The latest chapter in this story is the cane toad, an invasive species that is moving gradually across the country, threatening both ecosystem and biota.

Recent research by a group including the Queensland Herbarium, the NSW Royal Botanic Gardens, and the NSW National Parks and Wildlife Service on land-clearing rates in Australia paints a discouraging picture of land use trends. These studies indicate that Australia has the fifth highest land clearance rate, almost seven hundred thousand hectares per year, falling behind only Brazil, Indonesia, Sudan, and Zambia. This is changing in some positive and impressive ways, though, with inspiration for the American scene. Land clearance has been abruptly stopped in Queensland (as of January 1, 2007, it became illegal to clear any bush), and Australia now plants more trees than it clears, which is why the country is able to comply with Kyoto goals. Bush regeneration in cities and some large-scale landscape rehabilitation projects are now rapidly increasing and are considered in detail in this book.

The march of dryland salinity is astounding in its magnitude. Already some 5.7 million hectares have been affected, and estimates put the land area affected by the year 2050 at more than 17 million hectares, including 360 towns. Much of this problem results from the economic bind that farmers are experiencing. Heavy debt prompts farming for short-term return, without the luxury of thinking about longer-term landscape health. Reducing the portion of one's farm devoted to income-generating commodity production is difficult in the absence of some equivalent income source. (I discuss this issue in more detail in chapter 3.)

And so, like the United States, Australia is a land of contrasts— landscapes and ecosystems of immense beauty and productivity but under substantial stress and pressure (figure 1.2). It is a nation where, as in the United States, most people live in cities, and these cities overall have the same problems and face similar challenges: urban sprawl, car dependence, energy consumption, and air and water pollution. Yet, many creative and hopeful responses to these problems have emerged: creative efforts at conserving and protecting the country's landscapes and unique environments, and new and exemplary efforts at moving cities and urban populations in the direction of sustainability. Given the inherent similarities and extensive parallels between Australia and the United States, the potential to pro-

Figure 1.2 The Three Sisters formation, in the Blue Mountains National Park, west of Sydney. Australia has an immense antiquity of unique landscapes and spectacular biodiversity, faced with significant management and conservation challenges. *Photo credit:* Tim Beatley

ductively learn and apply many Australian models and examples is great indeed.

Recent national elections in Australia offer lessons and portend much about future political and policy shifts in the United States. The victorious Labor Party candidate Kevin Rudd is ushering in a far greener administration, providing a positive example for the United States. The 2007 federal election was fought largely over climate change as the previous prime minister, John Howard, stood out with George Bush in opposing the Kyoto Treaty. The first thing Prime Minister Rudd did after taking office was to sign the Kyoto Agreement and pledge to help develop the next global agreement—garnering in response a standing ovation at the United Nations (UN) Bali climate conference, which was occurring at the same time. Al Gore, in his speech accepting the Nobel Peace Prize, mentioned the Australian experience and, in particular, the grassroots adoption of climate change issues that became so critical to the 2007 election. Some of the stories in this book demonstrate how this understanding has built on other environmental projects and causes.

Even the election process itself offers useful instruction. In Australia, voting is mandatory, and as a result the 2007 elections saw an astounding (in comparison to the United States) 95 percent voter turnout. Holding elections on a Saturday and significantly reducing the length (and expense) of such elections (they lasted only six weeks!) are other examples worth appreciating and perhaps emulating. As Aussie journalist John Barron observes: "Because everyone has to vote, there is no need to spend a billion dollars to inflame passions and divide the electorate just so people will pick a side and care enough to fill in a ballot come November" (Barron, 2007, p. B01).

Certainly the United States is also a source of many very good ideas and exemplary efforts and initiatives. There is undoubtedly much that Australia could (and does) learn from the United States in return. But there are many local-level lessons to be learned from Australia that rarely make it across the ocean. This book is about Australia's state of practice in sustainability, its trends and challenges, and its many positive stories and lessons. The audience is primarily American planners, citizens, and elected officials looking for practical guidance and tested methods for moving their communities and states in a more sustainable direction as well as the inspiration and hope that such photos, stories, and profiles of good practice can provide.

Much of what follows is an effort at storytelling, an attempt to relate some of these best or better practices and special sustainability programs and initiatives. It derives from six months of living and traveling in Australia and numerous interviews and site visits. I make no claim that what I have done here is comprehensive or exhaustive. It is not based on comprehensive surveys of practice or on systematic analysis of aggregate data relating to the performance of Australian cities and states (though broader data and evidence have been enlisted where available). Instead, it emphasizes unique and special approaches to urban sustainability and landscape conservation and creative, compelling ideas and programs. Along the way, I attempt to place these stories and ideas in broader contexts (reviewing urban trends and sustainability patterns within and outside Australia), but the strength of what follows is the *particular* people and organizations and the innovative ways they envision a more sustainable and hopeful world.

Following this introductory chapter, the book contains five main, substantive chapters. Chapter 2 begins to tackle sustainability stories and efforts in Australia's cities, providing a detailed overview of the array of green urban tools, techniques, and planning ideas in use in these cities and how effectively they have been applied. This chapter more than the others is based on my interviews and site visits in Australia's five major cities: Sydney, Melbourne, Brisbane, Adelaide, and Perth. It examines a variety of urban sustainability programs and initiatives, including local sustainability plans and reports, green transport, urban greening (such as natural stream restoration), city farms and urban agriculture, solar and renewable energy projects, green building, and lifestyle and green living programs.

Chapter 3 extends this focus by looking at the same issues in the bioregions around the cities. It discusses some innovative efforts at landscape protection and conservation, ranging from an examination of efforts to conserve a magnificent fringing coral reef to new ways of seeing old growth forest to designing koala-friendly housing developments.

Chapter 4 examines innovative efforts at strengthening and nurturing the unique place qualities of Australian cities and towns and describes a host of specific policy areas, including efforts at promoting street life, public art, heritage planning, and initiatives for advancing place knowledge and place-based economic development planning, among others.

Chapter 5 considers closely the natural or bush qualities of Australia's major cities and the extent to which those cities have been able to preserve bushland and promote a sense of concern about and knowledge of the bush among their citizenry. Chapter 6 takes a hard look at innovative efforts at regional and state planning policy—specifically, the efforts to advance sustainability at these governmental levels.

The final chapter of the book, chapter 7, extracts overall impressions and broad observations from all of these Australian initiatives and experiences. It argues that many important insights and lessons derived from the Australian examples can be applied to landscape conservation and sustainable urban planning in the United States.

Following chapter 7 is a thoughtful afterword by Peter Newman calling attention to some of the things I have missed or underemphasized, and reflecting on the full significance of these Australian stories and examples.

2

Greening and Sustaining Cities

If the adage "think globally, act locally" still has currency today, as I believe it does, Australia represents a good model of how this might work. Partly a response to the lack of leadership at the national level (as in the United States), there is much energy and much activity at the local level in Australia, and sustainability is "front and center," in concert with state sustainability initiatives and programs. Municipalities and shires in Australia are doing much and generally have given sustainability higher visibility and greater importance than most American communities. In my travels throughout the country, and in numerous interviews with local officials, I found that sustainability was viewed not as a new or untested or foreign idea but as an important core value and that it was expressed as such.

Although the precise expression of what sustainability means, and how it applies operationally, varies, considerable agreement exists among localities that they aspire to profoundly reduce their ecological footprints, reduce their consumption of energy and materials, reduce their emissions of greenhouse gases, live within natural ecosystems (local and global), and move in the direction of becoming net producers of energy, food, and other urban needs—and all this while enhancing and celebrating life in cities. And while local councils and state governments are actively and ambitiously advancing a green agenda, sustainability resonates strongly with Australians as an important local (and now national) goal.

Australian cities are using a variety of planning instruments—usually including land use and community plans—to give meaning to sustainability. Some local councils call an overarching plan a structure plan, while others call it a strategic plan, but whatever the name these plans tend to extensively incorporate explicit discussion of sustainability and strongly stated and prominently featured sustainability goals and targets. Sustainability is a key theme emphasized in, for instance, Melbourne's *City Plan 2010* and is even included in the subtitle of the plan, which reads "Towards a Thriving and Sustainable City" (Melbourne City Council, 2005).

Creating an "Environmentally Responsible City" is one of the Melbourne plan's four strategic directions, and the plan identifies a number of specific opportunities for advancing this theme (dealing with a host of environmental issues, from water to waste to greenhouse gas emissions). Important strategic directions identified in the plan include reducing greenhouse gas emissions and protecting and enhancing the city's biodiversity. To advance the first direction—reducing greenhouse gas emissions— the plan endorses the target of achieving zero net greenhouse emissions by 2020, enhancing the city's (and region's) carbon sink capacity, investing in renewable energy technology, and working to develop business partnerships to reduce greenhouse emissions. To achieve the second strategic direction—protecting biodiversity—the plan calls for greening the city's parks, waterways, and rooftops and planting trees to connect parklands. For each strategic direction, the plan presents a key summary table, identifying indicators by which to monitor progress and the desired direction for such indicators (box 2.1).

Much evidence shows that in many Australian cities sustainability is finding its way into the core of governance and management. The City of Melbourne, for instance, has made sustainability important in many ways, including committing to the use of triple bottom line (TBL) reporting and decision making and enabling the recent design and construction of a world-leading green council building. Many other local authorities now regularly incorporate TBL thinking and methods into their general management plans. The concept of the triple bottom line entails judging the success of an organization or business according to not only the financial bottom line (i.e., profit levels) but also the environmental and social bottom lines, that is, according to the extent to which access and equity in service distribution and environmental sustainability are advanced. Melbourne has developed some unusual and creative procedural mechanisms for assessing the TBL and has, with the help of ICLEI (the International Council for Local Environmental Initiatives), actually developed a TBL toolkit. Among other interesting tools is a procedure for conducting sustainability assessments for council reports (City of Melbourne, 2002).

The City of Melbourne, initially with $5 million of its own funds, created a Sustainable Melbourne Fund and has been investing in local sustainability projects, including underwriting water and energy efficiency

Box 2.1

Indicators for an Environmentally Responsible City

The City's progress will be measured against the following indicators:

What We Want to Monitor	Indicators	Desired Direction
Air quality	The quality of the air	↑
Water Consumption	Change in the municipal-wide consumption of drinking water	↓
Water Consumption	Kilolitres (kl) of rainwater storage capacity	↑
Biodiversity	Number of native bird species observed	↑
	Number of species with viable populations	↑
Leadership in Sustainability	Number of projects funded by the Sustainable Melbourne Fund	↑
Leadership in Sustainability	Total $ invested in projects by the Sustainable Melbourne Fund	↑
Green Building	% of floor area of buildings that receive 3-5-star Australian Building Greenhouse Rating	↑
Green Building	% of floor area of new buildings that receive 2-6 Green Star Ratings	↑
Green Building	Kilowatt (kw) hours of renewable energy produced.	↑

Source: Melbourne City Council, 2005.

improvements for individuals and businesses. Many local councils in Australia have made significant strides to address and give attention to sustainability, both within their organizations and outside, marshaling public attention to environmental issues.

In 2007, the City of Sydney adopted an ambitious Environmental Management Plan that "establishes the environmental vision, goals and targets required to create a sustainable city" (City of Sydney, 2007, p. 3). The targets are ambitious indeed, including 100 percent offsetting of greenhouse emissions by 2008 for the council's operations and, by 2050, a 70 percent reduction for the entire local government area.

Other targets have been established for water, waste, and open space, as well as indicators, and the plan identifies a variety of specific actions the city must commit to in order to realize these targets, including further efforts to green its vehicle fleet, a bicycle strategy, support for green power, and efforts to further encourage energy efficiency improvements in commercial buildings.

An even more ambitious greening initiative has been underway in Sydney. Called "Sustainable Sydney 2030," it has resulted in a far-reaching vision and strategic plan (by the same name), unveiled in 2008 (City of Sydney, 2008). The result of extensive community consultations, including 30 community forums, the plan presents some bold ideas for moving the city in the direction of a sustainable future and calls for Sydney to become "Green, Global and Connected." Specific ideas for change include new pedestrian and transit improvements, new green corridors through the city, and intriguing new energy ideas (including so-called "green transformers," or neighborhood-based cogeneration plants that would, among things, convert waste to power, recycle water, and provide district heating and cooling). Many of the ideas generated from this community process are presented on the Sustainable Sydney 2030 webpage (www.sydney2030.com.au).

In the Sydney region, a number of local councils have adopted some form of sustainability "branding" that seeks to give greater visibility to environmental issues. Penrith Council, for instance, has developed a prominent policy division or track within its council organization called "Sustainable Penrith" and has adopted as its logo an image of an Eastern water dragon (*Physignathus lesueurii*). These beautiful lizards, found along the Nepean River, are local to the council and are viewed as a good indicator of the overall environmental health of the community (another "focal species"). Penrith gives tangible expression to this sustainability self-branding in some unusual ways. It hosts, for instance, a yearly "Solar Splash," a solar boat contest held on Lake Penrith that draws competitors from around the country. It has convened the first two "sustainability streets" in the Sydney region, an innovative neighborhood-based sustainability program (described further in chapter 4).

Many—perhaps most—Australian local councils have now prepared and adopted some form of explicit sustainability strategy or action plan. For example, Manly Council, also part of the Sydney region, has adopted a sustainability strategy called "Blueprint for Our Future." Other councils, such as Baulkham Hills, in the Sydney metro area, have prepared "holistic and integrated" local environmental management plans. The Blue Mountains City Council, on the western edge of the Sydney region, has similarly gone through an extensive public process preparing both a vision for a sustainable future and a more detailed blueprint or "map for action" for how to get there. The twenty-five-year vision for the city suggests that commitment to sustainability principles will be at the core of all future planning and policy. The vision states that in 2025, the Blue Mountains will be "recognized nationally and internationally as a centre of excellence for learning about sustainable living and sustainable communities" (Blue Mountains City Council, 2004, p. 3). The level of commitment to sustainability expressed in these local plans is remarkable; although implementation remains a challenge, the ambitious targets and strong incorporation of sustainability concerns into planning and governance are notable.

Local councils in Australia have instituted a host of policy actions and programs to implement these plans and tangibly express their sustainability aspirations. The City of Gosford, north of Sydney, for instance, has adopted an Environmental Management Purchasing Procedure (Gosford City Council, 2004). A number of other local councils have also adopted green purchasing standards, and some local governments, such as Manly, have prepared comprehensive sets of ethical standards against which all council tenders are to be judged (box 2.2).

Cities like Gosford, moreover, have placed a high priority on purchasing environmental vehicles (e.g., Toyota Priuses) and supporting new fleet technologies and fuels, such as biodiesel. Perth's efforts to support and demonstrate hydrogen buses and Adelaide's development of a solar-powered electric bus (both described below) are further examples of how sustainability is being translated into changes in other urban policy and management areas by Australian cities and local councils. Park and landscape management can also reflect sustainability goals. For example, the City of Melbourne has adopted *Growing Green*, a sustainability plan for managing its parks and open spaces in ways that enhance biodiversity and minimize resource consumption (City of Melbourne, 2003).

The city of Melbourne is a leader in finding new and creative ways to integrate sustainability practices. They are proud of being the first city to have participated in the UN's Global Compact, an effort to promote voluntary corporate citizenship around the world. Launched in 2000, the Compact encourages participants, mostly businesses and corporations (four thousand in more than 120 countries), to endorse and look for ways to follow the Compact's set of universal principles, aimed at human rights, fair labor, and protection of the environment. The Compact's principles and framework are generally written to help corporations build sustainability and corporate social responsibility into their plans, expectations, and accounting, and

Box 2.2
Manly's Ethical Charter

Council is committed to supporting the principles of Ecologically Sustainable Development (ESD) as defined in the Local Government Act 1993 and ethical business practices. Council believes that sustainability must be the guiding principle of our business, requiring policies that meet the needs and aspirations of the present generation without compromising the opportunity of future generations to fulfill their needs and aspirations. Council also supports the Earth Charter and recognizes that it is sets the grounding principles for sustainability.

We support and will act on the following principles in our services:

- **Equity and justice** - We will act fairly, seeking to ensure equity, tolerance and removal of discrimination and support democratic societies that are just, participatory, sustainable and peaceful.

- **Respect** - We will treat other people and the environment with respect and acknowledge and support the values of indigenous peoples and minorities.

- Sustaining the environment - We will act with care and caution towards the environment, protecting the biosphere, its biodiversity, and using its resources sustainably for present and future generations.

- **Creating and sharing sustainable prosperity** - We will seek to create and share prosperity in a way that helps sustain our business, the community and the environment, and support locally based businesses who share these ethics where possible.

- **Responsibility** - We will take all responsibility for our actions and for any harm or good we cause. We will account for our actions, evaluating our progress in implementing these principles, and seek to continually improve. We also commit to combat corruption in all its forms, and the obstacles to good governance. We will not associate with organizations who act in direct contradiction to these principles.

Source: Manly Council, 2006.

Melbourne—as a local government—has sought to act similarly. The City of Melbourne has also developed and disseminated the ten Melbourne Principles for Sustainable Cities, an aspirational manifesto of urban sustainability that was unveiled to considerable fanfare at the UN World Summit on Sustainable Development in 2002 in Johannesburg, South Africa.

In 2007, Brisbane lord mayor Campbell Newman unveiled a new package of green initiatives called "CitySmart," with the intent to make that city "Australia's most sustainable city" (http://www.brisbane.qld.gov.au/ BCC:CITY_SMART). Under CitySmart, the city has set the goal of being a carbon-neutral city by 2026 and has embarked on an array of sustainability and urban greening initiatives to move in that direction, including major new tree planting (1 million new trees) and habitat restoration in the city, a new sustainability grants programs for not-for-profit organizations, new efforts at incorporating sustainability curricula into the local schools, and new support for green building, among others (e.g., see Hammond, 2007; Williams, 2007; and Passmore, 2006). Public education and grassroots citizen action are key elements here; creatively, Brisbanites are asked to show their love for the city, and to commit to its sustainability, by placing a "green heart" on an interactive map of the city.

A number of local authorities in these Australian cities have developed new, dedicated funding sources aimed at sustainability programs and initiatives. Many local authorities have adopted "environmental levies,"

Figure 2.1 The skyline of Melbourne, Australia. Melbourne has emerged as an international leader in green urbanism, integrating sustainability into it governance and planning, promoting a vibrant pedestrian culture, and demonstrating commitment through projects like the Council House 2, its new super-green municipal office building. *Photo credit:* Tim Beatley

which are essentially elements of the local property tax, though the taxing amounts and purposes to which they are used varies from place to place. In Adelaide, local governments have been grouped into Urban Catchment Management Groups, which raise a levy through council rates to manage urban creeks, wetlands, and estuaries affected by ambient pollution or habitat destruction. In the city of Brisbane, a $30 per rate payer per year environmental levy has existed for several years. Known as the bushland levy, it is specifically earmarked for acquiring undeveloped habitat within the city. Most of the many Brisbane volcanic hillocks that were too steep for early development have now been purchased as part of the Brisbane open space system using this levy. In the Blue Mountains, a flat rate is charged to residents to support specific environmental projects, and in Manley, an environmental levy has funded more than eighty restoration and protection projects since 1987. A similar levy in Perth has been raised by the state government for more than fifty years and has been used for park acquisition and infrastructure land.

In New South Wales (NSW), all local councils must prepare a "State of the Environment" (SoE) report each year under NSW's Local Government Act of 1993. These reports, though variable in length, detail, and quality, are generally well-done (I have read many of them!) and provide an excellent snapshot of where the locality stands, what the main environmental issues are, and what trends are of concern. They also provide a useful summary of existing projects, policies, and initiatives as well as those newly under way. They provide a helpful degree of transparency to what local councils are (or are not) doing to protect and manage their local environments.

These SoE reports contain substantial amounts of information, commonly include community and sustainability indicators, document and discuss projects completed or under way, and identify actions for the future. In cities like Gosford, the SoE report (for 2004) has been expanded and broadened to take the form of a "Sustainability Report" (City of Gosford, 2004). This detailed report describes current sustainability trends and conditions, targets, and indicators; discusses management efforts that are under way (including extensive case studies); and includes very detailed actions to be taken in the future. Gosford has created a Sustainability and Education Team, which initially arose from public discussion around its SoE report.

These SoE reports also typically contain the locality's main statement of policy and usually some form of sustainability indicators. Many of these local sustainability reports and strategies thus become key policy documents, central to decision making and local management. In Gosford, the Sustainability Report is considered as one of eight documents that together comprise its City Management Plan. Actions from the Sustainability Report feed directly into the city's Corporate Plan, another of its key documents. These local government SoE reports feed into the SoE report done by the state government. This is now a sophisticated collection of core indicators with a sustainability basis for how its recommendations are made (New South Wales Department of Environment and Climate Change, 2006).

Re-imagining Cities

Australian cities are helping to profoundly shift our notion of what cities or urban centers might become. Few efforts in Australia to promote green urban ideas are more comprehensive or extensive than those in Adelaide, the capital of South Australia. A sunny city in a Mediterranean climate, Adelaide is the main urban center of the state of South Australia, with a metro area population of just over 1 million. It is famous as a planned city (laid out by Colonel William Light in 1837), and its economy is a mix of manufacturing (especially cars), tourism, bioscience and technology, and wine production, with increasing attention to the arts and the environment. Here, various creative efforts have been made to help "brand" the city as a green one. Perhaps in part a response to feeling second fiddle to Melbourne and Sydney, these efforts have sought to distinguish the city and its aspirations. Adelaide aspires to be "internationally recognized as a Green City by 2010" (McGowan, 2004).

Some of Adelaide's early innovations have been in helping to stimulate this new thinking about what the city is or could be. One unusual, catalytic initiative has been the "Thinker in Residence" program, created by South Australian premier Mike Rann. In its short period of existence, it has helped to stimulate discussion about the future of this city and to promote some useful self-reflection about current circumstances in Adelaide, the assets (acknowledged or missed) there, and the opportunities for the future. Thinkers arrive, meet with groups and individuals, listen and take stock (often for as long as several months), and then report back to the community about what they have learned, offering their thoughts and suggestions (as outsiders, to be sure) about the future, both in the form of a major public presentation and later as a published (and widely disseminated) written report. As the premier notes, Thinkers are "asked to challenge our beliefs, spark fresh ideas and set new directions," and this for the most part seems to have been the positive effect. One of the early Thinkers (in 2003) was creative cities expert Charles Landry, who set the stage for greening innovations by suggesting that Adelaide focus more on "greening issues, and noting the natural but missed opportunities here"—for instance, in the areas of green engineering, connecting the food culture with green production, and sustainable economic development generally (see Landry, 2003, especially pages 50–51, for more on these creative ideas).

The Thinker in Residence program is a unique and interesting effort at injecting new ideas and outside energy into local discussions and debate. It has brought a dizzying array of impressive experts and authorities from around the world, enticed in part by the evidence of a community and region committed to promoting the arts and exploring new ideas. Thinkers have been writers, practitioners, and theorists representing various disciplines and professions. Recent Thinkers have included climate scientist Stephen Schneider, homeless advocate Rosanne Haggerty, and green cities expert Herbert Girardet, as well as creative cities guru Charles Landry. The final reports or white papers that thinkers produce have all been stimulating and provocative and have helped to shape local discourse and debate commonly for months after the Thinkers have left Adelaide.

Herbert Girardet, an internationally known authority on urban sustainability from the United Kingdom, spent a jam-packed eight weeks in the city, meeting with people and groups, listening to and collecting ideas, and making presentations. At the end, he produced a sweeping, visionary report, *Creating a Sustainable Adelaide*, which contains thirty-three recommendations. Girardet had many good ideas and proposals, including creating green business incubators across the city, mandating installation of solar hot water heaters in all new and renovated buildings, drawing up detailed action plans for supporting new recycling industries in the city, and "waterproofing" Adelaide by encouraging water efficiency measures and rainwater collection in all households and businesses in the city (Girardet, 2004).

Many of the recommendations in Girardet's report have since been brought to fruition, as a recent state report documents, adopted either by local councils or by the state government (South Australia Department for Environment and Heritage, 2005). For instance, all new homes must now be plumbed to allow a rainwater collection tank, a new state mandate. Many of the ideas have been embraced by the city. One specific goal that developed from these recommendations is to become carbon neutral by 2020. Adelaide is pushing the renewable energy agenda by working closely with the state government and the electric utility, who between 2002 and

2006 managed to build and commission three major wind farms, representing 15 percent of the state's electricity requirements.

Adelaide has also made a strong push for solar energy. One of the city's more interesting projects is its North Terrace Solar Precinct, in the city center. Envisioned here is the transforming of the city's major "cultural boulevard" into a series of demonstration projects and examples showing the potential of solar energy. Photovoltaic (PV) panels have already been installed on the rooftops of the South Australian Museum and Art Gallery, and soon panels will also be found on the Parliament House and the State Library (figure 2.2). Other green city ideas are already making their way into the North Precinct, including the innovative stormwater management retrofit recently completed for the South Australia Museum.

The accomplishments, especially on the solar front, are already evident. Adelaide, and South Australia, boast almost half of Australia's grid-connected solar energy, for instance, even though the population amounts to only about 8 percent of the nation's total.

Adelaide's designation by the Commonwealth government as the first "solar city" comes with substantial financial assistance from the government and promises to greatly expand the installation of solar energy systems and the visible commitment to solar power. Under this grant, made to a consortium that includes (locally based) Origin Energy, BP Solar, and several local councils in addition to Adelaide, the installation of some 1,700 rooftop PV systems on homes and council structures is envisioned, as well as the installation of PV on at least seven "iconic" municipal buildings, buildings that are especially visible and important (for at least 2 megawatts of additional solar production). Also envisioned is the installation of seven thousand smart energy meters and the distribution of forty thousand energy information packages to residents and businesses.

Part of Adelaide's commitment to promoting solar energy has been to look for small but symbolically significant demonstrations. One example of this is the installation of distinctive new street and public space lighting that produces energy. Called solar mallees, because they take the form of native mallee eucalypts, they contain PV cells on their top (figure 2.3). They represent an interesting and different way to think about power production in the city—in terms not just of rooftops but every urban design detail or addition that might be reenvisioned as a small piece of a more sustainable distributed power production system. Each solar mallee actually produces seven times the power needed to provide the lighting, thus serving as a net exporter of energy into the city's power grid.

Figure 2.2 The City of Adelaide, in South Australia, aspires to be a solar city. The City has designated a solar energy precinct, and promoting installation of photovoltaic panels on public rooftops such as the South Australia museum shown here. *Photo credit:* Courtesy Adelaide Capital City Committee, Copyright of the Government of South Australia.

Figure 2.3 Solar Mallee Trees. These streetlights in Adelaide produce about seven times the power need for lighting, sending considerable electricity back into the city's power grid. *Photo credit:* John Hoare Architects

Many schools in Adelaide and South Australia are going solar as well. Under its solar school initiative, the state government encourages and financially supports the installation of PV panels on school rooftops. Already, 112 schools have participated, and the state has set an ambitious target of having 250 schools participating as solar schools by the year 2014 (South Australia, 2007). Adelaide's emerging reputation as a solar city was further solidified when Adelaide hosted in February 2008 the Third International Solar Cities Congress. As a preliminary for this event, an international solar school design competition was held, further building on this ambitious way of understanding the solar education students might be expected to receive in a solar city.

Adelaide's commitment to solar power seems especially strong and promising as a new model for thinking about green cities. It was the first Australian city to receive funding under the Commonwealth government's $75 million AUD Solar Cities initiative. Adelaide had a significant leg up on other cities in competing for funding under the Solar Cities program. Former prime minister Howard declared that Adelaide would be the first solar city, a sensible choice given the interest and local resources there. As Chris McGowan, who heads the Green City program, notes of these natural advantages: "Solar intensity in Adelaide exceeds that of many other cities and Adelaide receives nearly twice the sunlight compared with Northern Europe" (McGowan, 2006, p. 2). Thus it is natural to see the commitment to solar energy there; it is really an opportunity born from the intrinsic conditions of the place. Geothermal and wind also represent major energy opportunities there and are being considered as well.

The Commonwealth Solar City program, from which Adelaide is receiving funding, has distributed funding to four other communities that have now also been designated solar cities, and it holds the promise of further stimulating interest in and commitment to solar energy. With funding of $75 million AUD (or about $73 million USD), the program is implemented by the Commonwealth Department of Environment and Heritage and is a plank in the Commonwealth's efforts (even before the change of government and the signing of the Kyoto Agreement) at addressing climate change. The award to central Victoria holds a potential similar to Adelaide's. As with all of the participants, the award is to a consortium and will support, in this case, the installation of 2,500 rooftop PV systems; solar hot water heating systems; smart meters in homes, businesses, and schools; and the distribution of energy efficiency packages to residents.

Adelaide has taken a number of other steps to advance the green urban agenda there. The Adelaide Building Tune-Ups project, for instance, also under the auspice of the Green City program, is a unique effort at encouraging energy and water efficiency retrofits for commercial office buildings. It is a public-private collaboration in which private (and some public) buildings agree to participate for a modest fee. In three stages, buildings are "benchmarked" to estimate current energy and water consumption (against the Australian Building Greenhouse Rating, or ABGR, system), cost-effective retrofits are identified and carried out (sufficient to raise the

ABGR score by at least one point), and environmental benefits are evaluated. Stage one, which has benchmarked the energy and water demands of ten buildings in the city's central business district (CBD), has already demonstrated that the potential environmental and financial savings are considerable and that completing these retrofits represents a good investment (Energy Conservation Systems, 2004). Adelaide has also retro-fitted about half of its traffic intersections with high-efficiency LED (light-emitting diodes) lighting and has set the goal of retrofitting them all by 2010.

One of the more unusual outcomes of the Adelaide Green City initiative is the Eco-TV project. Spearheaded by a local businesswoman, Deb Lavis, and cosponsored by a number of public or private organizations, including the Adelaide Film Festival, the idea was to support and stimulate young filmmakers while at the same time helping to raise consciousness about the environmental problems facing South Australia. Filmmakers were encouraged to submit proposals for a thirty-second television commercial addressing one of four key messages drawn from the State's 2003 *State of the Environment Report*: water use and quality, climate change, species loss, and the marine water and coastal environment. A panel of judges then selected four finalists, who were each given a budget of $4,000 AUD to produce the commercials, which were aired at the Adelaide Film Festival in March 2005. The winning entry was broadcast on local channel 10 and awarded a cash prize (see http://www.ecotvc.com).

The project is in many ways a perfect merging of Adelaide's focus on the arts and media and its aspirations and emerging reputation as a green capital city. The commercials produced by the four finalists—creative if not necessarily polished—reflected strong artistic and environmental values. From an organizational and governmental perspective, Adelaide's approach is impressive and somewhat unusual. Born partly out of the view that a "greening" image will be good for the city's business and economy in the future, it also seems to reflect a strong commitment to environment and sustainability at the very top, starting with the premier, Mike Rann. And this initiative is a true collaboration between state and city. In fact, a special structure, the Adelaide Capital City Committee, has been created by an act of parliament to facilitate this collaboration. The committee is chaired by the government, with the local city manager and several city council members sitting on it, and with its own office and staff. Most of the funding for Green City projects, moreover, has come from the state government. Also impressive is the extent to which the Green City initiative has reached out to all sectors in the community, especially the business community. Partly on their own, but also clearly benefiting from the support and platform provided by the Green City program, many businesses and business organizations have been advancing on green issues also.

Adelaide exhibits an emerging green city culture and shows what can be done to help this along. Small startup funding has been made available for local neighborhood and grassroots sustainability ideas. For example, a small funding grant from the city was made to the Grote Street Business Association. As explained by the association's energetic and highly enthusiastic director, Deb Lavis, "the funding has provided the chance to do several key things, including the setting up of a system of shared recycling depots for cardboard and other business waste."

For a small initiative, the Grote Street effort represents a model for reforming and reimagining in small businesses. Under the program, training is provided for business staff, and to date some eighty businesses have signed on, agreeing to designate a work-environment officer in each establishment. It is really about shifting the business culture to be more aware of this footprint. There have been clear positive spillover benefits of a different sort, as the merchants and their employees have taken much of this green spirit back to their homes as well.

Green Transport and Land Use

Australian cities are, much like American cities, sprawling in their land use patterns and highly car dependent. Home-to-work trips in Brisbane, for instance, are made about 92 percent by car and only 8 percent by transit and other means. The present lord mayor, Campbell Newman, a member of the liberal party (Republican), is committed to building a series of five to seven auto tunnels designed to free up road traffic in the city center; however, most other mayors in Australia's major cities are trying to build up other transportation modes rather than infrastructure for car use.

There are differences between Australian and U.S. government control of land use. Australian metropolitan areas have a history of regional planning coupled with a generally stronger government planning system and framework that has resulted in a more compact urban form. These impressive regional and state planning efforts (discussed in more detail in chapter 6), which have gained in strength and emphasis on sustainability, are an important part of the story, along with a jurisdictional geography of relatively large state boundaries (that completely encompass metro areas). Newman and Kenworthy's global cities database suggests that Australian city-regions use about half the transport fuel of U.S. city-regions on a per capita basis (Newman and Kenworthy, 1999).

While public transit use in Australia's cities is closer to that of American cities than of European cities, in Sydney, Perth, and Melbourne major commitments have been made to strengthening "centres" and investing in the rail and bus services that make these cities transit oriented.

In Perth, this sprawling capital city is attempting—with a regional plan (Network City) and major new extensions of its rail system—to reduce dependence on private cars. Significant progress was made during the 1990s, when rail ridership grew from 8 million riders per year to 31 million per year (1991 to 2001), and that number increased to 47 million by 2005 (new metro rail)—a result of a $400 million rail investment (Kenworthy, Murray-Leach, and Townsend, 2005). The latest chapter is the seventy-four-kilometer extension of Perth's rail system to Mandurah to the south, which was completed in December 2007 and is expected to double the patronage again. This would mean that a city was able to go from almost no rail to around 100 million passenger trips per year in around fifteen years. The journey-to-work data between 2001 and 2006 show that Perth increased its use of rail by 44 percent and its use of cars by just 15 percent. Few cities in recent years have done anything quite as spectacular as this, and the possibilities for U.S. cities are clear because Perth is very like many U.S. cities in its commitment to car-based developments in its recent redirections.

These investments have been referred to as "transformative sustainable infrastructure":

> Perth's new rail system which has been built with substantial political input over the past fifteen years, is quite transformative. It has cost $2 billion and has given the city a 180 km modern electric rail system with 72 stations; it was built without a cent of federal funds, though the Freeway it passes down was funded almost entirely from federal coffers. This railway has been justified over many elections as a way of oil proofing the city. (Newman, 2005, p. 14)

The story of Perth's recommitment to rail is an interesting one because it tells us something about the role of civic society in Australia's green urbanism. The state government closed the rail line in 1979, but a strong civic movement emerged that set a new vision of what could be achieved. This has largely happened as the issues were made part of each political agenda over the past twenty-five years (Newman, 2002).

Some fantastic examples of emerging transit villages and transit-oriented development (TOD) can be cited from the development in and around Perth's rail system. Subi-Centro is one of the best examples, and most promising models, of transit-oriented development in Australia. This eighty-hectare former industrial site in the city of Subiaco has been transformed into a compact, walkable, relatively dense new urban neighborhood, with an underground Transperth rail station as its key mobility feature. The project created housing for two thousand new residents, three to four thousand jobs, and eighty thousand square meters of commercial retail. Directly above and adjacent to the station is Subi-Square, a mixed-use complex of office, shops, restaurants, and a full-service grocery store. A neighborhood commons, children's play area, and promenade are all within a few minutes' walk of new homes as well as close to Subiaco's existing (and fairly vibrant) commercial district.

The urban design guidelines of Subi-Centro have been rewarded in the marketplace, as prices have risen and demand for units is strong. The amenities and quality of life are impressive here. The planning instruments employed to bring about Subi-Centro are worth noting. An act of parliament created in 1994 the Subiaco Redevelopment Agency and (importantly) exempted it from local planning conditions and requirements. The national government's Building Better Cities program helped fund the sinking of the rail station, allowing more compact and intensive use of the land above and around the station (figure 2.4).

One measure of the success of the TOD neighborhood is the value of private investment here. From a state investment of $130 million AUD, $500 million AUD has been spent by the private sector. The Subiaco Redevelopment Authority (SRA) also developed an impressive set of urban design guidelines to ensure that a quality urban form results. Elements of these guidelines include the following:

- A form-based guideline ensures a visually coherent development although each building is different. The resulting medium-density urban form is now being called New Perth style. It is strongly urban in character, with buildings on the front property line creating a Brooklyn, New York, feel on the street (buildings close to the sidewalks with little or no setback); all garaging is at the rear, creating a more walkable feel to the street.
- A Housing Diversity Policy was adopted by the SRA in 2002, which sets the target of 10 to 15 percent of new housing (on SRA land releases) as affordable—for example, social housing or special needs housing (Subiaco Redevelopment Agency, n.d.).
- An extensive network of cycleways and pedestrian footpaths, as well as extensive public spaces, is also required. The popularity of Subi-Centro is testified to by the range of other developments

Figure 2.4 Perth, in Western Australia, has invested heavily in recent years in its electric rail system, which now extends 180 kilometers of track and includes 72 stations. It is a miraculous story considering the state closed the rail system in 1979, until public outcry and protest led to its resounding reopening. *Photo credit:* Tim Beatley

modeling themselves on this project, including new suburbs on the new southern railway.

Melbourne's impressive system of trams is both the most enjoyable and the fastest way to get around and is an iconic symbol of the city itself (figure 2.5). Dating back to 1885, the 245 kilometers of track are now operated by Yarra Trams. Some 1,800 tram stops are served by almost five hundred vehicles in the tram fleet. The trams, ranging from modern to historic, provide a distinctive look, feel, and sound to central Melbourne. The system has been extended and improved over time, with new platforms and stations added as well as such enhancements for riders as a system (called tramTRACKER) for remotely tracking where and when the next tram will arrive at one's station.

The Green Depot project in Melbourne has attempted to reduce the environmental effects associated with servicing and maintaining the trams

Figure 2.5 Melbourne is a city of trams, and its system dates back to 1885. The trams are essential way of getting around in this city as well as an important and unique quality of place there. *Photo credit:* Tim Beatley

at tram depots around the city. A number of green retrofits have been made to the East Preston Depot, including the installation of rooftop photovoltaics and solar hot water panels, rainwater collection, water-efficient vegetation and gardening, an integrated waste collection system, and waterless urinals. Water from the depot's three eighteen-thousand-liter rainwater collection tanks is the sole source for washing the trams as well as providing water for toilet flushing. Yarra estimates that these water elements will reduce annual water consumption by more than 3 million liters.

The greening of public transport vehicles is another area where Australian cities and regions are making significant progress. The increasing use of alternatively fueled vehicles is notable, particularly in Perth, where all buses now run on compressed natural gas and a hydrogen fuel cell bus trial has been under way.

Perth has been operating three of the DaimlerChrysler-made buses as part of an international trial, along with ten partner cities in Europe: Amsterdam, Barcelona, Hamburg, London, Luxembourg, Madrid, Porto,

Figure 2.6 Perth has been piloting the use of hydrogen fuel cell buses, such as this one made by Daimler Chrysler. *Photo credit:* Courtesy Simon Whitehouse, WA Department of Planning and Infrastructure

Stockholm, Stuttgart, and Reykjavík. Most of the funding for the Perth program was provided by the state with some support from the Commonwealth government. The European trials have been funded under a European Union (EU) program called Clear Urban Transport for Europe, or CUTE, and "cofunded" by the EU Department of Energy and Transportation. Operation of buses has been closely monitored and is being evaluated to assess the program's success. In the case of the Perth buses, the hydrogen is supplied by British Petroleum from its oil refinery at Kwinana, south of the city. Hydrogen here is a by-product of the process of refining crude oil and thus essentially utilizes a waste product. However, in a long-term perspective where hydrogen becomes a major energy carrier in our cities, it is possible to create such hydrogen by splitting water using solar energy (something in considerable surplus in Australia, especially Perth).

The buses are made by DaimlerChrysler (Mercedes-Benz Citaro buses) and the fuel cells by Ballard (PEM, or Proton Exchange Membrane, fuel cells) (figure 2.6). The buses are powered by an electric motor and are essentially emission-free. Water vapor and heat are the only emissions from this clean vehicle, so there are obvious benefits over other buses, such as diesel.

For Simon Whitehouse, project leader in Perth, the project has also given glimpses of how much must still happen before hydrogen buses became "commercially viable." In his mind, several things must happen: significant improvements must be made in the process of purifying hydrogen, fuel cell advancements must continue that would allow lower levels of hydrogen purity (currently, hydrogen must be 99.9 percent pure—much purer than currently produced), and perhaps most significantly, there must be ways to produce hydrogen from renewable energy. When asked about the availability of hydrogen or the source of hydrogen, Whitehouse has a strong response: especially in a state like Western Australia (WA), which is rich in natural gas, there is abundant hydrogen. Providing the hydrogen renewably is, in his words, "a different kettle of fish" and will require advancements in solar, wind, and wave energy, all of which, he is quick to add, are also abundant potential sources of renewable energy in Western Australia, though not yet very fully developed.

Whitehouse differentiates between the technology of the bus itself and the infrastructure needed to support it. He is very confident about the vehicle, and although improvements will be made in the next generation of buses, he feels this technology has proven its ability. He is less confident about the infrastructure needed to support an entire fleet of these buses. He mentions as one example the time needed to refuel a hydrogen bus. It presently takes a minimum of ten to fifteen minutes to refuel a hydrogen bus—and with all of the current safety precautions, perhaps longer. This is much longer than what it takes to refuel a conventional diesel or natural gas bus. He sees this as a "huge weakness in the supply chain."

The buses have already carried more than fifty thousand passengers and traveled more than forty thousand kilometers. On comfort, smoothness, and drivability, the buses have done quite well—drivers and passengers alike appear to like the buses a lot. They have generally proven to be reliable and have performed well on fuel efficiency. Whitehouse anticipates that, while the trial has been successful, it will likely be 2015 before the fuel cells reach a fully commercial level.

The Perth trial does prove convincingly that merit and value rest in small steps forward and small experiments that can, among other things, focus public attention and garner public support for other steps needed on the way toward sustainability. Whitehouse calls the buses an "iconic" project, and they clearly are. They are easily recognized on Perth's streets and give a sense of the long-term future with their "zero emissions" image.

Most citizens of Perth know something about the buses, having seen a story about them or perhaps having even ridden one of the brightly painted vehicles. Prince Charles, in a recent visit to Western Australia, was given a high-profile tour of the city in one of the buses. The project won a Banksia Award (the nation's most prestigious environmental award). A school-based education program centered around the bus. Surveys were conducted that found the buses were extremely popular, with no stigma associated with the hydrogen fuel. The buses have prompted useful debate and discussion, both inside and outside government, about sustainable transport and renewable energy ideas. They have increased visibility of green issues generally and are helping to shape Perth's own self-perception as a green capital. Thus important, and often underappreciated, public relations, educational, and community catalytic benefits flow from such initiatives.

At a broader policy level, the Western Australian government has now embedded the fuel cell bus trial in a broader Sustainable Transport Energy Program (STEP) and has been taking actions to promote this concept. The Department of Planning and Infrastructure has purchased some twenty hybrid cars; now has an official policy to buy four-cylinder cars over six-cylinder vehicles (unless a special justification can be made for the latter); and has committed that eventually all buses will be powered by alternative fuels.

The STEP program has run several events dramatizing the issue of peak oil, including a series of public meetings as well as a presentation by Ali Samsang Bakhtiari (a former Iranian oil minister who has become a global speaker addressing the reality of peak oil) to the state cabinet. (Trans-Perth operates more conventional buses, including a network of smaller, high-frequency buses that, remarkably, are free. In Fremantle, the Central Area Transport, or CAT, buses do a free loop through the city, which is very useful for getting around without a car.[1])

Adelaide has been supporting, for several years, the development of an entirely electric community bus and now boasts the operation of this bus on city streets, fully powered by solar energy. More specifically, the bus operates entirely through the use of a bank of Zebra batteries, which allows the bus to travel two hundred kilometers between charges. The bus is called the Tindo, the Kaurna aboriginal word for the sun. Electric charging of the bus is offset by the city's largest grid-connected PV array, located at the Adelaide Central Bus Station. These solar panels produce an estimated seventy thousand kilowatt-hours per year, further reflecting the city's commitment to installing solar and making its city operation carbon neutral (Adelaide City Council, n.d.).

As part of a larger set of green travel initiatives, North Sydney Council has put in place a sliding-scale parking fee system (from large sport-utility vehicles to fuel-efficient small vehicles) to favor smaller, more energy efficient cars. Its concerns in this area are largely driven by its geographical context—it often finds itself clogged with traffic as drivers use the city as an alternative way to access the harbor bridge into and out of the Sydney CBD. Other ideas explored by the council include placing restrictions on the availability of new resident parking permitted in certain areas, joining with several other councils to support car sharing (e.g., private council spaces for use by car-sharing companies such as Newtown Car-Share) as well as efforts to further encourage public transit.

When car travel cannot be avoided, options exist for offsetting at least some of the resulting carbon load by supporting tree planting. A Melbourne-based national nonprofit called Greenfleet, founded by Henry O'Clery, is the largest and best known in Australia (figure 2.7). The appeal

Figure 2.7 National nonprofit *Greenfleet* plants native trees to offset the greenhouse gas emissions of cars, including state carpools. To date, it has planted more than 3 million trees in hundreds of sites around the country. Shown here is Queensland Government Minister of Public Works, Robert Schwarten, helping to plant the 500,000th tree as part of the Qfleet offset program (along with the team from Australian Farm Forestry). *Courtesy:* Greenfleet

here is both to individuals and to companies and institutions. At an individual level, for a $40 AUD (about $38 USD) tax-deductible contribution, Greenfleet will plant seventeen native species of trees, sufficient, they calculate, to cover the average greenhouse gas emissions for one car for one year (4.3 metric tonnes of carbon). An online calculator provides another way to calculate more specifically an individual's emissions, but the key idea is to link the purchase and operation of a car with taking responsibility for its (hidden to the driver-owner) environmental consequences. Air flights can also be made carbon neutral through Greenfleet. For example, an around-the-world flight for three people can be made carbon neutral by a $261 AUD (about $250 USD) donation that will place ninety trees in the Western Australia wheatbelt. A certificate for the trip is awarded to the purchaser.

Greenfleet has planted more than 3 million trees in 270 sites since the program began in 1997. It has developed some impressive long-term relationships with public (and private) motorpools and car fleets. "Q fleet," the fleet manager for the Queensland state government, is their largest client, resulting in the planting of some 500,000 trees in that state (see figure 2.7). They will soon plant 12,000 trees in the Pimpana River Conservation Reserve, "reducing salinity and soil erosion, and providing essential habitat for native species" (Greenfleet, 2005, p. 1).

The planting will provide habitat for such rare and threatened animals as the square-tailed kite and the rose-crowned fruit dove and will act as an important buffer for the marine habitat of the false water rat—one of Australia's rarest animals. Other mammals that will directly benefit from the planting include the koala and the squirrel glider (Queensland Government, 2005, p. 2).

Greenfleet's philosophy is to plant trees as part of restoration projects, never solely in plantations but in ways that repair natural areas and landscapes. The trees that are planted are never to be harvested, and they utilize local species and local provenance stock.

In Western Australia, StateWest Credit Society launched its Green Choice Car Loan in February 2005. Borrowers receive a complementary subscription to Greenfleet, as well as a reduced interest rate when purchasing fuel-efficient cars, and staff can sign up their own cars with a 50 percent subsidy from the credit society.

Greenfleet has been growing in popularity in Australia. According to Henry O'Clery, subscriptions have increased each year since the nonprofit was formed in 1997. It seems to be picking up steam because, O'Clery believes, there is more awareness about climate change today as well as a greater corporate sense that something can and should be done. He now has relationships with managers of state fleets of cars in three Australian states. Greenfleet actually has a planting backlog. It still needs to plant some 650,000 trees and finds that the lead time to find appropriate sites and undertake the planting is considerable.

Men of the Trees, a nonprofit planting organization with historic roots in early tree-planting efforts in Kenya, is also very active in this area and actually has its own carbon-neutral program in Western Australia. Since 2002, when the organization started, thousands of trees have been planted. In 2006 alone, more than 235,000 trees will be planted in WA, offsetting emissions for about eleven thousand vehicles (Men of the Trees, 2006). Of this, more than 100,000 trees will be planted to cover emissions from WA's state government, and about 50,000 trees for the WA Water Authority. Among its "carbon-neutral heroes" are a variety of organizations, including local hospitals, consulting firms, several port authorities, an air taxi company, and a number of local councils who have sought to mitigate the greenhouse gas emissions of their municipal fleets (see http://www .carbonneutral.com.au). The interest on the part of local governments is especially promising in WA. Trees in WA are planted to support biodiversity and habitat restoration and, in particular, to partially address the increasingly destructive effect of dryland salinity.

One great sustainable transportation story from Australia is its experience with TravelSmart, the behavioral, dialogue-based marketing strategy to empower people to reduce their trips by automobile and to use transit and bikes and walking more often. Pioneered by a German firm, Social Data, run by Werner Brog, these marketing techniques have been used most extensively in Australian cities, especially Perth, and have now been formally integrated and enshrined in official transportation targets and plans across the country since a major federal grant was awarded for all Australian cities. While TravelSmart is now in use throughout Australia, it found its beginning applications in Perth in the late 1990s. The government of Western Australia has adopted a ten-year TravelSmart action plan, an element of its larger Perth Metropolitan Transport Strategy.

TravelSmart focuses specifically on that segment of the population interested in and potentially able to choose a noncar transportation option. Surveys by TravelSmart generally indicate that there is more interest than usually thought in sustainable modes of transport and that misinformation about these modes commonly occurs (e.g., respondents often underestimate travel time by car and overestimate travel time by transit) (WA Transport, 1999).

At the heart of TravelSmart is a targeted marketing approach, often referred to as dialogue marketing or community-based social marketing, where information is tailored to the specific needs and circumstances of individuals. Specific interventions include installing timetable information specific to particular bus stops, distributing wallet-sized timetables to households in that specific "catchment," and local mobility maps that show transit, bike, and walking routes and indicate common destinations. Through telephone surveys, interested households receive information and even home visits, if desired, and are given "test tickets" to try out transit. Households with children are especially targeted and are informed that walking, biking, or taking transit to school is better for children's health and maturation (especially their decision-making skills).

The use of TravelSmart in the Perth region has shown considerable success. In a pilot program focused on South Perth, the campaign resulted in a net decrease in car trips of more than 15 percent. This has been duplicated across Perth suburbs, with inner areas showing slightly higher and outer suburbs slightly lower outcomes. The program shows generally a 20 to 30 percent increase in bike/walk travel (from a low base) and a 9 to 14 percent decrease in auto travel. In 2007, more than one hundred thousand households participated in TravelSmart.

TravelSmart has been shown to make economic sense as an alternative especially to road building. Studies in WA show a cost-benefit ratio of 13 to 1 (much higher than what is usually estimated for transport infrastructure investments; see WA Transport, 1999). TravelSmart is now moving to work more with businesses and schools and in Perth is embarking in 2008 on an experiment to see how the approach can be used to help households on an integrated sustainability program involving water, energy, waste, and travel.

Other sustainable transport ideas, such as the use of bicycles and car sharing, are less developed in Australian cities, but there are some programs in place to help change that. The City of Adelaide has recently completed an Active Adelaide campaign, cosponsored by Bicycle SA and the Adelaide Green City Program, aimed at stimulating bike commuting to its downtown by offering participants a variety of benefits and inducements. These have included free bicycle safety workshops, access to bike parking and showers, free bicycle gear, and significant subsidies for purchasing a bike. The program took place over roughly a six-month period, with priority given to applicants (from a tremendous response to the call for participants!) who were currently inactive and who wished to be more physically active. Surveys of participants who have completed the program show it has had the desired effect: car travel among the participants went down sharply (about a 50 percent reduction), and trips by bicycles have risen sharply (about a tenfold increase!).

New ideas about curtailing city traffic and reinvigorating neighborhood streets have also been coming out of Australia. One creative Australian, David Engwicht, a former window washer turned road activist, developed walking school buses; neighborhood traffic treaties; the notion of neighborhood pace cars, where residents declare their intention to obey speed limits in traveling through neighborhoods; and, most recently, "mental speed bumps" (accompanied by a 2005 book by Engwicht of the same title). A mental speed bump is the recognition that slowing the speed of cars is mostly about psychology, or changing the social perceptions of drivers, and not about physical constraints or more signage or traffic-calming measures. These things often have the opposite effect, he believes, giving drivers license to drive even faster. Rather, creating elements of intrigue and uncertainty work profoundly better. Encouraging more socializing in and close to streets, blurring the boundaries between car space and community space, and working to make the street more like a room (with furniture, a sense of enclosure, public art, and activity areas like the "fish forest ruins" Engwicht has been building in his own front yard) are all important elements.

Engwicht's ideas and work have emerged in parallel with the "naked streets" movement in Europe, and the work of Hans Monderman and others to take away signage, intersection lights, and other physical traffic constraints, recognizing the value of shared spaces, more subtle social cues (e.g., changes in paving, trees along the streets to minimize the sense of wide open roads), and eye contact among motorists, pedestrians, and bicyclists moving through towns and villages.

Climate Change and Green Building in Australian Cities

Sustainability commitment finds expression in Australian cities and local councils in specific terms when it comes to climate change activities. Despite the lack of federal government support for signing Kyoto (until after the late 2007 election), local and state governments were some of the first in the world to begin coherent climate change programs.

An unusually high number of local councils (more than two hundred) have prepared climate action plans, covering more than 80 percent of the nation's population (Australian Greenhouse Office, 2007). Partly this is due to the involvement of ICLEI, which was formed at the UN Conference on Environment and Development (the Earth Summit) in Rio in 1992 to assist local governments with sustainability. ICLEI has partnered with the Australian Greenhouse Office (within the Commonwealth government) to deliver these programs, an unusual partnership (by U.S. standards anyway) that has helped to explain the success. ICLEI is active in all states of Australia, running its Cities for Climate Protection (CCP) program (in Perth, all forty of the local councils are committed to ICLEI's CCP program), and the Melbourne office is the largest in the world, with more than forty staff members (see http://www.iclei.org/oceania). Another organization, Environs, was formed from local governments in New South Wales as a training body on sustainability.

The city of Sydney and the city of Melbourne were two of the first global cities to join the Clinton Foundation's C40 Climate Leadership Group, which links the major cities of the world into a consortium for buying low-carbon technology, goods, and services. Both cities have been global leaders in this area, and Melbourne is now participating in one of the Clinton Climate Initiative's first major programs: its Energy Efficiency Building Retrofit Program aimed at accelerating energy retrofits for both public and private structures (Clinton Foundation, 2007).

Sydney has developed a new green community centre at Surrey Hills (a six-star building using geothermal water cooling for its air conditioning) and has adopted the impressive greenhouse gas reduction target of becoming carbon neutral for both its council operations and the entire local government areas involving energy efficiency, renewables, and their own urban forest (City of Sydney, 2007). It has developed an energy action savings plan for reducing emissions at key locations and has, with other councils, developed some interesting initiatives to address the commercial office sector, the largest source of greenhouse gas emissions in the city. Specifically, it has joined with North City and Parramatta City Councils to develop and implement the 3CBDs Greenhouse Initiative, an effort to encourage private commercial office tenants to adopt energy efficiency measures and, through commitment, education, and training, to significantly reduce the energy and greenhouse footprint of this community sector. While voluntary, already almost fifty businesses have committed, covering 8 percent of the office space among the three CBDs of the local governments (City of Sydney, n.d.). In 2008 this program went national as City-Switch Green Office (see www.cityswitch.net.au).

Some local councils have actually been at it for a long time. In the Sydney metro area, Leichhardt Council has been an early leader in renewable energy by promoting the installation of solar panels throughout that city, including on the rooftop of its town hall. Solar projects and installations can be found throughout Australian cities. A notable example is the installation of photovoltaics on the rooftop of the Queen Victoria Market in Melbourne (the "largest urban grid-connected solar photovoltaic installation in the Southern Hemisphere"; City of Melbourne, n.d.). Jointly funded through the Australian Greenhouse Office and the City of Melbourne, the project consists of 1,328 photovoltaic laminates, generating about 240,000 kilowatt-hours of electricity.

Many local councils support renewable energy through the purchase of a minimum amount portion of renewable green power. Bankstown Council (in the Sydney metro area) is typical, with a policy of purchasing 10 percent green power, which covers its street lighting. Leichhardt Council, also in the Sydney metro region, raised in 2007 its intention to purchase 25 percent from green power, and over time local councils seem to be similarly ratcheting up their green power purchases. The city of Sydney has declared its intent to buy 100 percent green energy.

While Australia has a long history of climate-sensitive design, the planning for the 2000 Olympics in Sydney marked a new commitment to renewable energy. Many of the Olympic Park's facilities and venues incorporated interesting energy production and conservation features, including the use of natural ventilation in the design of the Olympic Stadium, the extensive use of natural lighting in the Aquatic Center, and the installation of photovoltaic panels on the Sydney SuperDome roof, the Olympic Plaza lighting towers, and elsewhere. The Novotel Hotel was designed to reduce energy consumption and included a large solar hot water heating system on its roof (four hundred square meters in size, lowering energy consumption by an estimated 40 percent compared with a conventional hotel of its size). Most notable was the development of the Olympic Village at Newington, billed as Australia's first solar neighborhood. The homes, used to house athletes during the games, included a number of green features, notably solar passive design, cross ventilation, dual-water systems, solar hot water heating, and roof-integrated grid-connected PV systems. Now home to five thousand Sydney residents, the Village remains a model of how to incorporate energy and sustainability into urban design.[2]

Interestingly, climate change and renewable energy are now in Australia finding their way into many business sectors and social concerns not usually thought to be sensitive to or concerned about green matters. Theater is one place with emerging activism about what can and should be done. The Adelaide Film Festival in 2007 became the "first CO2 neutral arts festival in Australia," with the help of a locally grown company called

Carbon Planet (Adelaide Film Festival, 2007). Theaters and theater management groups in other Australian cities are similarly warming to their climate change obligations. In Melbourne, the Malthouse Theater has developed its Greenlight initiative, which is examining how it might reduce energy consumption (e.g., from the extensive lighting systems and air-conditioning) and produce much of the power it needs from solar panels. It is imagining itself as an "ecologically sustainable theater," and theater patrons will be asked to contribute by adding a small price to tickets to cover climate offsets. Other theaters are developing a similar climate change strategy, including a new performing arts complex in Perth and the Sydney Theater Company (STC), which manages among other facilities the iconic Sydney Opera House.

Sometimes these creative Australian ideas about responding to climate change hit the international arena and catch on with a vengeance. In March 2007, the Sydney region hosted the first ever Earth Hour, a campaign to get businesses and households to switch off their electricity for one hour during the evening. At 7:30 p.m. on March 31, Sydneysiders—some 2.2 million households strong, and some 2,100 businesses—turned off their lights for an hour. The brainchild of World Wildlife Fund–Australia, and in partnership with the *Sydney Morning Herald* (the city's main newspaper), the event was strongly supported by the city of Sydney and its mayor, Clover Moore. It was a resounding success on every measure. A large amount of energy was saved (a more than 10 percent reduction in consumption for that hour—the equivalent, according to organizers, of taking forty-eight thousand cars off the road), an important symbolic commitment was made by residents and businesses, and a strong message was sent around the country and world about the importance of conserving energy and addressing climate change.

Some fears about the event were not realized (no increase in burglaries seen, for instance), but perhaps more importantly, Sydneysiders captured back the evening sky and had some fun in the process. As Mayor Moore notes: "Instead there was the magical sight of stars appearing in the night sky, families picnicking outdoors, top-notch restaurants serving dinner by candlelight. . . . The spirit of camaraderie and goodwill was palpable, and the event was reported around the world" (Moore, 2007). The event has now gone global, and many cities around the world, including Chicago, Toronto, Copenhagen, and Manila, participated in Earth Hour 2008 (see http://www.earthhour.org).

Much of the long-term progress in reducing energy consumption and greenhouse gas emissions will result from the many exemplary green building initiatives and projects found in Australian cities. Australia leads the way in efforts to mainstream and institutionalize green building— ahead of the United States, I would contend—and this happens in many ways, through many different initiatives. Much of the current flurry of green building around Australia stems from a combination of new regula- tory and green building rating systems, some national, others state or local. One of the two national systems is the Australian Building Greenhouse Rating (ABGR) system, administered by state governments and nation- ally by the NSW Department of Environment and Climate Change. Under this voluntary program, buildings are awarded up to 5 stars (including half stars), based on actual monitoring of energy usage over a twelve-month period (and with yearly renewal required). A 4-star rating under ABGR de- notes "excellent" performance, while a 5-star rating denotes "exceptional." The ABGR has been embraced by public agencies and private companies and does seem to have stimulated buildings (and tenants) to use less en- ergy. The Henry Deane Building in downtown Sydney is one prominent example—receiving 4.5 stars under the ABGR and serving partly as the home for the NSW's Department of Planning. The building reduces con- sumption in several ways, including through high-tech, energy-efficient lighting ("T5 luminaries with electronic ballasts"), windows, and air- conditioning.

A second national-level green building rating system, the Green Star Rating System, is operated by the Green Building Council of Aus- tralia (GBCA; the equivalent of the U.S. Green Building Council) and awards up to 6 stars (prospectively) based on environmental impacts in nine categories (management, indoor environmental quality, energy, transport, water, materials, land use and ecology, emissions, and innovation). It is largely modeled after the American LEED (Leadership in Energy and Envi- ronmental Design) and British BREAAM (Standards for Building Research Establishment Environmental Assessment Method) systems. As of 2007, the GBCA was reviewing more than four hundred buildings aiming to be above 4 stars (a substantial increase over the one hundred buildings from the previous year), with one from Sydney (the Macquarrie Bank building by Multiplex) aiming to be the first commercial 6 star–rated building.

While it may be somewhat confusing to an outsider to see two such systems in use (one for design and one for actual use), there is no question that they have had a positive impact in helping to raise the green bar for new office construction. Many builders and designers are striving to reach the highest rating, but so far this has been difficult. Only two office build- ings, the CH2 office and 40 Albert Rowe (both in Melbourne and described below) have been awarded the 6 stars under the GBCA's system, while others are still trying to reach that standard. And, while the systems are voluntary, they have increasingly been incorporated into state building mandates and government leasing requirements.

New South Wales has gone the farthest of all the Australian states in terms of imposing green building standards. In 2004, the NSW Department of Planning (then the Department of Infrastructure, Planning and Natural Resources, or DIPNR) rolled out its innovative Web-based mandatory green building program called BASIX (Building Sustainability Index). Building designs are evaluated in this system against five indices: water, thermal/comfort, energy, landscape, and stormwater.

Two specific performance targets must be met: a 40 percent reduction in potable water use and a 25 percent reduction in greenhouse emissions (which rose to 40 percent in 2006), as compared with what an average structure uses. The system has imposed this requirement on a phased basis—single-family units were the first to have to comply, and all multi-family structures followed in October 2005. The mandatory system began with a first tier of Sydney metro councils in July 2004 and eventually became mandatory for the entire state in 2006.

Applicants generate the BASIX certificate, which must accompany applications for a development permit. Local inspectors ensure that at the time of construction, design features are actually constructed and realized. There is a unique do-it-yourself aspect to the BASIX system; architects and builders access the BASIX system online, plugging in design information about the house or building—such as its orientation, floor area, roof color, and type and extent of landscaping—as well as the location's post code number, which evaluates it against the particular microclimate found there. The system is thus able to take into account the hotter, drier climates encountered in building in the western Sydney suburbs, for instance.

By all accounts the requirements are working well, and most believe they are resulting in much better designed buildings, especially buildings that clearly exert a smaller ecological footprint. By NSW Department of Planning estimates, the ten-year environmental savings will be massive: 287 billion liters of water conserved, and 9.5 million fewer tonnes of greenhouse gas emission (estimated to be the equivalent of "taking 2.6 million cars off the road") (New South Wales Department of Planning, 2005b).

The system also takes account of regional environmental differences, such as differences in climate and rainfall in different parts of the state. "BASIX applies bonuses for well-designed naturally ventilated houses, recognizes that smaller homes use less energy and forces larger homes to be far more efficient." (New South Wales Department of Planning, 2005a).

Some twelve thousand BASIX certificates were issued in the first year of operation (New South Wales Department of Planning 2005b). No particular ecological feature, technology, or design is mandated—it is up to the designer to specify the package of things that will reach the mandatory targets. Preliminary compliance evaluation suggests, however, that most homes are including certain sustainability features, such as water-efficient bathroom fixtures, rainwater tanks, eaves for window shading, and (in one in four homes) a solar hot water heater.

Getting the developers and local governments on board and supportive took some convincing, but they eventually saw the benefits of having one uniform standard throughout the state. The politics of BASIX received a boost when drought struck the whole of Australia. Drought has certainly helped on the water side—there is a serious need to do something about water consumption all across Australia. Because the drought is seen to be linked to climate change, there is a real need to have governments doing something to respond to this global crisis and reduce carbon emissions. The Web-based system is also unique in that it looks at interactions among different design features, such as showing how water-saving showers can reduce greenhouse gases.

For a relatively small country, Australia has a high number of globally significant examples of ecological design and building. Perhaps the most striking eco-building anywhere in the world is Melbourne's CH2 building. Few local authorities have been as ambitious in sustainability as the City of Melbourne. Mention is made elsewhere of the city's innovations in urban design, sustainability reporting, and transport, but their global showpiece is their new Council House—CH2. The building was planned to be "visionary," so that it had the "potential to change forever the way Australia—indeed the world—approaches ecologically sustainable design" (City of Melbourne, 2004b). And they may be right, as this structure does incorporate some revolutionary ecological design thinking.

The building was given the maximum rating of 6 stars by the Australian Green Building Council. This has led to a rash of commercial buildings across Australia trying to match this high standard not just for its ecological value but for the associated increase in productivity being shown by workers in the buildings due to their improved daylighting and more healthy environment.

This new ten-story structure, built adjacent to existing city offices in the very heart of the city, incorporates some unusual design features, such as its wavy-concrete ceiling system, which stores "coolth" through thermal mass and also contains chilled beam panels for air-conditioning (a tech-

Figure 2.8 Melbourne's newly opened Council House offices—CH2—is a visionary green building. Its healthy work environment, including fresh air and natural daylight, has already led to a substantial increase in worker productivity. Image rendering courtesy of the City of Melbourne.

nology that uses between one tenth and one third of the energy of normal air-conditioning; see figure 2.8). One hundred percent fresh air is delivered to work spaces through a sealed-access floor plenum. Its north facade is its most interesting visually. Rooftop wind turbines and an induced stack effect draw air up through the structure, and "vertical gardens" provide shading and enhance air quality and working conditions. A series of "shower towers" send cool water to a Phase Change Material tank in the basement (described as a kind of cooling battery) and then to the chilled ceiling panels. A heat purging system opens windows automatically in the evening, on the north and south facades. Photovoltaics, solar heating panels, and a cogeneration plant are also to be found on the building's roof, within a roof garden.

The building has eighty bike spaces and twenty car spaces for hybrid and biofuel vehicles, and shower facilities for bicyclists are adjacent to the bike-park. Another interesting element is the building's water harvesting system, which takes sewage from Collins Street and runs it through a "multi-water treatment" plant, generating usable water for toilet flushes, municipal fountains, and other nonpotable purposes. This "sewer mining" is considered to be a major part of how a city can generate a more distributed water system, but until CH2 it had not been allowed. The role of new sustainable technologies is not just to demonstrate technical feasibility but to test the institutional system's flexibility in adapting to the new world of sustainability.

Together these creative design elements have produced new council offices that are much more pleasant to work in and that use tremendously fewer environmental resources. The goal of improved productivity from the workforce appears to be happening, and yet the ecological footprint from the building shows just how much less impact on the planet we can have. Reductions in energy consumption, compared to existing offices, may be the most dramatic advantage. Estimates are that, overall, CH2 uses 85 percent less electricity and 72 percent less water than a 5-star building (City of Melbourne, 2004b). With even a modest 5 percent increase in the productivity of council work, the annual savings is predicted to be as much as $1.12 million (and a relatively short, ten-year payback period for all of the extra environmental features of the building). Other commercial green buildings in Australia (more than thirty-eight buildings have been certified by the GBCA, with more than four hundred in application) have found that the highest economic benefits have been generated from the improved productivity of the workforce due to the healthy and bright work environment (see http://www.gbcaus.org/).

A recent analysis of the first full year of CH2 occupancy shows that personnel productivity is actually significantly higher than predicted (a more than 10 percent increase in worker productivity, or about twice the extent predicted). This higher-than-expected increase in productivity, a direct result of the positive green qualities of the building (more natural light and fresh air), has reduced the payback period for these green design features from ten years to only seven (City of Melbourne, 2008; Paevera and Brown, 2008).

On the edge of the Melbourne central business district is another exemplary green building, the 60L building. Now home to prominent environmental groups, including the main office of the Australian Conservation Foundation (ACF), it has set several green building precedents. It uses an estimated one third of the energy of a typical office building of its size. It includes a number of interesting energy features, including good solar orientation, daylighting, and extensive use of light shelves (rooftop and window devices that direct sunlight into interior building spaces); natural ventilation through four thermal chimneys; and an automated louver system that allows for night purging. Other green building features include a rooftop garden, use of nontoxic materials, waterless urinals and water-efficient fixtures, collection of rainwater in two ten-thousand-liter tanks, on-site wastewater and gray-water treatment, and reuse of water for toilet flushing and landscape watering. Extensive reuse of building materials and concrete was employed with 60 percent "recycled aggregate." The building also creatively preserves and incorporates an existing three-story structure in the front, including an 1800s-heritage facade.

The site for 60L was chosen to provide access to nearby public transit (rail), and the design also incorporates parking for thirty-five bikes and related shower facilities. Trees were planted in Western Victoria to compensate for the remaining greenhouse gas emissions of the building, making it a carbon-neutral office building.

Perhaps the most interesting feature of the project has been the effort to educate tenants about its green features and to ensure that they follow the philosophy behind the building. To this end, the notion of a "green lease" has been employed, which commits tenants to adhere to the building's energy management plan and provides them with an environmental manual and orientation kit (see http://www.60Lgreenbuilding.com).

Subtly encouraging its occupants to engage in a bit more physical activity during the day, the design includes two prominent stairways. There is an elevator, but a conscious effort was undertaken to make the stairs the clearly preferred option. The stairs are "unashamedly 'front-and-centre.' . . . We very much want to encourage people to use the stairs rather than the lift, which is placed more towards the back of the atrium," says Mike Krockenburger of the ACF (see http://www.60Lgreenbuilding.com/health.htm).

Sydney has not let its great competitor get away with leadership in the sustainability arena. Sydney's efforts have perhaps been just as significant because they have shown what the private sector can do using the latest in sustainable building technologies while ensuring they can remain financially competitive. The "30 The Bond" building was the first iconic sustainable building in Sydney (figure 2.9). It was built by Lend Lease on the

Figure 2.9 An innovative green building in Sydney, "30 the Bond," uses much less energy than a typical building of its size. Open, daylight stairwells have significantly reduced the use of elevators, and the energy needed to power them. *Photo credit:* Tim Beatley

former site of the Sydney gas works, into sandstone carved away by convicts; the remaining wall is a heritage-protected feature, creatively incorporated as a key characteristic of the building. When entering on the ground level, the wall is the most dramatic presence and comprises a character backdrop for the life of this structure. The wall, which can be seen from the open floor plan from several levels, seeps and drips water from the hill above and is itself an important part of the energy strategy, providing thermal mass cooling the air. There are usually around six hundred people in the space, but it is very pleasant and cool. It is "cool" in other ways too— the open spaces and corridors were designed in collaboration with the workforce, who asked for something akin to a city structure with planned meeting spaces in each corridor to ensure that staff interact accidentally as well as in planned meetings. There are two "chill-out" areas per floor— separated common rooms where workers can crash and relax by windows that can be opened to the outside. Lend Lease uses the benefits of the workspace to help attract and keep young talent.

Other important features of the building include the use of chilled beam technology (the first time in Australia it has worked very well) as well as outer spaces that have blinds and louvers to block sun (these are automated but can also be controlled by the occupants). The design has had great success in reducing energy consumption, with estimates that the building uses about one third the energy per square meter than the previous buildings did. Elevators stand next to beautiful, open stairs—with the latter intentionally designed to make them look more enticing (this has worked as intended). Elevators have consumed just half the projected energy, so they are hardly used. The building is one hundred meters long, thirty-five meters wide, and nine stories high.

The building has a beautiful rooftop garden, with native plants arranged in the shape of a bar code, and two "grass benches" for sitting on. One hallmark of the project is the extensive community outreach process to engage the surrounding neighborhood. This has been very successful, among other things helping convince the Sydney Council to allow a "trafficable roof"—that is, one that can actually be walked on.

The Kogarah Town Square project, in the southern suburbs of Sydney, offers a marvelous example of integrating land use and good urban form with sustainability principles and design (figure 2.10). Here, a downtown redevelopment project on a council carport has brought a fairly dense mixed-used neighborhood, literally across the street from the city's main train station (and a relatively short commute to Sydney). It includes 194 apartments, retail and commercial space, and a community library. Intended to serve as a new model of a "vibrant and sustainable urban village," the development's energy and water systems are its most impressive elements, though it has also acted as a catalyst for creating a more walkable town center. It was designed from the beginning to take advantage of solar orientation, with northern orientation for most apartments, design for cross ventilation, and use of awnings, overhangs, and movable louvers to block the hot summer sun. Shiny metal awnings called "light shelves" are placed over windows to both act as shading devices when the sun is high in the sky and enable deeper natural light penetration into each room through reflection.

Most of the rooftop area of the Kogarah Town Square is producing power, as roof-integrated PVs essentially take the place of traditional roofing materials. Some 1,659 PV cells are employed, resulting in an annual reduction in carbon dioxide emissions of 143 tonnes (Kogarah Council, n.d.). The solar panels are estimated to produce about 60 percent of the energy needs of the development and have been funded through a grant from the Commonwealth's Australian Greenhouse Office. Energy-efficient appliances, low-energy lighting, and gas cooking are used to further reduce the

Figure 2.10 Kogarah Town Square, in the Sydney metropolitan area, is a transit-oriented development with many other green features. An innovative water management system collects and reuses some 80% of the water falling on the site. *Photo credit:* Tim Beatley

energy impacts. An interesting effort was made to make the energy and water features a visible part of this new urban neighborhood. Ground-level awnings, seen by those walking in and through the neighborhood, have eye-catching PVs in them, spaced in a way to let daylight pass through (figure 2.11). The portico of the library also incorporates similar highly visible PVs. A prominent feature in the project's public courtyard is a meandering stream and water feature, its design based on the work of Herbert Dreisetl, noted water designer and artist.

The town square's water system is perhaps its most unusual element. Described as an example of "integrated water sensitive urban design," it incorporates a dual pathway for stormwater, emphasizing collection, treatment, and reuse. So-called dirty stormwater from parking and street-level surfaces is collected in a cistern and used for landscape watering. The grass and landscaping are used as a natural system for cleaning and filtering contaminants. Rainwater collected from roofs—considered "clean" stormwater—follows a different path: it is also collected in a tank

Figure 2.11 The entire roof area of the Kogarah Town Square produces electricity, and PVs have even been installed on the awnings such as this one, producing power but also shading (and allowing some light to penetrate) pedestrian and shop spaces below. *Photo credit:* Tim Beatley

but is used instead for toilet flushing, for car washing, and for the project's notable plaza-level water feature. Signage explains the project's unique water feature and educates about the seriousness of the water problem and the need for conservation.

It is estimated that 85 percent of the water falling on-site is reused, resulting in a yearly savings in needed potable water of about eight thousand kiloliters (from the rainfall alone). The units are also designed to limit the amount of water consumed, through low-flow shower heads and other water-efficient appliances, reducing even further the extent of potable water use. The Kogarah project represents a partnership among several agencies, with the Commonwealth's Australian Greenhouse Office providing $1 million for the PVs, and with additional funding coming from NSW state agencies (Kogarah Council, n.d.).

Exemplary case studies also exist of local authorities applying green building standards to the retrofitting of existing municipal facilities. In Marrickville, in the Sydney metro region, an impressive example can be seen in the major rebuilding of the Tillman Park Children's Centre (a "children's centre and early childhood clinic"). It incorporates a number of green features, including passive solar (and internal design of rooms to maximize exposure of the children to daylight), natural ventilation (use of ventilation slots in doors, and a creative modification of acoustic louvers in the roof to facilitate convection), thermal mass and insulation, low-flow water fixtures and dual-flush toilets, avoidance of paints and material that off-gas, a heat pump water heater, and incorporation of a fifty-thousand-liter underground water tank fed by the building's roof and used for toilet flushing and landscape watering (Marrickville Council, n.d.-a). Permeable landscaping and use of native, low-water plant species were also part of the retrofit. Perhaps its most dramatic feature is the 4.8-kilowatt PV system on the roof. The panels add a visible amenity to the adjacent Tillman Park and are estimated to result in a reduction of 6 metric tons of carbon emissions each year.

There are also exemplary examples of green retrofits in other Australian cities, including the impressive office refurbishment of 40 Albert Road, in Melbourne. The headquarters office of technology company Szencorp, this five-story, 1,200-square-meter office structure underwent a comprehensive greening in 2005, including the use of a number of green technologies new to Australia. Along with CH2, it is one of only two structures to have received 6 green stars under the GBCA's rating system. Among the green elements are operable windows and cross ventilation, attention to bringing daylight into the structure (double-glazed windows, skylights, light sensors), an atrium that utilizes the thermal chimney effect to draw air through the building, a central vacuum system, and on-site electricity production from a combination of ceramic fuel cell, waste energy for hot water production, and rooftop photovoltaics. Low-flow water fixtures, waterless urinals, and rainwater harvesting reduce potable water demand by more than 8 percent (compared with a conventional office structure), on top of a 70 percent reduction in energy demand. Use of low-VOC (volatile organic compound) paint, carpets, and other materials; an innovative desiccant dehumidification system; and a central vacuum system have all significantly improved the indoor air quality of this building, and together these green features are likely improving worker comfort and productivity as well (Green Building Council of Australia, n.d.).

Christie Walk is an inspiring, sustainable infill project located not far from downtown Adelaide. Designed by Paul Downton of Ecopolis Architects, and named after a local environmental activist (Scott Christie), it is sensitively nestled into a T-shaped urban lot. A mix of townhouse homes, apartments, and straw bale cottages, it has an unusual look and feel. The project has the full complement of green ideas and features: solar orientation, design for natural ventilation, solar hot water heating, gray-water recycling, a rooftop garden, rainwater harvesting, and the use of vines and vegetation to shade living spaces. Use of straw bale in a more vertical urban site is unusual. The common spaces outside are especially noteworthy, including a community garden and common places to sit and socialize. It has zero parking because residents can walk to everything they need in the city. It has become a positive model of how to design and fit considerable density onto an oddly shaped, leftover urban space. And best of all, it is within the city, where one can walk and not need an automobile.

Christie Walk is the most tangible outcome of a visionary nonprofit organization named Urban Ecology Australia Inc. (UEA), which proposed in the early 1990s one of the most ambitious ecocity districts anywhere, called the Halifax EcoCity Project. Downton and his colleagues at UEA, with the direct engagement of much of the community, developed a truly visionary scheme for redeveloping a 2.4-hectare site. It imagined a new urban community of about a thousand people, with an organic green architecture, solar and renewable energy integrated into its fabric, other green features (such as a solar aquatics system for sewage treatment), and an ecology center. It was to be a mixed-use and very pedestrian environment, with a central village square, and very distinctive expansive rooftop gardens on the two- to five-story buildings.

Among the design products generated through the project was a bird's-eye plan of what the community would look like, the skyline of this organic community with its interesting architecture, rooftop spaces, and (labeled) mosaic of green ideas and technologies (e.g., see Urban Ecology Australia Inc, 1993). This rendering especially depicted a view of the future that was at once utopian and tangible. To Downton's regret, however, a more conventional development was eventually built on the site. Yet, the design of the Halifax Ecocity Project continues to inspire and to serve as a model vision of what might be possible. Downton observes that Halifax has "attained a vaguely legendary status as one of the great unbuilt visions of urban ecological design," similar to many of the concepts of Richard Register in the United States (Downton, 2005).

One of the best Australian examples of an eco-house is the creative retrofit of an older inner Sydney home by environmental lawyer Michael Mobbs and his family. They sought to incorporate some bold and ambitious green features at the time of a significant home renovation, resulting in a story and a model that at least many Sydneysiders (and indeed many Australians) are aware of. In the renovation, they aspired to produce all of the energy they needed (indeed to be a net energy exporter—a goal they have nearly reached); to retain, treat, and reuse all wastewater on-site (through an innovative filter bed system located under the home's back deck); and to provide all their potable water needs through collection and storage of rainwater (another goal they have mostly met).

In the process, they achieved these green goals through creative design (e.g., an ingenious enclosed gutter and drainpipe system that collects rooftop rainwater). Michael has written a widely disseminated book about the house, *Sustainable House* (Mobbs, 2000), and has started a green building consultancy. Many tours of the house have been given, and the house has done much to spread the word about what is possible, with modest financial investment, on an existing, compact, attached, inner-suburb home, a style and type quite common in that part of Australia.

Model sustainable new homes have been sponsored and built in several Australia cities as a way to demonstrate the green building and living possibilities. In the close-in city of Subiaco, near Perth, is a very recent example of this idea, with an effort to "green" a fairly standard home in a new, emerging development. Sponsored by the Subiaco Redevelopment Authority and the Subiaco city council, the house has been a very popular place for visits, including one by Prince Charles, who compared it favorably with projects he is promoting in the United Kingdom.

The exterior of the house is not visually dramatic, a bit drab and plain, and one is a bit underwhelmed when seeing it for the first time. This was part of the exercise of designing and building a model sustainable home: to blend this house in with existing homes and to demonstrate that any home can be sustainable. The interior, by contrast, is quite nice and interesting—light penetrates in from the upper level through a high-pitched roof and windows that send light down the house through a rammed-earth stairwell, providing extensive daylight throughout the home. Much of the construction material for the house had been recycled, including recycled concrete crushed into the rammed earth walls, and wood from plantation timber. Energy savings are impressive, with as much as 50 percent less energy use than for a regular home of its size. A study by the Commonwealth Scientific and Industrial Research Organization (CSIRO) compared this home with other model green homes and found it to be the most energy efficient.

One of the more unique elements of the home is its creative landscaping, particularly the edible landscaping, which includes the planting of an almond tree and grape and passionfruit vines. A creative, built-in system of elevated plant and herb beds provides extensive areas for growing vegetables and flowers. One aim was to include enough space to provide for the vegetable-growing needs of a typical West Australian family. Because of the universal design goals of the home, these gardens can be tended easily by someone in a wheelchair.

Managing Water More Sustainably

Already the driest continent, Australia has been in the midst of a devastating drought. With climate change expected to make matters worse, Australian cities and states face a future of increasingly severe water shortages. Already, there are a number of creative local examples and exemplary practices to report. Developing more distributed water systems that seek to design in stormwater collection and water conservation features at the neighborhood and building scales can help close the cycle in a local area. This is a growing goal in Australian cities, especially given the reductions in water flow in the twenty-first century. Distributed water systems are becoming standard practice in most new Australian subdivisions (see chapter 5 in Newman and Kenworthy, 1999, which sets out this concept, although no real demonstrations were available at that time).

The Sydney region, while facing major water supply issues, has also been an early leader in sustainable water planning. A joint initiative called Riverlife, begun in 2002 among the Marrickville, Canterbury, and Strathfield Councils, forms an umbrella to support a variety of restoration, education, and watershed planning activities related to the Cooks River. There are now walking and kayaking tours of the river, riverbank restoration projects, and a streamwatch program that works to involve schools in river monitoring and conservation.

Community-based sustainable watershed planning is one of the more interesting elements of Riverlife, and the methodology and process for this have been piloted in the Illawara Road subcatchment, in south Marrickville. The site of significant flooding and stormwater management issues, this community has been directly engaged in the planning process and has developed a water vision for 2050. The council, in collaboration with researchers at Monash University, has developed a master plan for the subcatchment that identifies and uniquely models different mixes of stormwater management options and configurations in the community. The model and decision support system, referred to by the acronym *MUSIC* (Model for Urban Stormwater Improvement Conceptualization), allows for the assessment of different combinations of measures (different bioretention systems and options) against different water quality targets and has potential for use in other communities and watersheds (e.g., see Marrickville Council, 2003, 2004).

Some of the most impressive and leading-edge examples of water reuse and reclamation technology can be seen, not surprisingly, in Australian cities. A Water Reclamation and Management Scheme (or WRAMS) is a system for collecting and treating stormwater and wastewater and re-using it in toilet flushing, landscape watering, and so forth. It was put in place in the Sydney Olympic Park, for instance, and to many it represents a leading model (figure 2.12).

In most Australian cities, 95 percent of potable water is used for nonpotable purposes, according to Nicole Campbell, environmental director for the Olympic Park. Hence, the initiatives in the Park are designed to steer reuse water into these nonpotable functions, especially flushing toilets and watering gardens. The giant roof of the Olympic stadium is in fact a water-collecting device that channels rain into a large tank under the sports field. This is used to water the pitch and surrounding grounds. Also, recycling of water in the surrounding suburbs of Newington has been achieved by being connected to the WRAMS (originally the athlete village).

In the Olympic Park and in Newington Village, 40 percent of reused water is used for toilet flushing and the other 60 percent is used in irrigated/operational washdown. WRAMS, plus other water conservation measures, saves 850 million liters of drinking water each year.

Much recent emphasis has also been placed on the concept of water-sensitive urban design, generally known to all by the acronym *WSUD*.

Figure 2.12 The Water Reclamation and Management Scheme (or WRAMS) collects, treats and reuses stormwater and wastewater in the Sydney Olympic Park. *Photo credit:* Tim Beatley

This concept, first developed by a team in Perth, was seeded in the 1980s but has taken ten to twenty years before finally being recognized. Water-sensitive urban design in Australia has come to refer broadly to efforts at including water as a central design element or concern in the design of homes, buildings, and neighborhoods. The philosophy is one of emphasizing the small scale and decentralized, often applied to stormwater collection and treatment through a variety of techniques from bioswales to rainwater tanks to permeable paving to tree planting and revegetation, among many others—many of the practices that in the United States would be commonly referred to as LID, or low-impact development. But Australian WSUD is often more comprehensive, more holistic, and just as likely to include water conservation, reuse, and reclamation measures.

Victoria Park is a new water-sensitive development project in the suburb of Zetland, in inner Sydney, that illustrates well the value of WSUD model projects—in this case designed and built by LandCom, the State's land development corporation (figure 2.13). Here, a mixed-use neighborhood with many sustainability qualities has placed water issues and

Figure 2.13 Victoria Park, in Sydney, is an example of water sensitive urban design (or WSUD). Here, roadway surfaces are designed to direct stormwater into vegetated swales where it is kept onsite and allowed to percolate back into the ground. *Photo credit:* Tim Beatley

creative management of stormwater at the core of its design. Extensive use of bio-retention swales has been integrated into the formal parks and roads, along with extensive vegetation throughout (one hundred thousand native shrubs and one thousand trees). Along all major roadways, sawtooth drainage openings allow water to drain into vegetated swales. The major parks and recreational spaces in the community are all designed to serve as rainwater collection points and to allow natural retention and percolation of rainwater.

Given the critical nature of water and the semipermanent drought conditions that exist in Australia, much thought has been given to how the country's water demand can be reduced and its water reused. A new, green three-bedroom home in Clovelly (near Sydney) is equipped with three rainwater tanks that collect and store water from the roof (together, the tanks provide nine thousand liters of storage) (figure 2.14). The collected rainwater is then used to supply the bathrooms and showers and the home's small swimming pool, so a separate set of water lines is incorporated.

Figure 2.14 A new house in the Clovelly neighborhood of Sydney incorporates a number of green features, including this unusual three-level green wall for treating and reusing the home's graywater. *Photo credit:* Photo by Nick Bowers, Courtesy of Steve Kennedy Architects

The house's most interesting water conservation feature, however, is its gray-water system, which collects and treats gray water and sends it back to the house for toilet flushing and washing machine use. Most innovatively, the architect, in collaboration with an environmental engineer, designed a three-level green wall, with gray water filtered through these layers of vegetation. The wall is 2.1 meters high, 6 meters long, and 400 millimeters wide (Veale, 2006). Steve Kennedy believes this green wall is "the only greywater treatment system of its type in the world" (Kennedy Associates Architects, n.d., p. 5). Also of great interest here is the way that water has been designed into the home as an explicit effort to "reintegrate" water and climate into our lives.

Creative efforts have been undertaken in many of the local councils and state agencies in Australia to reduce water consumption. Waterwise is an initiative in West Australia to promote low-water, native gardens. Waterwise also seeks to get the message out through garden centers, a place with considerable opportunity to reach residents and at a time when it might influence their gardening choices and plant selections.

There are now twenty-four garden centers in Western Australia that have been "endorsed" under the Water Corporation's Waterwise Garden Centre Program, as of 2008 (figure 2.15). To get the endorsement, the garden centers must meet certain minimum criteria, including training staff in waterwise plants and planting techniques and how they can relate to other waterwise programs run by the Water Corporation, such as their rebate on showerheads, front-loading washing machines, groundwater bores, water tanks, and gray-water recycling schemes.

The educational component of Waterwise reaches to classrooms (kindergarten through high school). In Western Australia, there are, as of 2008, 368 public and private schools participating in the parallel program Waterwise Schools. Here, schools are required to undertake a series of steps, including devising and adopting a school water policy and developing and incorporating a water curriculum into the school. In participating schools, not only do students now learn about water but they undertake a series of projects and activities aimed at understanding and reducing water use in the school itself. At one participating primary school in Fremantle (the school attended by my then-six-year-old daughter), a beautiful interior courtyard had been planted in native, low-water species of plants and flowers, a daily, beautiful reminder of the need to conserve water.

Despite the availability of material and demonstrations on low-water gardening, the cultural perception about gardens is slow to change. One developer, Multiplex, at Vale in Perth, has tried to help facilitate this change

Figure 2.15 An initiative of the Water Corporation in Western Australia, the Waterwise Garden Centres Program works to educate, train and certify gardens centers about water conserving plants and gardening. At this center in Perth, plants are labeled according to how much water they are likely to need. *Photo credit:* Tim Beatley

by creating an incentive of a $2,000 landscaping package that must include low-water-using native plants and only 20 percent lawn. In the first stage of their development, 90 percent of people did not follow the guidelines because contractors and householders found the change too difficult. But a series of workshops from TV gardening expert Josh Byrne were helpful, and the next stages saw the take up improved to around 80 percent. Now they are trying to coordinate planting so that in each street there will always be at least one native flowering species with nectar available for birds at every time of the year.

Lifestyle and Green Living

Little long-run progress will likely be achieved in promoting green urbanism and sustainable cities without concerted and systematic efforts to instill a new ethic of sustainable living among the larger public. Spending time in Australian cities, one sees unusual evidence of creative efforts and real commitment to influencing these broader patterns of consumption and lifestyle. It happens in many different ways in Australian cities and states, but the extent to which serious importance is given to educating, empowering, and providing practical guidance about how to live more sustainably is commendable. Promoting and facilitating green urban living and lifestyles is viewed as a necessary role to be played by local councils.

Community education and sustainability resource centers, for instance, have been established in a number of cities, with some creative and impressive efforts to reach the community. The City of Fremantle has sponsored several green living initiatives under the label of "Living Smart," a partnership among the City of Fremantle, Murdoch University, the Meeting Place Centre, and Southern Metropolitan Region Councils. The intent is to empower individuals through education to move their behaviors and lifestyle in the direction of sustainability. Living Smart enables households to examine their use of energy, water, food, waste, gardens, and transport, with an emphasis on household and neighborhood solutions. The program involves families in a series of talks and workshops as well as some field trips in the community to see households where sustainability innovations are in place.

Preliminary evaluation suggests that this program has changed behavior and also increased knowledge about the community and feelings of being part of the community. Some 91 percent of the participants reported that "they felt more a part of the community" as a result of the program (Raphael et al., n.d.). Such green living education programs suggest that through them it is possible to build community bonds and a sense of community, as well as the other obvious sustainability gains. An expansion of this program in partnership with TravelSmart will now be instituted on a trial basis as a model for state government involvement in reducing household use of water, energy, waste, and car travel.

Gosford, as a further example, has adopted and is implementing an Environmental Education Strategy to help the city move from "simply raising awareness of environmental issues in the community to developing education programs aiming to change the behaviors of our community towards the environment" (Gosford City Council, 2004, p. 25).

It is also common for local councils to sponsor major community events that focus on environmental and sustainability themes and messages. In June 2005, for example, Randwick Council, in the Sydney metro region, held its EcoLiving Fair, which included various exhibits, distribution of free native plants grown in the council's nursery, and talks by prominent environmental experts (including University of New South Wales dean of science Mike Archer, author of the provocative book *Going Native*; more on that in chapter 5). The City of Sydney's Live Green event at Victoria Park in 2007 drew 10,000 visitors. Randwick also puts on a series of sustainability workshops for its residents, an element of the council's Sustaining Our City initiative. The most recent topics addressed in these free workshops include household strategies to reduce environmental impacts, creating native gardens, organic techniques for weed control, and creating sustainable permaculture food gardens. Similarly, in Kogarah Council, "Earthworks Courses" are offered to citizens on such topics as recycling, waste management, composting, and worm farming. These are just a few examples of what can be seen as a common, consistent goal of Australian cities to promote environmental awareness and to facilitate ecological living and more sustainable lifestyles. This is viewed as a legitimate and important local government role.

One of the more interesting public education projects in the Sydney region is the "ecological footprint challenge." A joint initiative of three councils in northern Sydney, and with funding from the NSW Department of Environment and Conservation, twenty-five participants took part in this unique idea for promoting sustainable lifestyles. More specifically, participants were grouped into teams of seven to eight members each, with each grouping done by geographical area or neighborhood. Participants in the twenty-to-forty age-group were targeted. Initially, the participants were taken on a field trip to a local museum and asked to calculate their current ecological footprint. As a base measure from which to start, the challenge is to see which team is able to go the furthest in reducing their footprints. Along the way, the participants receive training, go on field trips, and generally learn about the sustainable living options available. Each week, the staff presents the team with different themes to consider, most recently "feeding frenzy," a unit focused on options for more sustainable food and eating.

Interestingly, many of the participants have kept online journals documenting their experiences and revelations along the way. Several of the more skeptical participants have now become the biggest supporters of sustainability, and the process does seem to have had a transformative impact for many of them. But the organizers see the potential impact beyond the twenty-five participants; the program has received good press (a nice article in the green supplement to the *Sydney Morning Herald*, for example), and each participant is expected to reach out to others in his or her family, network of friends, and community. The Web site and journal entries provide potentially powerful educational opportunities for the broader public, although it is not clear at this point what the larger community impact will eventually be.

· A reality TV show in Perth, produced by Australian network SBS, followed the struggles of two families, the Edwardses and the Shepherds, as they sought to substantially reduce their consumption in four areas— energy, water, waste, and transport—and to bring their ecological foot- prints closer to sustainable levels, all with the help of an eco-coach assigned by the show. The show, called the Eco House Challenge, was quite popular, watched by many viewers who were encouraged to play along online and who, presumably, through this visceral reality style of TV, would consider how they might also make changes to their own lifestyles. A similar ABC show, *Carbon Cops*, has followed, and reruns are planned for both shows. The demand for relevant household-scale information on how to be more sustainable seems to be exploding, especially after Al Gore's tour and film, which led to a rash of neighborhood-based climate change groups being formed; in Melbourne, there are more than seventy that have formed into a loose coalition.

North Sydney has also been exploring the development of a new sus- tainability learning center, to be located on the site of former coal-loading tunnels. Perhaps a Duisberg Landscape–style park, it would serve as a demonstration site for many sustainability ideas and technologies (Beatley, 2005). Such sustainability education centers are already quite common in Perth and southwest WA, with centers at Rockingham, Fremantle (two), Maylands, Melville, Bibra Lake, and Denmark (see http://www.istp.mur- doch.edu.au/ISTP/casestudies/casestudsmain.html).

Many of the eco-centers visited for this book are not only important meeting places and educational venues but also impressive green buildings and facilities themselves. The Piney Lakes Environmental Education Cen- ter in Melville (in Perth) is a terrific example of a exemplary green building that provides space, exhibits, and programs for community education about the environment while also providing a building that teaches by example. Designed by noted Perth green architect Garry Baverstock, the building incorporates principles of climate-sensitive design and generates most of the power it needs from an on-site wind turbine and PV panels. Beginning with a reference to the aboriginal history of the land, the building assumes the shape of a boomerang and is solar oriented to the north, with a long east–west axis. "Solar verandahs" allow in the winter sun but shade the more intense summer sun, and a number of other intelligent design fea- tures take advantage of (and teach about) natural cooling and shading (such as the use of eaves, solar pergolas, windows in strategic locations, and a high thermal mass from its three-hundred-millimeter rammed earth walls). One dramatic feature is a map of the Beeliar Wetlands Chain, of which the site is a part, painted on the concrete floor of the main hall. The building and adjacent nature reserve have extensive space for group meetings and school visits, and the center puts on a variety of workshops, lecture series, environmental festivals, and night walks through the bush.

These exemplary community eco-centers commonly emphasize helping residents and visitors understand the native landscapes and ecology of the places they inhabit. The Rockingham Regional Environmental Center, in the city of Rockingham (south of Perth), is a case in point. Known as Naragebup, a combination of words from the aboriginal Nungar language, this center features an impressive green building (walls constructed of straw bale, reclaimed materials such as roofing beams from old telephone poles, and energy produced mostly from wind and solar) as well as extensive landscape exhibits that educate about more harmonious relationships to land (including a nature trail highlighting the ecology of the coastal dune system, a bush tucker garden, and a demonstration rotational organic garden). Most interesting is the center's site adjacent to Lake Richmond, one of the few locations of thrombolites, or living rocks, which are living assemblages of ancient microorganisms. Visitors learn about this unique (and threatened) ecological community and its connection with the early history of the earth (thrombolites helped generate the oxygen that created conditions for life) and then can stroll along the lake and see the real living thing.

The Port Phillip EcoCentre, in the Melbourne metro area, is another exemplary case. Located adjacent to the St. Kilda Botanical Gardens, its main building, the EcoHouse, serves as an important demonstration for many green design ideas (rooftop solar, rainwater harvesting, use of recycled and sustainably harvested wood) and as a meeting and staging point for local environmental and community groups. It is also the site of a model sustainable garden. The center is also a point of distribution for green products and technologies (e.g., recently offering a water-efficient showerhead exchange program). Not far from the center is a unique feature, a resident population of the world's smallest species of penguin, the little or fairy penguin (*Eudyptula minor*), which has taken up a home at the St. Kilda breakwater. These penguins are a breakaway group from a much larger colony on Phillip Island. The EcoCentre has taken on the task of educating and advocating for the penguins and has started an interesting ecotourism service called Beach Buddies (using as a logo an image of the penguins against the skyline of the city), which is financially supported by several local foundations and offers a walking tour that ends at the penguin colony.

The Manly Environmental Center, in the city of Manly, is another long-standing and similarly effective community-based institution. Created in 1991 and located above the city's food co-op, it is a knowledge distribution point (with hundreds of reports and books) and an important platform for environmental advocacy and volunteerism in the city. The center has been active on many fronts, especially in pushing for the protection and conservation of its two notable local animals, little (fairy) penguins and long-nosed bandicoots. Ecological centers such as Manly's and Port Phillip's become points of advocacy and staging points for efforts at protecting flora and fauna. Piney Lakes has undertaken a research and conservation initiative aimed at the rare Quenda, and the Rockingham center serves as a rehabilitation center for young Loggerhead turtles who have been swept too far south as a result of the Leeven current. These eco-centers and environmental education facilities serve multiple important functions and become community beacons of conservation and hope. Every community needs a beautiful place like this that embodies its environmental commitments, and seemingly every Australian community has one.

Another way sustainability education is manifest is through the high degree of activity in bush regeneration in Australian cities, especially in Sydney, where techniques for bushcare are often an integral part of environmental education centers (see chapter 5).

Conclusions and Lessons Learned

In both the United States and Australia, much responsibility and initiative devolves down to the local level. In Australia, this has translated into real local commitment and innovation in sustainability. Local councils throughout the country are integrating sustainability into plans and actions, and sustainability has been mainstreamed in Australian local governments to an impressive degree. It is both a meaningful concept (meaningful to elected officials, council staff, and citizens alike) and an operational tool.

It is also notable how in many Australian cities this commitment to sustainability is finding creative application in parallel policy and management sectors. In transport, commitments to sustainability are resulting in the development of new green vehicle technologies (e.g., the hydrogen fuel cell bus in Perth and the solar electric bus in Adelaide) as well as new operational strategies (e.g., Melbourne's green tram depot). Sustainability and green urbanism in these progressive Australian communities is viewed not as a stand-alone or isolated value or commitment but, rather, as one that is productively spilling over into other areas in some very interesting ways.

These many exemplary programs and efforts also show convincingly that sustainability ultimately requires multiple actors and many different strategies. Not only is there much value in mandates—for instance, in the area of green building—but much can also be accomplished through education and outreach and through the partnerships seen in innovative programs like the Waterwise garden centers and schools. Ultimately, changing the direction of a culture and an urban population will require efforts on many different fronts by many different individuals and organizations. And cultural movement will require some explicit commitment at the local level to long-term education and awareness building and to efforts to facilitate and empower local residents to live more sustainably. The importance given to supporting sustainable living—through a variety of creative efforts, from visiting those who have newly arrived in a neighborhood to sponsoring and funding sustainability fairs and festivals—is encouraging indeed.

States invariably provide the context and specific funding programs for these innovations, but in many ways local councils have led the states into these programs. The specific stories from such cities as Adelaide, Brisbane, and North Sydney offer marvelous creative ideas, from designating solar precincts to changing parking fee structures to favor smaller environmental and fuel-efficient vehicles. The local governments in Australia also offer important insights about ecological and sustainable governance. The preparation of state of environment reports, sustainability action plans, environmental levies that provide new specific funding, and efforts at educating and actively engaging and involving citizens in the hands-on work of urban ecosystem restoration all speak to a profoundly different way of operating and all provide a glimpse of a different way of living. The inspirational examples of sustainability projects—from the Kogarah Town Square to Christie Walk to the carbon-neutral campaigns and initiatives like Greenfleet—have much to teach American communities, despite the differing climate and social contexts.

The practices of green Australian cities offer special insights in several key areas—water and energy in particular. As drought conditions and water shortages become more prevalent in the United States, many of the creative water-conserving projects and strategies described here will become especially useful. Water reclamation schemes, such as the WRAMS at the Sydney Olympic Park; creative efforts at promoting more water-efficient gardens and plantings, as in the case of Waterwise; and building designs that utilize less water and creatively capture and reuse water will be compelling models of what will be needed in a future world of diminishing water supply. Future buildings and urban neighborhoods in many American cities should consider the water reuse standard of a project like the Kogarah Town Square, which reuses and recycles an impressive 85 percent of the water falling on that site.

Equally true, integrating solar and renewable energy into community planning and design will be needed in the United States in the future. Such efforts as Adelaide's move to reenvision itself as a solar city and to redefine every space and aspect of the cityscape as an opportunity to produce power from sustainable, renewable means, and New South Wales's BASIX system, which has shown how to reduce 40 percent of energy and water in all new houses in a relatively painless way, show that innovation in governance can indeed be considered both essential and feasible.

3

New and Hopeful Perspectives on Ecological Assets

A visit to Australia is a wondrous experience of breathtaking landscapes and unusual flora and fauna—in many ways an unparalleled natural heritage. But as a nation and a culture, it has not always adequately conserved or shepherded this special patrimony and in the future clearly faces some extreme challenges in protecting and restoring its environment. The pace of land degradation from dryland salinity continues at a fast clip, biodiversity continues to be degraded, and threats such as the invasive cane toad present new dangers. The ecological footprint of Australians is high, and in many ways like the United States, its population and culture have not really faced up to the need for fundamental lifestyle and behavioral changes. Dependence on fossil fuels, water shortages, the likely impacts of climate change—these and other trends cause one to be less than optimistic about the long-term sustainability of Australian society.

Nevertheless, there are signs of positive changes, and good examples and hopeful stories of efforts to confront these problems, often in very creative ways. In this chapter, I review several of the more impressive examples of creative attempts to profoundly shift the way resources and environment are considered, a shift generally away from a short-term extractive view to one that sees the need to nurture, protect, and restore the intrinsic qualities of Australia's incredible landscape. In most cases, these examples are both imperfect and incomplete, the former because they perhaps do not go far enough or fast enough, the latter because they are still unfolding, still evolving. Yet, they are inspirational stories that provide positive guidance and lessons for similar efforts in other parts of the world.

Repairing the Southwest's Unique Landscape

There are few places as biologically wondrous as the Southwest. For a visitor such as myself, the diversity, the biological uniqueness, was an incredible and special surprise. Knowledge about and appreciation of this biological diversity, especially the amazing floristic diversity, have become more widespread in recent years in part because of the work of Russell Mittermeier and his colleagues at Conservation International assessing global biodiversity; they have declared the Southwest to be one of the world's biological "hotspots"—a region rich in biodiversity and substantially threatened. Originally one of eighteen hotspots globally (the most recent update puts the number of global hotspots at thirty-four), the Southwest remains the only place in Australia to make the list (Mittermeier et al., 2005; see http://www.biodiversityhotspots.org). Formally known as the Southwest Australia Botanical Province Hotspot, it covers an area of more than three hundred square kilometers (about 12 percent of the very large state of Western Australia).

In the words of Steve Hopper, former CEO of Kings Park in Perth (and now head of Kew Gardens in London) and one of the most eloquent supporters of the region's diversity, it is a landscape with "few parallels." An ancient landscape, never subject to marine inundation or glaciation, with no mountain building to speak of, it has been a harsh, nutrient-deficient environment that has required unique biological adaptations for survival.

> The absence of glaciation and significant mountain building for such immense periods has meant that the southwestern soils are deeply weathered. Rainfall over the last 270 million years has leached mineral nutrients and left sandy soils that are very poor compared to those of recently glaciated or mountainous terrain. It is little wonder that plant life in the southwest exhibits some of the most sophisticated root systems and partnerships with subsurface fungi and bacteria known for obtaining scarce nutrients from impoverished soil. (Hopper, 2003, p. 1)

There are several reasons for the immense diversity. It is an extremely old landscape, a part of the original Gondwana, or mega-continent, formed of ice some 300 million years ago but not volcanically active for 3 billion years. The geology and geography has given rise to a peninsula that functions biologically more like an island—with the Indian Ocean on two sides and with the dry desert inland to the east. Hopper talks about this unique environment of the Southwest as the result of "rampant evolution-ary forces swirling around us" (Hopper, 2003).

In the 1960s, only 3,600 plant species were recognized, while today the number is around 8,300. Astoundingly, some 75 to 80 percent of these are endemic, meaning they are found nowhere else. Each year brings the number higher as more are discovered, named, and studied, though there is some sense that the ultimate number of plant species will likely level off at about 10,000. The ecological gradations and variations of the region have produced considerable evolutionary adaptation across the region, and quite substantial "morphing" of species from east to west. Single species, such as the white-tailed black cockatoos, show signs of landscape adaptation—one beak shape east of the Albany Highway, a different beak shape west of the highway to match its different food sources there.

The diversity of reptiles is also especially high, and the area is home to a number of other unusual and interesting fauna (figure 3.1). These in-clude the Quokka (a small kangaroo found especially on Rottnest Island), the numbat (the emblematic species for Western Australia, though now quite rare), the honey possum, and the western swamp tortoise, all what Mittermeier, Myers, and Mittermeier (1999) refer to as "flagship species," or species that are seen as representative of an ecosystem or bioregion and its habitats and that help to garner public attention and support for con-servation.

In the face of this immense diversity are a host of real threats—some expected to observers from the outside, others more novel. Habitat de-struction has happened through a number of means, but especially through land clearance for agriculture. As recently as the 1960s, the state govern-ment had a major program to clear 1 million acres per year of bush, to expand the agricultural economy and populate the region, although this abruptly stopped in 1974 at the rabbit-proof fence, which now acts as a bar-rier to farmers but not to rabbits! Other significant threats have included timber harvesting; invasive species, especially rabbits, feral cats, and foxes; a particularly destructive root disease ("Jarrah dieback"); and dryland salinity (a significant problem, especially in the area's "wheatbelt," dis-cussed further below).

While there are a number of conservation efforts under way, few are as ambitious as Gondwana Link. Only about five years old, its vision is grand indeed—reconnecting and patching together a land mosaic over a seven-hundred-kilometer arc from Karri forests in the wet regions to the west through heath and dryer woodlands of the Stirling Range and

Figure 3.1 The Stirling Range in the South West Botanical Province is a notable geologic feature and important core area in Gondwana Link.
Photo credit: Tim Beatley

Fitzgerald River national parks and then connecting even farther east to vast areas of the Kalgoorlie gold field woodlands, which have never been cleared and connect through to the vast outback interior (figure 3.2). Although seven hundred kilometers of intensive conservation area are involved in reestablishing the ecological connections, the result will be a continuous link of natural bush stretching several thousand kilometers.

It is an umbrella project and a vision that the Gondwana Link project shares with six other partner organizations—Greening Australia, Fitzgerald Biosphere Group, Friends of the Fitzgerald, the Mallee Foul Preservation Group, the Wilderness Society, and the Australian Bush Heritage Fund—and they are aware that it will take several generations to complete. What elements explain Gondwana Link's success so far? Having a passionate, likable leader of the cause seems essential in this case, and Keith Bradby is not (and is not seen as) an outsider—a raving greenie from a big city. Keith was at the heart of the movement that stopped agricultural expansion at the rabbit-proof fence, a self-taught botanist who has found many new plant species and at various times served as an advisor to government on environmental matters. He is seen essentially as a local boy,

Figure 3.2 Gondwana Link Map. Gondwana Link envisions conserving and repairing land and habitat in a connected ecosystem spanning a 700-km arc from Karri forests in the west to the Kalgoorlie goldfields in the east. *Image credit:* courtesy of Wilderness Society

with community roots and connections; it is not a big outside environmental group coming in and lecturing the locals about what to do. He seems at once to be liked, respected, and trusted.

The Gondwana Link's focus extends well beyond a few species or a narrow geographical area. In Bradby's words, the partnership is focusing on

> restoring fundamental ecological processes across a broad swath of South-Western Australia. We are moving beyond a single-minded focus on saving a small section of rare species or specific areas. Our vision is: reconnected country in South-Western Australia, from Kalgoorie to the Karri, in which ecosystem function and biodiversity are restored and maintained. (Bradby, 2005, p. 18)

Much has been accomplished on the ground in a relatively short period of time. A number of properties have so far been secured (at a rate of about two per year), with the focus on the Stirling-Fitzgerald area (an area lying between the Stirling Range and the Fitzgerald River national parks). This has already amounted to protecting about 3,200 hectares of land and revegetating 400 to 450 hectares of this land. Through its grants and funding successes, Keith's full-time staff has grown to about six, with a number of others working part-time.

The project works closely with farmers who are needed to restore their land or cede it for that purpose. This builds on the work of the Fitzgerald Biosphere Group, which has focused on getting farmers to change farming practices over the past twenty-five years, after it was formed to emphasize the special natural features of the area.

The Gondwana Link project receives help from large companies like Shell Australia, who see it as a way to contribute to an enduring legacy for the state. This has not been an easy process for Gondwana Link as there is no strong philanthropic tradition from large companies in Australia. However, the Gondwana Link project felt that the size of the project and its grand vision would appeal to large companies and that if it had been a purely government project it would have been much harder to convince farmers to work closely with the project. Individuals also help support the project by buying areas to restore.

In addition to revegetation and habitat restoration work, the project is about building a new biodiversity-friendly economy. To this end, Gondwana Link has gained funding to test a variety of new tree-planting regimes that promise to provide restorative benefits and also hold commercial potential. Much of this has to do with rethinking the use of plantation forests and looking for new combinations of trees that provide wildlife and habitat benefits as well as commercial wood fiber. Some ways native bush is used in the economy include: brown-bush garden fences, Moort poles for fine wood and structural timber, and wildflowers, which are a growing industry. As one approaches Albany from Perth to the north, numerous plantations can be seen along the way; some planted with blue gum have been highly successful. Because of tax benefits that allow investors in such plantations to shelter income, there has been a significant flow of investment capital here. And most believe the blue gum plantations to be highly successful from an environmental perspective because they are especially good at helping to curtail the serious salinity problems of the region. In the Denmark catchment, where extensive blue gum has been planted, salinity levels have actually declined, reportedly the only catchment in Australia where that has happened.

Trials include sandalwood, a parasite species that actually requires a host tree on which to grow and so is especially well suited for bringing in extra diversity (it is also proving to be a highly commercial species). The Gondwana Link project is presently helping support a six-hundred-hectare proposal for a biodiverse sandalwood plantation.

Bradby supports these commercial enterprises not only because they have the potential to generate income and jobs but also because they provide a way, as he sees it, to revegetate at no cost. Revegetation, much of what this project and its partners do, is indeed costly, and its per-hectare cost is almost as high as the per-hectare cost of land acquisition (revegetation currently runs about $700 AUD per hectare; acquisition, between $800 and $1,000 AUD per hectare).

Other trials have focused on brushwood (good fence building material), Moort species to be used for mallet production (e.g., rail posts for vineyards), wildflower growing, and even bush food. Carbon sequestration is also a very promising economic venture, and a number of plantations are negotiating to receive carbon credits. One main revegetation species is oil mallee—a local bushy tree that yields a valuable oil from its leaves, carbon black from its branches (as well as electricity from a biopower plant trial), and carbon credits from its deep rooting system because they can continue absorbing (growing for two hundred years). The tree coppices, or sprouts again, after cutting each year, allowing sustainable and renewable cutting (harvesting) of this tree growth. These plantations are spreading across the region, offering important biodiversity and salinity benefits while also providing an economic return for farmers.

Other economic elements include forms of ecotourism to the region, including the potential for an Appalachian Trail type of walking or cycling trail along the entire corridor. A similar trail runs eight hundred kilometers from Perth to Albany. Called the Bibulman Track, it has spun off ecotourism ventures at various points along the track.

One of the most important accomplishments of the Gondwana Link project is to change the way people in the region think about the surrounding natural habitat. For example, many residents of Perth are now looking to acquire land in places to help fill in and repair the ecological mosaic of the landscape. This buy-in creates a tension that Bradby recognizes between a tightly controlled project ("this is Gondwana Link") and what a colleague of Keith's has called the "contagion hypothesis"—that is, the notion that once a good idea gets attention, it spreads around on its own, strengthening and building momentum. And that seems to be where Gondwana Link is today. The idea has spread to the eastern states as well, where several large corridors are being planned, such as Kosiosco to the Coast in Victoria.

Getting such good ideas going is always a problem. In the case of Gondwana Link, some critical points of help occurred early in the process. These included an official at the U.S.-based Nature Conservancy who saw merit in what Bradby wanted to do and provided important start-up funds. Another apparent element of the success is the inclusive nature of the project. All are welcome to participate and are encouraged to help in some way, and Bradby's strategies have been contrary to the divisive way some landscape restoration projects have unfolded. He seeks funding in lots of places, and recently the Urban Development Institute of Australia (UDIA) in Perth, which represents property developers, has even been involved. A member of UDIA's board, Martin Bowman, was entranced by the Gondwana Link Project and has enabled a number of developers to get involved personally or to have their developments invest in Gondwana Link as part of their social responsibility obligations.

Official government policy has been schizophrenic on this issue, however. On the one hand, the conservation agency has been purchasing land for reserves and national parks. On the other, the Department of Agriculture has historically worked at odds with biodiversity protection in this part of Western Australia, and Gondwana Link is still dealing with the consequences of this history.

New Ways of Seeing the Forest

While Gondwana Link envisions reconnecting and restoring a vast (and largely degraded) habitat belt from the Stirling Range to the Nullarbor Plain, the Southwest also contains some of the oldest intact forest systems anywhere: majestic Jarrah, marri, Karri, and tingle forests. These large and old forests, historically some in state parks and protected areas and others privately owned, have been subject to extensive pressures from logging and clearance. But their status, and the views held of them by the public and politicians alike, has been changing—and in some very positive ways in recent years.

In 2001, the WA state government was elected after a campaign that focused mostly on stopping the logging of old growth forest in the Southwest. Subsequently, the area with old growth has been declared as thirty national parks. The story of this remarkable conservation victory, however, began many years earlier, in the mid-1970s, when public opposition to woodchipping began to emerge and the campaign to save the giant trees and ancient redwoods of the Karri Forest started. The struggle took twenty-five years or so, and the work of many individuals and groups, to raise public consciousness, as Schultz documents well (2003). Formation of an umbrella organization—the Western Australia Forest Alliance (WAFA)—to coordinate different conservation groups involved was crucial, as well as the strong public support of individuals, such as local "folk hero" and West Coast Eagles coach Mick Malthouse, who came out for the forest in the lead-up to the 2001 election, thus freeing many closet conservationists to declare themselves and join the campaign.

Growing media coverage given to the forest conservation side (especially from the *West Australian*, Perth's daily newspaper) was instrumental is informing the public about the threats to the forest. Public opinion polling showed overwhelming public support for protecting old growth forests (some surveys indicated up to 92 percent support). Together, these pressures culminated in the 2001 election promise from the Labor Party to stop old growth logging in the state.

The outcome from local activist and furniture maker Murray Johnson's perspective is equally positive, certainly. He notes there are now forty thousand hectares of old growth forests near Pemberton that are classified as national park, and the future of the region's ecotourism and woodcraft industries is largely secure. But Johnson believes a broader assessment of WA forests is needed and that a considerable amount of work remains in shifting from the state's historical "quarry mentality" to one that emphasizes careful conservation and value-added use of the state's forests resources (Johnson, n.d.-a).

The government's forests commitment, as expressed in the white paper *Protecting Our Old-growth Forests*, is implemented in its comprehensive forest management plan, adopted in 2004. This document, entitled *Forest Management Plan, 2004–2013*, codifies the intention to protect old growth forests, essentially reclassifying most of them to national parks or forest conservation areas. Together these areas now comprise an impressive 1.26 million hectares (about 3 million acres). Another 1.2 million hectares remain in state forests and timber reserves, where logging is permitted, but under new, tighter forest management standards and lower allowable harvest levels (Conservation Commission of Western Australia, 2004). While not all are happy with how old growth forests have been defined, and how the other forests in the state's system are used and managed, these steps to protect old growth forests are nevertheless remarkable, given the context of Western Australia.

In the campaign for the forests leading up to the 2001 election, the timber companies used their staff to demonstrate in the streets that their jobs were threatened and that local towns in the forests would be devastated if the green agenda was adopted. No one in the forest movement ever suspected that this would happen, especially after the ALP (opposition party) pledged a fund for retraining and redeploying loggers. However, few would have predicted the remarkable turnaround of these towns as they grasped their new green agenda instead of being monocultural logging towns. Diversification of the economy has followed the recognition of biodiversity, and a far more sustainable future appears to be developing for these forest towns. The long term value of recreational use of the old growth forest is many times greater than the short term dollars from cutting the forest down.

Visitors from around the world come to see large old growth forests and to buy artisan works in stores like the Fine Woodcraft Store in Pemberton. The senselessness of former harvesting practices is even more apparent in this context. According to Murray Johnson, owner of the Fine Woodcraft Store, old growth bought for charcoal brings about $6 per tonne, while wood artisans are able to produce fine furniture at a retail price of about $35,000 per tonne. According to Johnson: "The highest return yet achieved was $1 million per tonne for a highly figured ground salvaged log which was veneered by the artisan, and used to make finely inlaid and veneered furniture pieces" (Johnson, n.d.-b).

The conventional approach to harvesting forests is also incredibly wasteful. Many tree species that are of value to artisans are simply destroyed in the "initial scrub rolling operations, or bulldozed and burned in coupes after logging operations have been completed." These lost species include banksias, peppermint, sheoak, and native pear trees, which all have value to artisans though not to the traditional timber industry, which is used to dealing in huge-scale structural uses of wood rather than these more aesthetic, high-value uses. It should, of course, be relatively easy to accommodate both uses in the productive forests (now that the majority of the old growth areas are in conservation zones). However, the old cultural divide between the loggers and the greenies appears to still be there, sometimes threatening the viability of the fine wood craft industry.

Part of the obstacle for small artisan wood users is having some officially condoned and legal access to the forests. Not until 1986 was there a mechanism, in the form of a craft wood license, something Murray Johnson helped to negotiate. Under this type of permit, artisans can negotiate to have access to particular kinds of wood considered to be waste by the timber companies. Before this license, artisans were not legally able to access the forest.

In the timber town of Dwellingup, about a hundred kilometers south of Perth, is a unique facility called the Forest Heritage Centre, now about ten years old. A partnership between CALM (the state Department of Conservation and Land Management), the fine wood industry project, and federal, state, and local governments, as well as a number of private donors, the Forest Heritage Centre clearly demonstrates the benefits—economic, community, and ecological—of searching for common sustainable uses of forests and wood. The building is itself a dramatic image, designed in the shape of a Jarrah leaf and constructed of rammed earth. It contains both a forest interpretive center, with extensive exhibits about flora and fauna native to the area as well as the history of logging and the forest industry, and a fine wood craft training center.

The training center is called the Australian School of Fine Wood. It is a teaching unit where typically twenty students are enrolled full-time in a course of study on how to design and build high-value, upscale furniture. The students are apprenticed to master artisans for their training. The students' work is showcased each year in galleries and exhibitions and published in a glossy collection guide. Many of these works are works of art, rather than utilitarian objects. Much of this student work is on display and for sale in the Centre's wood gallery.

The Centre is a tremendous community resource. Groups of schoolchildren frequently visit for educational field trips, and many woodworking and craft classes are offered for residents and students to experience the joys of making products from native Australian timbers.

The landscape of the Centre is remarkable as well, with an educational emphasis, including a Timber Getters Trail, where visitors can see what a 1800s-era timber camp actually looked and felt like, and an Aboriginal bushlife trail. Interpretative stations are found along the trails, with many hands-on items (such as cross sections of trees that can be picked up and touched, and stations where student visitors can have their guidebook "stamped"). A Jarrah Forest Lodge provides accommodation for conference or course participants.

Oil Mallees, Dryland Salinity, and Renewable Energy

Innovative solutions are being pursued in Western Australia with the potential to simultaneously address some of the state's (and country's) worst environmental problems—dryland salinity, reliance on greenhouse gas (generally fossil fuels), and loss of economic vitality in rural communities.

This effort will require not only saving remaining forested land but repairing and restoring them. And increasingly, those restoration efforts will have to accomplish other things as well, such as growing saleable products, sequestering carbon, and helping to generate needed electricity in a renewable way. The promise of oil mallee trees to do all of this as well as help to recover economic vitality in rural areas is being tested in other parts of Western Australia (figure 3.3).

Planting mallee trees, a broad classification of eucalyptus trees that do not have a central trunk, is viewed as a potentially potent response to the salinity crisis. Farms are planting the trees in the so-called wheatbelt,

Figure 3.3 Oil Mallee trees provide many potential benefits at once: they restore habitat and help ameliorate salinity problems, they sequester carbon, and they produce products that can be sold (eucalyptus oil) or burned in a renewable cycle to produce electricity. *Photo credit:* Tim Beatley

in rows or strips of three or four trees wide, interspersed with land left in wheat production or for sheep and cattle grazing (these are called "mallee alleys").

Mallees are amazing trees, with a sizeable and spreading underground root system that soaks up water, helps to keep salty groundwater at bay, and stores considerable carbon. The trees can be coppiced or harvested periodically, with the branches regenerating quickly and the roots remaining unaffected.

Commercial use of mallees is another promising dimension. A pilot energy plant is now under way in the wheatbelt town of Narrogin, about 150 kilometers south of Perth, which will help to show the extent of these possibilities. The plant—a joint project of the Oil Mallee Company, CALM, and Western Power—has received substantial Commonwealth funding. Its innovation is in the multiple products that will be produced from the mallees. Officially known as the Integrated Wood Processing (IWP) Plant, it will yield three main products: (1) the mallee leaves will be distilled to produce eucalyptus oil (producing perhaps one thousand tonnes of oil annually, with a market in pharmaceutical and industrial solvents); (2) the wood itself and spent leaves will be gasified and used to produce electricity in a small-scale one-megawatt gas turbine; and (3) some of the wood will be converted to charcoal and then to activated carbon (with several commercial and industrial uses, including filtration and purification). As a smaller pilot plant, it is designed to be about one fifth the size of a fully commercial operational plant, though it is not beyond reckoning to see a niche for one-megawatt biofueled electrical power systems as the world turns to distributed, renewably powered settlements.

The production of activated carbon relies on a unique fluidized bed technology developed by the Commonwealth Scientific and Industrial Research Organization, or CSIRO. The environmental benefits will be considerable, with this pilot plant producing enough power for about a thousand homes (most of the energy that is needed, for instance, by the town of Narrogin). It will result in a 7,300-tonne reduction in carbon emissions and the sequestering of 4,300 tonnes of carbon annually through mallee plantation growth. It will serve to generate local jobs and income and will also help to address, through tree planting, the serious salinity crisis that exists especially in Western Australia.

The IWP Plant model represents a compelling alternative vision, one that promotes a decentralized, locally based form of energy production, landscape restoration, and economic development. Western Power has identified the possible location of another ten plants, in an arc running

Figure 3.4 The pilot Integrated Wood Processing (IWP) plant in Narrogin, in Western Australia. This plant can produce a number of products at once, including eucalyptus oil, electricity (by burning leaves and oil), and activated carbon. *Photo credit:* Tim Beatley

from Geraldton, north of Perth, to Albany in the south. Access to the existing energy transmission system and tree plantings are the only requirement (the Narrogin plant will require about 2 million mallee trees) (Western Power, undated).

The processing plant itself is compact, occupying a relatively small site (figure 3.4). It is surrounded and visually buffered by rows of mallees, though the supply line will, of course, extend to farms throughout the region. The plan is to keep plants to a fifty-kilometer hinterland to transport the new material; otherwise, the energy balance from transport fuel begins to diminish the value of the project. This kind of thinking is quite visionary in an era when oil production is peaking and transport fuel will be an increasing issue.

To promote the planting and commercialization of mallees, the Oil Mallee Company was formed. The company has played a significant leadership role in promoting the industry and now represents some one thousand mallee growers, with an estimated 25 million mallee trees in the ground. The targets for the future call for planting 50 million trees per year, with a goal of 500 million planted by the year 2025 over an area of more than 1 million hectares. The commercialization has been slower than hoped, and the Oil Mallee Company honestly divulges that their resources are limited. The slow start is partly due to the need for funds to reach the point of commercial production—for example, developing a harvester that can chop and harvest the mallee trees economically, though a prototype of such a machine now exists.

There may be more opportunities for the use of mallee trees. For example, recent research has shown that mallee trees may also be an effective source of ethanol—some researchers have estimated that mallee trees will produce more than forty times the energy needed to grow and process this fuel. The inter-cropping way they are grown, allowing farmers to continue to grow other traditional crops, is another clear advantage. Thus oil mallee trees may have a strong future in a world looking for sustainable solutions with multiple benefits.

The potential economic (and restorative) benefits of carbon sequestration have been shown convincingly in the case of a recent deal with one of Japan's largest power companies, Kansai Electric Power Company Inc. The company has funded a major mallee tree planting project in WA through the help of the Oil Mallee Company. Specifically, the project resulted in the planting of 2.5 million mallee trees on one thousand hectares of farmland in Western Australia, sequestering significant carbon in the process while helping to address the salinity and land degradation problems there. Under this arrangement, the land is leased to Kansai for tree planting, with farmers getting an annual payment.

The Oil Mallee Company estimates that some 2.9 billion tons of carbon dioxide could be sequestered in WA. This means WA has the potential to be a major carbon sink and suggests that serious economic income is possible from this function. Syd Shea, the former, founding leader of CALM, states: "In terms of major environmental problems like salinity, I am convinced you are not going to find a solution unless the solution is profitable. The Greens hate that idea, but governments just don't have the money to address all these problems" (*Atticus Informer*, 2001). Shea is a major advocate for an oil mallee economy. Asked to head up the commercial side during his retirement, he does so while also teaching and researching sustainability.

Although the market for carbon sequestration is tremendous, the main obstacle had been that Australia had not signed the Kyoto Protocol and so could not get credit for plantings in Australia for the international market set up through Kyoto. The Kansai power plant happened pre-Kyoto, and they are still living off the profits of this deal. The state government had created the legal mechanisms to generate carbon credits through a Carbon Credits Bill. However, the federal government had not enabled this to be required internationally. As in the United States, the power of the fossil fuel lobby, especially coal, a major Australian export, had stymied signing on to Kyoto. However, all this is changing as the newly elected Rudd government has now signed Kyoto. Oil mallee plantations now seem to have a more assured economic future.

The state government in WA also is not blameless on climate change. Despite developing a greenhouse strategy, it has not done much for renewable energy or energy conservation. This could be due to the political dominance of the natural gas, coal, and minerals industry as well as the dominance of Western Power, which has not allowed innovative renewables projects into the power grid unless it controls them. This is changing as competition rules have led to an opening up of the power system in WA. Thus the number of wind farms is expected to increase beyond the two main ones, and a number of biofuel projects are developing similar to the oil mallee project.

Sandalwood represents yet another promising economic form of wood production, one with the potential to be extended beyond the monocultural plantation approach of blue gum. There is a sandalwood (*Santalum spicatum*) native to WA that was the basis for the first major export from the state in the nineteenth century. Sandalwood exports to China, where the fragrant wood is highly valued, have occurred for more than a hundred years. An interesting tree, sandalwood is actually a parasitic species that requires a host tree on which to grow. Sandalwood plantations have in the past typically utilized a single host species, but researchers are increasingly showing that there are many advantages—economic and environmental—to using many different host species.

The rub for landowners is always the hesitation to take out of production, wholly or in part, their best lands. Commercializing species like sandalwood, which can generate profit while providing habitat and landscape restorative benefits, may make this much more likely. As Woodall and Robinson write: "It is the authors' experience that landholders are more likely to consider creation of habitat or corridors if there is the long-term prospect of some commercial gain through the production of sandalwood" (2002, p. 132).

Adding to the viability of sandalwood is a value-adding industry similar to the fine wood craft industry. For example, the Mount Romance pharmaceutical company makes perfume and health products from sandalwood and emu oil. This business, based in Albany in the Southwest, has become an international exporter of Australia's bush products in the past twenty years. One of its innovations has been the development of an Indigenous Protocol with the Aboriginal people who produce the sandalwood and emu products in the desert. This protocol, developed with Aveda and Estée Lauder, is the first of, it is hoped, many more agreements between industry and indigenous communities that will guarantee sustainable harvesting and a fair return to those who produce the raw material but typically have no intellectual property associated with its pharmaceutical benefits. Thus the Mt. Romance Indigenous Protocol is being watched with interest by American companies under pressure to be more socially responsible and sustainable (Renne, 2008).

Living Landscapes: Conserving the Biodiversity of the Wheatbelt

A recent biological survey of Western Australia's 250,000-square-kilometer wheatbelt, a region of intensive wheat and agricultural production (located due east of the Perth metro area), found remarkable diversity and also tremendous potential loss from dryland salinity, if left unchecked. Twenty-five new invertebrate species were discovered, as well as 6 new plant species and a new family of crustaceans. Conducted on one thousand sites across the area, the survey predicts that 450 flowering plant species and 400 species of spiders, scorpion, and aquatic invertebrate are at risk for extinction from salinity. As Dr. Judy Edwards, the minister of environment for Western Australia, said at the time, even more is at risk: "In addition to species extinctions, all remaining remnants of many valley-floor wetland, scrubland and woodland communities could disappear because of salinisation" (Vance, 2005).

Various projects have been tried over the past thirty years to stem the tide of salinization, which is caused by the replacement of deep-rooted perennials with annual species, thus causing groundwater to rise and bringing salts to the surface. Most of these projects involve planting trees, but only in recent times has it been possible to see where the most strategic planting should occur.

Natural resource management (NRM) zones have been established by federal and state government grants based on the major river catchments across Australia. These NRM groups have each produced an NRM Strategy, which specifies the priorities for action based on an understanding of the groundwater hydrology, the soils, the biodiversity, and the land use history. Action strategies are worked out on the scale of small subcatchments, which generally means farmers in a community that share a valley or creek system.

It is on this basis that the group Greening Australia (GA) was able to create a Living Landscape project that works with the local community in priority areas. Thus, instead of isolated farmers doing demonstrations, as has mostly occurred up until recently, it should now be possible to work at a community scale. Nevertheless, it is always hard to bring a whole community into such a project working on concerns for the long-term common good, so GA has a number of social innovations to help guarantee success.

Greening Australia was created more than twenty years ago in response to a Commonwealth initiative in the 1980s to plant a billion trees. GA was formed essentially as a delivery mechanism under this program, but the organization and its work have matured over those years, recognizing that it is not just about planting trees but also about restoring ecosystems and engaging and working with local communities.

Beginning in 1998, initial work began in the Avon catchment to the east of Perth, working with families in five subcatchments. The number of families participating range from eleven to twenty (Smith and Penter, 2005). With funding from Alcoa, the Natural Heritage Trust (a federal government fund), the Avon Catchment Council, and Greening Australia, as well as local governments, an innovative approach to catchment management and biodiversity has emerged. An initial gift of $1.4 million from a private individual actually helped start the Living Landscape program; this catalytic funding was then used to secure an equal match from Alcoa.

The Living Landscape initiative has embodied much of this new approach of GA. This initiative involves working at a community level, directly with farmers and landowners to engage them and enlist them in stewarding over remnant habitat. A methodology, largely developed by Robert Lambeck, involves choosing a set of key processes of concern in a particular catchment (e.g., salinity change), selecting a certain number of key species that are most sensitive to these changes, and then beginning to look at land use changes through the lens of these umbrella or focal species. Through community meetings, farmers are shown maps of remnant habitat and are engaged in a collaborative discussion about what is actually happening on the ground and how their own practices might result in a better outcome. Lambeck calls this "focal species planning." (see Lambeck, 1997).

Living Landscape is distinctive in its emphasis on working directly with farmers and their families, in developing with them a shared understanding of the ecology and ecological management needs of the landscape. This is done in some very creative ways, including through group processes that encourage discussion about values and vision for the future, group events and activities that facilitate experiential learning about the landscape ("action-learning"), and, in the end, a process that moves farmers from a narrow single-farm view of the world to seeing their land and management actions in a larger landscape or ecological community context (South and Penter, 2005).

The process often begins with informal (and fun) processes for building knowledge of ecology and for active learning—such as excursions and field trips, bushwalks, picnics, and "campouts"—that also help build group trust and buy-in. Emphasizing the "fun" aspect, and involving entire families, has been critical. More focused meetings follow, in which participating families are presented with focal species maps—vegetation maps, bird distribution maps, and so forth—and helped to reach their own conclusions about conservation needs. Living Landscapes represents a positive and realistic partnership approach to conservation. Farmers and biologists together explore what will be needed to restore and re-patch this highly fractured and fragmented landscape, while the social activities build community and trust.

The focal species approach is based on the idea of planning for that species that is likely to be most vulnerable to the land use changes or habitat pressures experienced. In the case of the central wheatbelt, birds have been chosen, but the species might be different when the process is applied to other ecosystems or regions. These focal species are usually iconic local species with well-known stories about them in aboriginal and local history. Thus communities see their vital responsibility to ensure that these species do not disappear.

The small, highly accessible book *Birds of the Central Wheatbelt*, produced as one aspect of the Living Landscape program, is a model of what might be done. The guidebook is "local, relevant and its color pictures of 73 birds don't trouble someone who could be put off by hundreds of pictures of unfamiliar (and irrelevant) birds" (Smith and Penter, 2005, p. 13).

So far, almost 2,500 hectares of native vegetation in the Avon catchment have been protected, and 676 hectares have been revegetated through the Living Landscape program. (Smith and Penter, 2005, p. 2). More than 750,000 seedlings have been planted, seeding and revegetation work has been done on hundreds of hectares of land, and extensive fencing and other conservation work has been implemented, all through partnering with farmers—some seventy-six farm families over five years.

While the initial five years of funding from Alcoa has ended, the program continues in the Avon catchment. The program's success has also meant that it is being applied in other parts of Australia, notably in several catchments in the state of Victoria. GA is piloting the process in four other catchments and has plans to expand the number by an additional twelve catchments, to be rolled out in a phased schedule. This will be conducted under a new label, "Ecoscapes."

Saving Ningaloo Reef

There is an expression some Australians use: "Beautiful one day. Queensland the next." It reflects the worries many Australians have about the loss of their environment, particularly beaches and coastline, as has happened along some of the more popular parts of Queensland (perhaps the Australian equivalent of Florida). The battle over the fate of Ningaloo Reef in Western Australia reflects this concern.

Ningaloo Reef is a magnificent, unique fringing reef that extends 260 kilometers. Unlike the Great Barrier Reef, it doesn't require a long boat ride to get there; it is directly next to the shore. Home to an incredible diversity of life, its most famous visitors are the huge whale sharks—the largest fish in the world—that linger three or four months of the year, feasting on the coral plankton. Visitors come from around the world to swim with these gentle giants. Other marine critters call it home as well, including manta rays, dugongs, sea turtles that nest on these beaches, two hundred species of coral, and five hundred species of fish. The reef has been described by Australia's most popular author, Tim Winton, as "one of the nation's last great coastal wilderness areas" (Winton, 2003a).

In the late 1980s, the state government set in motion a conflict that would last for nearly fifteen years. The town of Coral Bay, it was believed, needed an influx of private capital (in the form of new resort development) to help solve some of its environmental problems (e.g., leaching sewage) and sagging tourist economy. The state government issued a tender calling for proposals for a new resort there.

By 2000, the winning bid, a $180 million AUD Coral Bay resort called Maud's Landing, seemed set to move forward. Slated to include a 240-boat marina, 710 hotel rooms, and another 200 units of permanent housing units, it was to be a large development, with substantial housing as well as five-star hotel accommodation. However its major problem was its location, beyond the town and not a direct contributor to the local economy. It was located close to a natural opening to the ocean, perhaps the most ecologically sensitive portion of coastline, described by Tim Winton as a "marine mammal highway" (Winton, 2003a).

The story of how the resort was turned down despite years of building momentum, and nearly coming to a final stage, is useful for anyone involved in battles over conservation. It shows the power of protest, of citizens and concerned groups working through the political system to stop something seen as clearly wrong and clearly the wrong direction, although a process had been followed to facilitate it. More than anything, it signaled a new and different tack, a different way of understanding this incredible natural asset that is Ningaloo. To make this shift required a deep, cultural change that would carry over into political action.

The Campaign to Save Ningaloo Reef was able to enlist several prominent marine cinematographers, who with stunning underwater footage were able to convey to the public the majesty of this wondrous place. They were also able to involve a passionate local celebrity—writer Tim Winton. The media helped to get the word out, and eventually every car in the Perth region seemed to have a "Save Ningaloo Reef" bumper sticker (Denis Beros, the campaign coordinator, estimates that as many as one in ten cars, did but my own experience would put the number even higher).

A watershed event in the campaign was a rally in Fremantle that drew an estimated fifteen thousand people. Politicians and others pay attention when things like this happen. It showed the deep concern the general public held for this issue. "This was no shadowy, mythical elite. This was rate-paying Australia, school-going Australia, suburban Australia" (Winton, 2003). Other elements of the campaign included an e-mail writing campaign (with twenty thousand people writing directly to the state premier on one weekend, causing a meltdown in the government computers), hiring planes to carry banners along beaches, and a variety of other "stunts," such as volunteers dressing up as ninga turtles, to gain media attention.

Key to the success of the campaign was shifting the perception of the opposition to Maud's Landing from yet another overreaching cry of a handful of elitist environmentalists to a popular grassroots campaign. At the Fremantle rally, Tim Winton gave a masterful speech, one that very effectively contrasted the positions on the issue and characterized the resort proposal as "old thinking, old school."

For Winton, and for the other campaigners and citizens, whether to allow the resort to happen was fundamentally a question of ethics and values. Winton makes this clear in his speech:

None of us made Ningaloo reef. We inherited it. The family silver, our precious heirloom. Our common asset. And we have a sacred responsibility to hand it on intact. To take all precautions to ensure its security. The precautionary principle. What on earth would induce us to risk something so valuable? It's hard enough entrusting it to our public officials who are at least somehow accountable, so why the hell would we hand it over to a bunch of business-men? . . . Why would we rob our own descendents unless we were greedy or gullible? Or asleep! (Winton, 2003).

Not only has this one contentious project been knocked aside, but to its credit, WA has dealt more systemically with the larger management challenge and has put into place new planning and a new management framework that bodes well for the future of the reef. Among the elements of this new management regime has been the establishment of a Ningaloo Sustainable Development Office to "proactively coordinate and facilitate appropriate nature-based tourism developments on the Ningaloo and to service the WA Planning Commission" (Western Australian Planning Commission, 2003, p. xi). A Ningaloo Sustainable Development Committee (NSDC) has also been formed. The committee, consisting of all relevant state agencies, is well represented by local stakeholders as well.

Coastal development in WA after Ningaloo must now follow a low-impact model, which is embodied in the newly prepared planning documents. Future coastal development along the Ningaloo Reef and extending all down the coast will, impressively, be restricted to very small (and very specifically delineated) areas.

As with many planning issues, there is a need to create an ongoing statutory base to the planning decisions that have essentially come from a political process. In Western Australia, planning has a strong statutory base, with the state (WA Planning Commission, or WAPC) having all the necessary land use powers to manage regional planning decisions (devolved to a local government for most detailed planning). However, a regional planning strategy must be developed first. This is now in place through the Carnarvon-Ningaloo Coastal Strategy. The NSDC now have the power to recommend decisions to the WAPC on how any development can meet the sustainability criteria and guidelines set in that strategy.

Equally impressive is a new model for ecotourism emerging in the wake of the Ningaloo conflict in which the new guidelines are shaping where camping sites can be placed (and where some need to be removed) as well as where resort-style accommodation can occur and how it should look and operate to fit the environment. The first proposals under these guidelines are now appearing, including a much more acceptable resort facility at Coral Bay.

Most locals thought that economic development would suffer in the region with the resort being rejected. But, ironically, the focus of attention on the region has led to much more money flowing into the region. This includes an estimated $19 million AUD associated with expanding the Ningaloo Marine Park. Prior to the campaign and resort conflict, CALM was spending only about $300,000 AUD a year there. However, the interest of the public in the area was so heightened by the campaign that it has become a major destination—while still retaining its low-key status.

The economics of ecotourism generated by new interest in whale sharks further confirms the virtue of this new planning strategy. The public's interest in and desire to experience the whale sharks directly is increasing. One can join one of the many boats based at Exmouth that take visitors to the reef, find whale sharks (with the assistance of trackers from the air), and be deposited close enough to swim with them—by all accounts a profound experience.

Marine researchers report that the whale sharks they're encountering on the reef are getting smaller, likely a result of the harvesting of whale sharks in Indonesia. The killing of the sharks responds to a strong demand for shark meat and shark fins in Asian restaurants. The Australian view is that the whale shark fishery has far greater economic value as an asset for ecotourism than as a short-term harvestable or extractive resource. Much discussion in the local media focused around how to provoke a similar shift in the Asian nations to the north.

About the same time, controversy began to rage over Japan's announcement of its proposal to the International Whaling Commission to expand its scientific whale harvesting and to, for the first time, begin to "harvest" a number of endangered Minke whales instead of just taking scientific "samples." This set off protracted lobbying on behalf of the strong Australian view that preserving the whales for their tourism value is the only sensible future path. In May 2005, front-page coverage was given to the beaching of three hundred false pilot whales in the Southwest. The personal efforts of hundreds of volunteers was a fitting retort to the Japanese plans, as the volunteers tried desperately to keep the whales alive in the shallows before the tide rose again. The change of attitude in the community from a society that was founded around whaling (there was a whaling station at Ningaloo and at Albany), which only stopped in 1975, to one that now views them as natural wonders is dramatic. A calculation recently made in Western Australia showed that more people now make a living from whale watching than were ever employed in the whale butchering business. Who said sustainability doesn't pay?

Other actions have been taken by the state to protect their precious marine resources. A Ningaloo Marine Park was established; following the Coral Bay decision, the state expanded the park and also expanded the size of the conservation zone (no-take zone) to encompass about one-third of the park.

Koalas: Revaluing an Iconic Species

If ever there was an iconic species in Australia, it is the koala (figure 3.5). It is ubiquitous as a symbol and as a logo for everything from local car rental companies to Qantas Airlines. The numbers of these beloved animals in the wild, however, have been gradually declining. The threats are many, but gradual habitat loss and urbanization are primary factors (along with the resulting increased car traffic and road kills, dogs, and loss of food trees).

Although koalas have not been given protection under federal legislation, there have been a number of protections granted at state and local levels and a number of attempts to plan and conserve in ways that will ensure the long-term survival of this species. Under NSW planning law, local councils are subject to a series of State Environmental Planning Policies (SEPPs). SEPP 44, "Koala Habitat Protection," has been the main planning law giving rise to the preparation of local koala management plans. Under SEPP 44, such plans must be prepared (before development approval can be given) where the council finds the presence of "core" koala habitat, meaning "land with a resident population of Koalas, evidenced by attributes such as breeding females (that is, females with young) and recent sightings of and historical records of a population" (4 definitions, SEPP 44). Councils do sufficient biological survey work to determine whether core habitat exists and whether land meets the criteria of "potential" habitat, defined as native vegetation where at least 15 percent of the trees are feed tree species (e.g., forest red gum and swamp mahogany).

The SEPP is vague on precisely what form the management plan must take; what implication the presence of core habitat has to development activities within the jurisdiction is also not clear. But part 4 of the SEPP does state that councils should incorporate core habitat into their local environment plans and "give consideration to preparing an appropriate development control plan for land that is or adjoins a core Koala habitat."

Figure 3.5 The Koala is an iconic Australian species, but one experiencing serious threats from urbanization and habitat loss. *Photo credit:* Tim Beatley

In many ways, this koala habitat regulation is designed to alert people to the problem of retaining sufficient habitat and ensuing that surrounding land use is compatible. The main idea is that developers and landowners must take the presence of koala habitat into account. If local authorities prepare comprehensive plans, approved by the NSW planning minister, then they are relieved of preparing individual management plans. This is obviously a new area of conservation planning, and the jury is still out on whether it is possible to integrate koalas into urban and urbanizing areas. But evidence is developing that humans and koalas can coexist just as humans and whales can.

Preparation of local plans has been slow in NSW, but some exemplary efforts have emerged, with promise for enhancing the current position of the koala. A plan in Port Stephens merits a special look. It is an experiment in green urbanism that the world will be watching.

In Port Stephens (on the northern coast of NSW), the plan has clearly resulted in an extra level of habitat analysis in the development review process. This has been positive, as developers have become more aware of the implications and in some cases have modified their designs to minimize impacts.

The plan has also set in motion a number of revegetation and habitat restoration projects, mostly on public land, in areas that represent important linkages and buffer areas for koalas. Considerable funding has come from the Hunter Water Corporation and through the Commonwealth government's Green Corps program (a project to use unemployed people in greening projects). It has yet to fully assess the cumulative biological impacts of these restoration projects, but they are positive steps certainly (e.g., see Westing, 2002, program reports, July 2002–2004).

Guiding the overall direction of community development in Port Stephens is an ambitious and sensible "Urban Settlement Strategy." The strategy opens by reflecting on the beauty of Port Stephens's natural setting, the charm of its pattern of small villages, and the need to grow in ways that build on this strength in the future. The first guiding principle of the settlement strategy states this well: "Port Stephens is cherished as a series of villages nestled in a beautiful environment. To the best of our ability this should be maintained, by actively encouraging urban growth around and linked with, existing villages, and protecting the natural environmental quality of the surrounding areas" (Port Stephens Council, 2002, p. 6).

Conversely, the strategy states clearly and strongly that continued rural residential growth outside existing towns is "not a sustainable form of development." The strategy goes on to flesh out "settlement opportunities" within the town, by planning district. For the Tomaree peninsula, where my koala encounters occurred, and where so much good koala habitat exists, the strategy identifies promising infill opportunities in Nelson Bay/Salamander Bay town centers and through expansion of the existing town of Anna Bay. Mixed-use development, clustered around these centers and within a short walk, are to be given preference. The plan strongly conveys these ideas in a settlement strategy map—"Opportunities for creating safe sustainable and attractive places"—which identifies, through a series of circles, where future development and growth (again building on its existing village structure) could and should occur.

Koala Beach is a housing project located along the Tweed Coast, in northern New South Wales, not far from the Queensland border (figures 3.6 and 3.7). It is an unusual project, and to Deborah Tabart, the charismatic and energetic head of the Australian Koala Foundation (AKF), it represents a positive model for future koala conservation. It grows from the recognition that knee-jerk opposition to all future growth in and near koala habitat is neither productive nor realistic. A more collaborative and cooperative approval between conservationists and developers, she believes,

Figure 3.6 In the Koala-friendly development Koala Beach, residents are forbidden from keeping dogs and cats, the former an especially serious threat to Koalas. *Photo credit:* Tim Beatley

Figure 3.7 Koala Beach has been designed to protect and nurture its resident population of Koalas, including the inventory and protection of important feed trees, reducing speed and impact of car traffic (and road kill) in the neighborhood, and a prohibition on owning dogs and cats. *Photo credit:* Tim Beatley

is essential, while acknowledging the importance of also moving forward on a variety of other koala management fronts.

Koala Beach, now in its final phase of development, began as a series of discussions between the AKF and the Roy Group, with the spirit of co-operation and potential for mutual benefit. The result is a carefully master planned community that incorporates many unusual, one might say even radical, koala conservation elements (figure 3.7).

The layout and design of the project was preceded by an extensive, two- year biological survey and analysis of the koala population. Koalas were radio tagged, and their movements were recorded and analyzed. With this information, their home ranges were identified and important food and habitat trees were recorded.

Considerable habitat has been set aside for koalas—an estimated 200 (out of 360) hectares (AKF, n.d.). Although land clearance did occur, great

effort appears to have been made to protect existing trees and native vegetation. Through restrictive covenants that run with property titles, important additional requirements are imposed—fences (which are generally
discouraged) are to be raised to provide a minimum of three hundred millimeters of ground clearance to permit koala movement (they need to
move between trees, mostly at night), the removal of specifically identified
home range and food trees is generally prohibited, and all pools must include a rope, which permits koalas to pull themselves out of the water. Traffic calming (speed humps) and reduced speed limits are also imposed (forty
kilometers per hour throughout; twenty kilometers per hour near blossom
bat habitat).

Perhaps most surprising is the prohibition on residents having cats and
dogs as domestic pets, and indeed a prohibition even on these pets visiting
the neighborhood. This is, moreover, not a hidden or obscure restriction; it
is a front-and-center key and very visible element of the community, noted
on a prominent sign as one enters the neighborhood. This is a residential
development where the koala is the iconic driver of the style and character
of the development.

Protecting essential food trees for resident koalas is another important management step. The primary food trees were identified and protected on-site, including tallowwood (*Eucalyptus microcorys*), forest red
gum (*Eucalyptus tereticornis*), swamp mahogany (*E. Robusta*), and small-
fruited grey gum (*E. propinqua*), as well as other hybrid species (Australian Koala Foundation, 2004).

While the Koala Beach effort has been focused especially on the koalas,
the biological work and management actions also address a variety of other
important species on-site, including wallabies, planigales, blossom bats,
glossy black cockatoos, superb fruit-dove, and black bitterns. The overall
management plan for Koala Beach contains numerous actions aimed at
protecting and improving habitat conditions for these species as well. This
is a "focal species" conservation plan for an urban development.

Long-term management of the estate is guided by an appointed
Wildlife and Habitat Management Committee, funded through a special
environmental levy, and a comprehensive set of management guidelines
(Australian Koala Foundation, 2005). The committee is responsible for
overseeing the planting of new food trees and trees required as replace-
ments for the limited number of trees allowed to be cut during construction.

The koala population at Koala Beach appears to be doing well, and residents are actively consulted about sightings, of which there appear to

be many (AKF, 2004). Important food and shelter trees are surviving, as are new plantings. There have been no reports of koalas being hit by cars or attacked by dogs, the main threats in a conventional development (AKF, 2004). Evaluation reports by the AKF along the way generally indicate that the project and its management and design appear to be working and that without such a comprehensive management plan and regime, koalas "would be highly unlikely to survive residential development" (AKF, 2004, p. 28). While additional habitat restoration work is needed and constant vigilance in the future will be required to ensure that covenant restrictions are respected, the overall picture appears optimistic one, at least here.

While the jury is still out on the long-term effectiveness of design efforts like this, they do represent a positive directive. Ultimately, long-term survival may require more—at both the federal (including endangered species protection and recovery efforts) and local levels. At the local level, more concerned and active individuals and groups of individuals will be necessary. Ultimately, part of the answer will likely be neighbors and neighborhoods directly taking responsibility, *personal* responsibility, for looking out for, guarding over, and improving the habitat conditions for koalas.

A similar and interesting story can be seen in one of the other NSW communities with a remaining population of koalas, Campbelltown, and with similar conclusions. Here, local awareness of and care about koalas has been the result of the work of one particular advocate, Dr. Robert Close of the University of Western Sydney. Close represents an interesting model of how a university professor works on behalf of local biodiversity and in the process helps to build local awareness of and support for conservation. He has enlisted the Campbelltown populace to help in his monitoring of local koala—he operates with his graduate students a call line that residents are encouraged to use to report sightings of koalas. Close even writes a weekly column in the local newspaper about koalas and about other species of interest locally and environmental issues more broadly. The koala is clearly the hook, but Close uses his pulpit to raise awareness about much of threatened nature. In one column, he asks readers to report sightings of platypuses in the Nepean River; in another, he asks about a rare bird. The public seems always willing to help.

Dr. Close has been involved for a little over a decade in Campbelltown koala issues. It began for him in 1993, when he joined the fight to stop a large development project proposed for the Wedderburn, a relatively large habitat area east of Campbelltown. He has been a defender and researcher of local koalas ever since.

Close is on personal terms with many of the resident koalas, especially Shirley, who is known to like to sit by a particular tree along a particular road. He describes the koalas he has tagged or radio collared over ten years (about 110) and speaks almost like a proud father of the offspring of these koalas. He has mapped their movements and their sometimes overlapping home territories. Close's research suggests that over time the numbers of Koala have grown and that the population has been able to disperse and repopulate other areas. In Campbelltown, the main threats to koalas are dogs and cars, equally lethal. In fact, it is often hard to tell without careful examination which is the culprit. Koalas come down from their trees only occasionally but are not very fast at ground level.

Close's interest in and activism on behalf of the local koala population make him at once a resource, a point of contact, an educator, and an exemplar of urban biodiversity conservation. "Mac Koala" is his byline in the local paper, and he in a sense represents a kind of biological docent (a "bio-docent," for short?), an individual extremely knowledgeable about a particular aspect of local biodiversity who is then able to lead others in seeing the wonder and value of a species or landscape and to provide guidance about how and in what ways a community should nurture or work to save something, in this case a resident population of koalas.

In other parts of eastern Australia, in Queensland and New South Wales, the plight of koalas is similarly precarious, as deforestation and urbanization take their toll. Legal protections matter, to be sure, but having local friends and bio-docents like Close, and the Port Stephens neighbors who care about and look out for their local koala, is invaluable.

Conclusions and Lessons Learned

These inspiring stories of efforts to conserve and protect landscapes and indigenous biodiversity, though not perfect, together contain the kernels of a new conservation paradigm, one borne from the unique environments of Australia but relevant everywhere, I believe. As these cases vividly demonstrate, there are common critical elements: an emphasis on the long-term public values of ecosystems and the ecosystem benefit they provide (as in Ningaloo Reef); resisting the appeal of markets based on the shorter economic gain to define new markets based on immense long-term economic benefit (as in preserving old growth forest, marine mammals, and koalas); and the importance of developing visionary and highly participatory frameworks through which conservation and protection can happen as the basis for these economic opportunities. Ningaloo was safeguarded in the end through an amazing and unusual outpouring of citizen concern and political activism. Of equal importance in these stories is the need to put in play long-term management frameworks that extend these protections beyond simple, discrete decisions or victories. Actively involving those who are closest "on the ground" to the resource under threat is another lesson. In the case of the Living Landscape project, the obvious step (though infrequently done) is to directly and personally engage farmers in conservation, and in the case of Koala Beach, to involve residents and landowners and, of course, the developers of the housing project in the first place.

Shifting mind-sets is a key lesson. Old growth forests and the Ningaloo Reef, for instance, are appropriately viewed as, in Tim Winton's words, the "family silver," and a new understanding that preserving and protecting them in their natural state makes much more long-term economic sense than does short-term extraction or the "quarry mentality" (to put it in the words of Murray Johnson). It is also a matter of ethics and protecting the public interest, of guarding public assets against short-term private gain. In a word, this new view is about sustainability. Admittedly, as these stories demonstrate, the mental shift has not been easy. In the case of old growth forests and Ningaloo, the ability to activate a public on behalf of conservation, to educate and challenge them, through some creative methods has been the basis of this mental shift. These methods and strategies could work in the United States as well. All of these stories show the importance of leveraging discrete project victories into support for changing the management framework that is in place and ensuring that it is established in a statutory framework.

Other critical lessons from these stories include the importance of directly and personally involving landowners in conservation (Living Landscape), engaging developers and homeowners (Koala Beach), and looking for conservation solutions that address several long-term sustainability problems at once (e.g., mallee tree planting to generate local power, address dryland salinity, and sequester carbon). These long-term public good options then become "owned" by those who drive the economy rather than just insisted on by governments.

The conservation models and approaches described here are not without their risks, of course. Koala Beach could be criticized for permitting or facilitating damaging growth in habitat areas that should ultimately be set aside for koalas. Allowing any development at Ningaloo could be seen as a compromise. And working with farmers, as in the Living Landscape initiative, could be cast as a poor substitute for adopting more stringent state restrictions on land clearance. The overall relevance of most of the cases presented, moreover, might be questioned because they address dramatic, highly visible (and, for the most part, highly valued by the public) environments and environmental resources: a large fringing coral reef, koalas, old growth forests with spectacular biodiversity. However this would suggest that human beings cannot adapt to living within these highly biodiverse landscapes, that the concept of sustainable development is ultimately barren. The impression I have from these case studies is that the ethical base, civic infrastructure, and governance for such cohabitation *is* being developed and that the possibilities of a greener kind of settlement that is far more aware of its biological content may be unfolding. These examples are not just "green"; they are "green urbanism" because they integrate people and environments in a new kind of sustainability partnership.

As the stories in this chapter certainly convey, Australia's immense biodiversity and landscape beauty have come under extreme pressures. But equally true, the Australian experience has been one of searching for new and different methods of conservation and for different and very creative public and private strategies for stewarding over this immense legacy.

4

Strengthening Place, Building Community

During my months in Australia, and over the course of many community site visits and interviews, I uncovered an impressive array of programs, initiatives, and ideas used to nurture and strengthen a special sense of place, to build new connections to place and to one another, and to generally enhance appreciation of the many special qualities of a community or region. In many cases, this was about renewing and relearning things about a community already known and protecting those important historical, environmental, and cultural qualities that make a place unique or special. In other cases, it has been about assembling new community overlays, about creating new experiences—whether through public art or new forms of community engagement or participation—that also help make a place distinctive.

This chapter describes some of the most interesting and unusual ways that place-building and place-strengthening has happened in Australia. These dimensions of place are an essential aspect of green urbanism and play an important part in developing a sustainability strategy.

It Takes a Sustainable Street

Part of building community and social capital is ensuring a robust set of community organizations and institutions. It often takes a village *and* a street. Sustainability Street is an innovative approach being taken in many cities in Australia. It can be found in more than one hundred cities in Victoria and New South Wales, and it is spreading to other parts of the country. Created by (and a registered trademark of) Melbourne-based environmental educators Vox Bandicoot, Sustainability Street is essentially a process of educating and empowering streets and neighborhoods around the notion of sustainability and the undertaking of tangible projects and steps to reduce ecological impacts. Neighbors learn about the environment, they are helped to understand their own impacts, and they set targets and goals for change. As the Vox Bandicoot Web site notes: "At its simplest, the Sustainability Street Approach is a basic training program in Sustainable Living around home and in the neighborhood" (see http://www.voxbandicoot.com.au).

And while the organizers are quick to point out that the "Street" is simply a metaphor—it might actually be the neighborhood, a block, or several streets or any other socially relevant spatial unit—sustainability takes on a highly personal and localized meaning.

Sustainability Street's appeal is indeed that it is highly localized and tangible—it is about saving the world certainly, but in visible ways in one's own neighborhood and community (figure 4.1). It is largely about building connections with and among people, strengthening place, and taking steps to a collectively reimagined community.

Figure 4.1 Sustainability Street is an innovative program by which neighbors join together to understand and monitor their environmental impacts, to commit to living more sustainably, and to undertake tangible community projects that promote living more lightly on the planet. Here the Iramoo (in Victoria) Sustainability Street village crew is restoring habitat to protect the endangered legless lizard. *Photo credit:* Courtesy Vox Bandicoot.

A first step for participants is to install an actual street sign—to have a "sign raising," as it were—that makes their participation in the program and their commitment to sustainability publically visible to an unusual degree. There is often a neighborhood party, a parade, or a celebration of some sort that accompanies the installation of the sign and the kickoff of a street or neighborhood's efforts.

The Sustainability Street process usually takes place over an eighteen-month period and follows a series of stages. A series of program "books" lays out an extensive Sustainability Street process. The Sustainability Street approach consists of six building blocks, four stages, eight principles, seven beacons, key foci, sustainability shortcuts, and community building (see Vox Bandicoot, "book one," for much more detail on these building blocks; Vox Bandicoot, 2003). Most important are the following four stages that groups cycle through, roughly analogous to the process of growing something: stage 1, Mulch (learn); Stage 2, Sow (plan); Stage 3, Grow (do it); and finally, Stage 4, Harvest (teach others and grow a new culture). It is in the last stage, Harvest, that some of the most interesting and tangible things occur. Here the group collectively decides on a culminating project or undertaking that will have a lasting value and impact and will carry forward the sustainability agenda.

What appeals to many about the Sustainability Street approach is its emphasis on the local and its commitment to building and strengthening community. Building block 6 is explicitly about community building and presents a number of specific ideas and suggestions, acknowledging the thinking of Robert Putnam (American political scientist and author of the seminal book *Bowling Alone: America's Declining Social Capital*), about how to expand and grow social capital. Its tenets include the following: "Say G'day to strangers," "Organize a local group," "Get involved in local politics," and "Get involved with your neighbors."

Sustainability Street also clearly emphasizes the importance of keeping things informal and of having fun in the process. "Doom and gloom" is discouraged (it is actually principle 2 in the second blocking block!), and celebrating "good stories" is encouraged. Socializing and having a good time together seem an essential ingredient here.

In Penrith, the first council in the Sydney metro region to participate in Sustainability Street, two streets have been chosen: John Jameson Circuit Street and Banool Avenue. Here, with funding support from the Australian Greenhouse Office and Integral Energy, special focus is being given to energy and water. The residents have already been very active by holding meetings, hosting energy and water lectures, organizing to apply for funding to secure rainwater tanks, and setting some ambitious environ-mental targets for themselves (such as a 30 percent reduction in green-house emissions over their current levels). Each street is also pursuing its own specific project ideas; one street wants to convert a vacant parcel of land in the neighborhood back to native bushland, while the other wants a mulcher to handle green waste from the neighborhood (see http://www.penrithcity.nsw.gov.au).

A 2005 evaluation report documents some main benefits of the pro-gram. Three main outcomes were seen: (1) a significant reduction in waste and resource consumption (in the range of 20 to 30 percent); (2) "extraor-dinary, locally devised and developed group projects"; and (3) "wonderful new connections and friendships with neighbors and other local groups." (Vox Bandicoot, 2005, p. 1).

One key assumption behind the program is that a kind of community snowball effect will develop, that one group on one street or in one neigh-borhood will in turn reach many other communities with the Sustain-ability Street message.

Let's Have a Party

In Port Phillip, in the Melbourne metropolitan area, the council efforts to help build a sense of community have come from a public health per-spective, recognizing that strong solid relationships are an important ele-ment in any community health strategy. More specifically, the city—as part of its health plan (all councils in Victoria are required to prepare such a plan)—has taken several initiatives under its Social Cohesion Project.

One main initiative of this project has been Streetlife, launched in 2003. Inspired by a program begun in Perth in 1979 for the 175th anniver-sary of the state, the idea is to help neighborhoods to hold street parties where neighbors get to know one another and begin to build some social bonds. It is about sparking an interest and removing obstacles, and it is al-ways neighborhood (and community) led. In the first year, the city helped hold eighteen street parties (scheduled during the summer months); in the second year, twenty-five parties were held. The city does several things to help organize these events and to help overcome some obstacles that commonly hinder neighborhoods doing this. Street parties typically re-quire a street closure permit and usually incur expensive costs for liability insurance. Under StreetLife, the city has partnered with the Port Philip Community Group, which provides the insurance for free. Street clos-ure barricades are also provided gratis by the council's main construction contractors. The council has also purchased a barbecue and loans this out when requested.

The council has advertised the program, gotten good press coverage for it, and held a council event to give it visibility. The response has been positive, with quite a bit of interest expressed in organizing parties, as the increasing numbers show. About half of the initial streets held a similar party in the second year, so the initiative is creating some good continuity and staying power for some neighborhoods. Now a number of other councils have been calling to learn about Port Phillip's experience and to consider starting up similar initiatives on an ongoing basis.

The city has produced a "toolkit" of good ideas about how to get started as well as a listing of "tips from the experts," extracting key lessons from the organizers of the first-year events. The listing also contains tips about researching one's street and provides sample invitations. An evaluation of the first year of Streetlife shows considerable positive benefits, a sense that the block parties and other activities have helped to make these neighborhoods more sociable and livable.

Imaginative efforts at nurturing new street life can happen in many ways. The city of Wodonga, in the state of Victoria, has recently taken some creative approaches to reinvigorating its public spaces and taking back its main downtown commercial street (its *high* street). First, it hired David Engwicht (mentioned in Chapter 2 and famous for his mental speed-bumps and walking schoolbuses) as their central business district *place-maker* and empowered him to think creatively about how to draw residents back to the city center after 5 p.m., when most of the businesses close. The most important of these initiatives has been Wodonga's Lounging on High, held every Friday evening during the summer months. In dramatic fashion, Engwicht and his colleagues from the city close off and reoccupy segments of the streets, rolling a couch and lounge chairs into the street itself. The events resemble festivals or fairs, with music and lots of activities for kids and families, including face painting, storytelling, clowns, and a circus. One of the creative games for kids is something called Spot the Misfit, in which kids are given an adventure map and tasked to identify the item in storefront shop windows that is out of place. Oversized games are also a prominent feature, with a giant chessboard occupying roadway space. The city's iconic water tower is also lit up with LED lights, part of a series of high street revitalization investments.

For David Engwicht, the challenge is getting residents to mentally (and physically) take back the street, overcoming the historic tendency to psychologically retreat from streets and roadways. David himself exemplifies the mood, directing these events in a green clown suit, funny glasses, and a vivid red party hat. These events have been very popular indeed and have become significant opportunities for residents to reconnect to their city, to rekindle a sense of community, and to have fun in the process. Wodonga has taken other creative place-making steps as well, including the formation of a group of citizen volunteers as High Street Hosts (to provide information and assistance to visitors while adding a personal face to the city), which is now more than three hundred strong; the program Tales From Within: Borrow A Living Book, which provides the opportunity on Saturdays to hear the real-life stories of residents (who become "living books" for the event); and, perhaps most impressive, the fact that Wodonga actually has a "placemaker" on staff.

New Neighborhood and Community Institutions

Place-strengthening can also happen by creating new places in which to be and learn, and new community institutions that facilitate sharing and sustainable living, such as community centers and neighborhood embedded learning and resource centers. The Sydney metro region has several exemplary models of community environmental centers that serve these purposes. In the Newtown neighborhood, for example, the Marrickville and Sydney councils have joined together to fund and create the unique Watershed Center, a storefront environmental center (figure 4.2). The Watershed's location is significant, right on busy King Street, in the midst of a very active, pedestrian-frenzied business district. Walking in off the street, one can find a knowledgeable staff person to advise on a host of environmental matters. The center contains an extensive set of books and other resources and also holds a series of free sustainability workshops on such subjects as natural cleaning, no-dig gardening, and conserving energy, among other topics. The center also sells things like worm farms, composting bins, and natural cleaning kits. The list of free sustainability workshops for 2007–2008 included composting and worm farming, natural cleaning and "home detox," growing food in containers, and ecochoices for sustainable living, among others.

The Watershed is also a major networking center, pulling together individuals and groups interested in sustainability, and working with local businesses. Each year, the center announces a series of green business awards and eco-home awards, for instance. It also runs campaigns (e.g., a "bagbusters" campaign) and supports the activities of an extensive pool of volunteers.

Figure 4.2 The Watershed Center, located in a storefront along a busy street in the Newtown district in Sydney, offers sustainability workshops and educational materials and advice about living more sustainably. *Photo credit:* Tim Beatley

One of the center's more unusual campaigns has been a collaboration with real estate agents to reach those newly arrived to neighborhoods (as well as those about to depart) to inform them of reuse and recycling opportunities and resources. The center has produced a magnetic, postcard-size handout, "Welcome to the Neighborhood," with environmental tips, such as where to take materials for recycling or reuse. The postcard issues both a welcome and a call for greener behavior and consumption, declaring: "As a new member of this community we need your help." New residents are encouraged to consider not only recycling but also composting, managing waste responsibly, supporting local businesses, and purchasing locally made products with limited packaging.

Perth has a number of environmentally oriented community centers as well many neighborhood centers. The Meeting Place Community Centre, for example, is located on Fremantle's main drag, South Terrace, toward the sound end. A converted nineteenth-century home, it provides an unexpected array of educational and community services ranging from a children's crèche to adult skills education, meetings of the Bipolar Disorder Support Association, and various recreational classes. Memberships are

Figure 4.3 Marrickville's Community Nursery is a volunteer-run facility that grows much of the native plant stock needed for local restoration projects. Many local councils in Australia operate or sponsor such community nurseries. *Photo credit:* Tim Beatley

available that provide discounts on the fees charged for courses and other services. The spaces in the building are used for community gatherings, including the monthly meeting of the South Fremantle Precinct (which offers advice on planning matters to the council). The Autumn 2005 program lineup was a diverse and rich one: Italian for children, Mozambique-African dance, creative sewing, seniors outings, homeopathy, and kinesiology, among others. It is also where a dads-only play group convenes and a movie club meets and where counseling and private tutoring happens. The spaces are widely used and quite valuable to the community. It is a building and a community institution aptly named! Heavily dependent on volunteers, the Meeting Place has created a kind of bartering system called Community Points. Volunteering earns you credits that can be used to sign up for classes and to take advantage of the services that might otherwise require cash, such as babysitting.

Many of the local councils in the Sydney metropolitan region have their own community plant nurseries, which both promote local biodiversity conservation and build social capital. Marrickville's community nursery grows and sells native plants and provides plant stock for community revegetation projects, such as its major restoration project at Tempe Reserve (figure 4.3). The nursery operates with a small paid staff (essentially a

director) and relies heavily on volunteers. Many such nurseries are operated by volunteers or run by councils.

One pleasant surprise for my family in Australia was the discovery
of a toy library. A concept completely foreign to us, coming from the less-
than-sharing culture of the United States, it struck us as a terrific idea,
holding the promise of both strengthening our sense of community and
our collective bonds (through sharing with others a common good or resources) and helping (at least in one small way) to dematerialize our lives
(figure 4.4).

As members of the Fremantle Toy Library, we learned how this concept works in practice, an extremely positive experience. Each week or so, a
new cache of toys was transported to our temporary home, eagerly greeted
and delightfully enjoyed by our two young daughters. The toys—Legos,
rolling stock (including tricycles), pushable cars, puzzles, and so forth—
were returned mostly intact about the time the kids lost interest (that is,
relatively quickly). The Fremantle Toy Library is operated by the council,
but many toy libraries are private, volunteer operations, run by dedicated

Figure 4.4 At the Randwick Toy Library, shown here, residents can check-out
(as with books) a variety of toys and play items. Toy libraries offer the chance to
de-materialize a bit, sharing a common stock of toys, as well as reducing the cost
of toys to parents and families. *Photo credit:* Tim Beatley

parents who see the need to share these useful but transitory play things. In Fremantle, the toy library is so popular that there is a waiting list (we were given special dispensation because of the temporary nature of our stay). It is lovingly shepherded over by its council staff person, who helps in many unexpected ways, including pushing the shopping cart (when needed) full of that week's new bounty to the car, an especially useful personal touch when kids are in tow.

In WA, there are some 110 toy libraries and even a WA association of toy libraries, formed in 1981. There are hundreds more throughout Australia. (There are also more a thousand toy libraries in the United Kingdom, where the idea originated.) Toy libraries represent a modest but not insignificant way to reduce material consumption and (like conventional book libraries) to give tangible expression to our public values. Most toys typically are purchased and fairly quickly forgotten within a family, and the act of checking out and later returning toys might, in this small way, help nurture a concept of sharing and temporary use rather than one of consumption and conventional ownership. It is also clearly fun for kids, who have access to a variety of toys far greater than their families would likely be willing or able to purchase. "Each week is like Christmas!" was the usual attitude of our kids.

Food in the City: Urban Agriculture and City Farms

Australian towns and cities provide many creative examples of integrating food production into urban life and of forging new ways to think about sustainable food. And of course food—specifically, the production of sustainable and local food—helps to address many other elements of the sustainability agenda discussed so far (including energy and climate change). Community gardens, urban farms, and other examples of neighborhood and community food production can be found in each of Australia's major cities. There is even an Australian City Farms and Community Gardens Network, which, among other things, convenes a popular annual meeting and publishes a journal called *Community Harvest* (see http://www.communitygarden.org.au; Australian City Farms and Community Gardens Network, 2007).

The many positive examples include community and neighborhood gardens, city farms, school gardens, intergenerational gardening, permaculture demonstration gardens, food co-ops, farmer's markets, and community food celebrations and festivals. While some community gardens have come under threat in recent years (e.g., several gardens in the eastern

Figure 4.5 The Perth City Farm, shown here, is many different things: a community garden and permaculture demonstration area, an orchard and commercial farm, a community arts center and neighborhood meeting place. It is also an excellent example of creative urban regeneration. *Photo credit:* Tim Beatley

suburbs of Sydney), their numbers have increased in many places (such as in South Australia; see Community and Neighborhood Houses and Centres Association, 2006). Some cities also have terrific models of year-round markets, including the Central Market in Adelaide and the Fremantle Market.

Australian cities contain some of the most interesting working models of city farms, impressive attempts to reenvision urban environments as places of bounty and renewal. One of the most striking examples can be seen in Perth. Visiting the Perth City Farm, one arrives almost in disbelief (figure 4.5). Stepping off at the Claisebrook train station, adjacent to downtown Perth, and walking down the steps from the elevated platform, the lush, green, and relatively small (one-hectare) block looks at once a bit out of place and an enticing oasis. Formed in 1994 and the idea of Roseanne Scott, the Perth City Farm defies easy definition or description. It is at once both a community garden and a city farm in the obvious ways—

food is organically produced; it has an on-site nursery; fruit trees are integrated throughout the site, even flanking the property along the perimeter street; and chickens and other poultry are being raised here. It demonstrates sustainable production and permaculture while also producing a considerable bounty.

But the place is much more than this. A former metal scrapyard and battery-recycling site, it demonstrates well the possibilities for creatively reusing contaminated sites in the city. In this case, the land was provided on a short-term lease from the East Perth Redevelopment Authority and substantial cleanup was required, including taking away about a meter of contaminated topsoil.

The farm operates as a not-for-profit, with few paid employees, and relies heavily on volunteers. Some workers are paid employees, some are supported by the government under welfare and back-to-work initiatives, and others are there to fulfill court-mandated community service.

Education is another important function of this unusual place. The city farm hosts many school tours and also conducts a variety of school-based workshops, building environmental awareness as well as a tangible sense of how to give practical daily expression to one's environmental ethics. The city farm is also a staging ground for extensive tree-planting and bush regeneration efforts.

Yet another aspect of the city farm is its nurturing of local artists and musicians. Visiting the farm, one immediately sees this support. Artistic values and impulses permeate the place, from the art forms that grace the gardens to the large wire and paper-mâché creatures hanging and under construction to the graceful graffiti out on the building walls, art is everywhere interspersed with the plants and greenery. The farm has also served as a venue for musicians and hosts numerous community events and performances. The site also serves as an all-purpose community meeting venue and a place where anyone can come and hang out.[1]

The farm, while producing much, is clearly not operating on the model of a commercial farm, though one has the sense that it could. In large part because of the many other dimensions and aspects of the farm—its arts and music as well as its social and educational functions—it is difficult to devote the single-minded attention that would be needed to turn a profit on the agricultural side. Roseanne knows and understands this, and she realizes the trade-offs here. Nevertheless, substantial income is produced through the produce, sold mostly at the Saturday morning organic market (others do drop by during the week to purchase and often pick up produce).[2]

Urban farms have taken a different form in other Australian cities. On a four-hectare site along the Merri Creek in the Brunswick suburb of Melbourne is one of the most ambitious city farms of a similar sort. Called the CERES (the Centre for Education and Research in Environmental Strategies) Community Environment Park, it was created as a garden and has now blossomed into a place with a vibrant mix of ecologically sustainable activities and practices. The Community Environment Park is an apt description given the range of activities there, which includes a certified organic farm, an organic market, a café that serves organic and biodynamic foods, and a permaculture and bushfood nursery that grows and sells local plants and provides horticultural services. This project has an educational mission (for example, offering courses in biodynamic agriculture and gardening) and is where many people recovering from mental illness have found a productive and therapeutic activity in the community. It is a place where community festivals and celebrations occur (such as the Return of the Sacred Kingfisher Festival), a place where new sustainability ideas and technologies are tested and exhibited, and a staging area and locus for networking, community-building, and volunteering activities (see http://www.ceres.org.au).

One major project has been the design and planned construction of the CERES Sustainability Centre. Stage one of the Centre (a visitors center and permaculture and bushland nursery) opened in May 2008. Additional planned stages include a performing arts hall, workshop spaces, offices and a community kitchen. When fully completed, the Sustainability Centre will represent an impressive cluster of green buildings and landscapes and a hive of sustainability practice, thinking, and education.

CERES has spawned other interesting community-building ideas and initiatives. One with special promise is its Urban Orchard Project. More than 180 households in Melbourne now participate in what is essentially a fruit-sharing effort. The project was borne of the recognition that many residents of (northern) Melbourne neighborhoods have extensive fruit trees in their yards and often too much fruit to eat or use on their own. So participants sign up and then bring their extra fruit (and now herbs and vegetables) to the CERES organic market to trade them for other fruits (with the assistance of volunteers). As Ferne Edwards reports: "Lemons are swapped for apricots, apples for tomatoes, basil for nectarines, and recipes for compost; all on a completely informal and friendly basis" (Edwards, 2007). This community orchard group is also able to share experience and tips about caring for fruit trees and serves as an advocate and resource for planting more fruit trees in the city.

The power of community gardens has been demonstrated convincingly in Sydney at the Waterloo Public Housing Estate. Beginning in 1996, several community gardens were installed adjacent to these large high-rise housing projects, providing opportunities for residents to grow food, flowers, and medicinal herbs. The project is a collaborative of the NSW Department of Housing of South Sydney Council and the University of New South Wales (UNSW). Researchers from UNSW evaluated the impacts of these gardens through a series of individual and focus group meetings with gardeners. The reported benefits are considerable indeed. Resident gardeners report a greater sense of belonging and sense of community, and that the gardens have helped to foster new friendships. Much sharing of produce, recipes, and gardening tips has been reported and seems to further cement friendships and build trust among residents. Considerable physical and emotional benefits from gardening are also reported. According to the UNSW study: "The garden acts as a catalyst for conversation, breaking down social barriers so that people feel they can speak to strangers. Seeing someone regularly working in the gardens is a means of identifying them as trustworthy. In turn this leads to friendship formation" (Bartolomei et al., 2003, p. 37).

The gardens have also helped to promote a greater understanding of and among the different cultural groups living in Waterloo and are viewed as "multicultural places," where some cultural and social barriers are overcome. Overall, the UNSW study concludes that the gardens "play an important role in enhancing community and social life on the Estate." These stories show the compelling role that community gardens, orchards, and other forms of local food production can play in forging new personal relationships, enhancing health, and deepening roots to place.

Heritage and Place-making

Australian cities and towns, despite their relative youth, often possess considerable architectural heritage, which contributes greatly to a strong sense of place and strong place character. Newtown, in the Sydney metro area, has taken impressive steps to protect and manage that heritage. King Street and Enmore Road, which comprise the heart of Newtown, represent an unusual and exemplary concentration of Victorian-era structures (figure 4.6). Not a sleepy museum atmosphere, these streets are extremely busy and vibrant with mostly small, street-level retail and housing and offices above. The architectural detail (such as the parapets with lions) is exemplary and breathtaking when taken as a whole.

Figure 4.6 The Newtown area, in Sydney, is home to unusual concentration of Victorian-era structures, and efforts have been made to protect the special historic nature and place qualities there. A special Heritage and Urban Design Development Control Plan has been prepared to guide and regulate any proposed changes (e.g. to building facades) there that might jeopardize the historic integrity of the district. *Photo credit:* Tim Beatley

The heritage controls in place in Australian cities, and the efforts at protecting and ensuring development consistent with the look and feel of these places, are considerable. In the case of King Street and Enmore Road, a special Heritage and Urban Design Development Control Plan (DCP) has been adopted jointly by the South Sydney (now Sydney) and Marrickville councils. The plans provide detailed standards and design criteria for facade alteration and infill development or redevelopment taking place there (South Sydney and Marrickville Councils, 2003). A Heritage Impact Statement is required for any development proposal involving an exterior alteration.

This important regulatory layer provides guidance about such things as building massing, windows and facade features, setbacks, and permissible signage, among others. There are very specific limits on the type and design of signage, but modern signage, consistent with a very active and vibrant commercial district, is allowed and adds to the energy of the streets and the dynamic blending of new and old.

This Newtown DCP is also a place where planners are required to analyze and state clearly what elements contribute to the special feeling of these streets, and this step is done well. In this case, it is a combination of the topography and directions of the streets as well as the street layout, subdivision pattern, and building form (Marrickville and South Sydney Councils, 2003, esp. p. 17).

Some special attention has been given to exterior paint colors, with an extensive inventory and database of colors and color combinations undertaken and a suggested paint scheme put forward. Meant to be helpful, it gives a number of color combinations for each architectural period (late Victorian, federation, and interwar), with detailed illustrations indicating appropriate colors for a structure's different architectural elements. As the council-commissioned study makes clear, building owners are certainly not required to paint their structures, but if and when they're ready to do so in the future, they are encouraged to follow the color scheme recommendations. The result is a pleasing visual harmony, with colors evocative of the historic period of the buildings.

The South West region of Western Australia provides other compelling examples of distinct and colorful towns. The town of Margaret River, for example, is now quite well known for its charm and character, but just a generation ago it was struggling economically. Now a center of a burgeoning wine-based and arts and crafts economy, it is a popular tourist destination. The town is a compact, walkable place, as many smaller towns and cities outside of major metropolitan areas in Australia often are. It is a mixed-use setting, with cafés, restaurants, a grocery store, and more and more housing all in close proximity.

Margaret River's main commercial road stands out for how different it is from its typical American counterpart. The commercial heart remains in the center—here a downtown Target, an ever-present chain store in Australia, which sits at the center of town rather than on a highway commercial strip (these are generally harder to find in Australia) some distance out of town. The town plan for Margaret River strengthens this focus by building up new residential areas within walking distance of the town and preventing sprawl through greenbelts (figure 4.7).[3]

The story in Fremantle is a hopeful one, but one that could have gone the other way. There was a time in the 1960s and early 1970s when downtown Fremantle was seen as a not very desirable place, where the popu-

Figure 4.7 Margaret River, in Western Australia, is a charming town, with a strong sense of place. *Photo credit:* Tim Beatley

lation and the city were in sharp decline and where there were serious and active plans (unthinkable today) to tear down some of the city's most beloved historic structures. One of the first structures proposed for razing was the Fremantle Arts Centre and Maritime Museum, a convict-built building from the 1850s that had been abandoned in the 1960s. Only by a narrow vote was this building preserved, and through concerted efforts and political organizing a heritage preservation era began (figure 4.8). An organization was formed called the Fremantle Society, which successfully fielded council candidates who supported this heritage agenda.

Fremantle did more than passively protect what it did not want to see destroyed. The city created a special fund to purchase and protect important buildings, and it offered financial incentives for preservation by the private sector. It also took active steps to promote the kind of new development and city center renewal it wanted to see take place, instead of sitting idly by and hoping private developers would simply do the right thing on their own. The council financially underwrote several influential projects that set the tone, including the Norfolk Row terrace homes (highly successful, demonstrating unequivocally that downtown housing was possible

Figure 4.8 Fremantle is a charming historic port city, in Western Australia. It is exemplary story of preserving and celebrating its heritage, and nurturing a pedestrian and café culture. *Photo credit:* Tim Beatley

and indeed profitable) and a mixed-use commercial project called the Fremantle Malls, which extended in positive ways the pedestrian-commercial district of the city.

Many observers point to the America's Cup, which came to Fremantle in 1987, as critical in providing the dramatic influx of capital that transformed the city to what it is today. The Cup brought substantial financial capital to bear in redeveloping Fremantle. The $800 million of redevelopment that took place over eighteen months could have removed all trace of its historic past, but instead it was used to enhance these qualities and build in a fifty-year future in terms of infrastructure and new economic opportunities. Such work required an active city council in close touch with its community. For instance, steering away a proposal to raze the historic Esplanade Hotel (and to put up a large modern hotel in its place) required considerable strength of purpose. A major renovation and expansion of the existing historic structure, all built in heritage style, proved to be the right decision, and the hotel is now one of the most popular in the Perth region.

These Australian examples show the importance of heritage planning. The language of "heritage" is interesting and useful to take note of here. In the United States, the tendency is to speak of efforts such as those in Newtown and Fremantle under the label of "historic preservation." But heritage is both more inclusive and more indicative of the values implied—that these are critical elements of the culture and history that require passing along.

In some communities, the heritage protections and philosophy extend to elements more natural than built. In Brisbane, for example, the city several years ago embarked on an interesting project to celebrate its historic fig trees, as part of the city's centennial celebration. Entitled "100 Years of Fig Trees," the program selected a number of the more notable fig trees in the city to highlight and present on an Arbor Day poster. For each of these trees, the city collected personal stories and recollections as well as historic photographs associated with the trees. There is the weeping fig salvaged by a city street sweeper, now known to family and friends as "Pop's fig." There is the Hills fig, planted by schoolchildren and remembered as a "wonderful climbing tree." There is another weeping fig remembered as a shady spot from which to watch factory cricket matches, or the small-fruited fig planted in 1919 to commemorate the men and women who served in World War I. These figs have grown to be massive trees, broadly spreading to fill the landscape, and have become important community icons and gathering spots. They connect generations (photos and memories were collected in the Brisbane project, for instance, of the aging grandson who remembers the grandfather who planted the fig trees he sits in front of) and infuse a sense of historic continuity and meaning (figure 4.9).

Other Australian communities have also sought to systematically understand the extent of heritage trees and to list and protect them in a manner similar to buildings.[4] The City of Sydney, for instance, has adopted an extensive Register of Significant Trees. Through a methodology of identifying trees that includes both cultural and natural criteria, nearly two thousand trees, or groups of trees, situated on both public and private property have been identified and described (City of Sydney, 2005). As part of this heritage process, members of the public are also able to nominate significant trees, and many have. Councils like Sydney understand and are committed to a broader, more inclusive understanding of heritage, which recognizes that there are stories and important layers of social meaning that attach to elements of the natural environment.[5]

Figure 4.9 Trees are important features of place in many Australian cities and towns, and they almost always have community history and personal and family stories attached to them. These Norfolk Pines are a distinctive feature in the Esplanade Park in Fremantle. *Photo credit:* Tim Beatley

Place-strengthening Icons

Trees are, then, significant place-strengthening features, examples of place *icons*. What we remember about a place, what is special about a place, is of course a function of a complex mix of sensory experiences, smells, and sounds as well as human relationships and personal memories that are bound up with these experiences. Icons are of various sorts, including visual icons—prominent things (though not necessarily large or even singular objects) that stand out in importance. Icons might be elements of the built environment or aspects of the natural setting. In Australian cities such as Fremantle, a number of natural environment icons, including trees and shoreline, are critical in shaping experiences and memories.

Port Phillip, in Melbourne, has commissioned an urban iconography study that has thoroughly identified some three hundred icons in the city, organized by neighborhood. More specifically, the study classifies things as icons (e.g., specific objects, such as a clock tower, a theater, or a prominent piece of public art), iconic collective features (such as a style of architecture), or iconic settings (such as a street or an entire precinct). These include both natural features (e.g., a Moreton Bay fig tree) and built features. The St. Kilda neighborhood is an excellent example of how these icons cumulatively add to a very special and significant sense of place. The neighborhood's icons include Luna Park, a historic amusement park with a visually dramatic clown face for an entrance; the Palais Theater; the St. Kilda Pier, a distinctive set of tramline poles; the Copper Domes at Seabaths; and a beaux arts drinking fountain (the Sali Cleve drinking fountain, circa 1911), among others. Perhaps my favorite visual object to make the icon study list is the public art display on the roof of the Hairroom hair salon on Acland Street (figure 4.10). The display consists of an assembled group of sculptures—described as "cartoon people"—that gets one's attention while walking along the wonderful street, partly for the piece's composition but mostly because of its unexpected location.

Iconography studies like this have several benefits. First, they represent a systematic effort to disentangle and identify the individual visual elements that yield a distinctive feeling to a place. Second, by doing this, there is at least the possibility that we (residents and visitors alike) might pay better attention to these features and qualities and thus work to protect, nurture, and add to this stock or pool of community distinctive elements, those features that together contribute to a distinctive place, quality, or character. It is not only a way to analyze and understand but also a guide to planning action. Finally, such a study also has the potential to help introduce a neighborhood and to help its residents know that neighborhood

Figure 4.10 This unusual piece of community art, called Hairroom Rooftop Art, is an extremely distinctive visual landmark in the St. Kilda district in Port Phillip. *Photo credit:* Tim Beatley

better than they otherwise would. Some icons may have been overlooked by those living nearby, remaining underappreciated for their significance or simply forgotten. Iconography studies such as this might help the residents to strengthen their personal knowledge of and connections to place.

An outcome of the iconography study has been the commissioning of "character statements" for several of Port Phillips's neighborhoods. The statements' format and structure are interesting. A precinct description is first written, followed by a statement of community values and a "preferred neighborhood character statement." A second page presents more specific design guidelines that show with text and graphics how important character elements in the neighborhood might be protected and strengthened (e.g., Edwardian architecture, specific types of building materials, scale and setback of structures, and additions to structures, tree canopy, and vegetation).

Distinctive Place-economies

The Blue Mountains, which rise approximately one hundred kilometers west of Sydney, are a designated World Heritage site and a place of immense beauty and biodiversity (figure 4.11). Commerce in the small, charming mountain towns is at once dependent on this resource and needs to be profoundly consistent with its long-term protection and nurturing. The Blue Mountain Council has focused much of its energies in promoting sustainable local economy and businesses.

The Blue Mountain City Council has adopted a twenty-five-year vision and action plan for advancing sustainability—Towards a More Sustainable Blue Mountains—with a priority goal to "enhance the distinctive qualities of our towns and villages to strengthen local identity and sense of place." (Blue Mountains City Council, 2004, p. 25). The plan also

Figure 4.11 The Blue Mountains, west of Sydney, have been declared a World Heritage Site. Concerns about the impacts of growth and development there have resulted in some unusual community efforts to recognize and protect the special nature of this region, and to envision a sustainable economy that nurtures and protects the special qualities of this place. *Photo credit:* Tim Beatley

states strongly the need to nurture the Blue Mountains as a "model for sustainable business and industry" (Blue Mountains City Council, 2004, p. 13).

One of the most interesting initiatives, spearheaded by Paul Heath of the Blue Mountains Council, has been an effort at "branding" businesses in the region that are operating consistently with the sustainable development principles and philosophy of the council and the special natural qualities of the place. In 2003, the Blue Mountains Business Advantage initiative began. As of the end 2005, fifty local businesses had gone through the sustainability training and certification process. Once completed, these businesses can display or use in other ways the Business Advantage's distinctive blue logo.

Although, according to Heath, participation has been slower than hoped, another eighty local businesses are in the process of becoming certified. In the end, Heath has strong hopes that the branding will indicate a meaningful commitment of the business sector for the whole region—signaling a commitment not only to resource protection and sustainable development but also to quality products and service and attention to the needs of customers (something he feels may be lacking in the experience of many visitors to the area today). The branding is viewed as a way to leverage the area's amazing natural bounty while at the same time protecting it, and to further market the region's ecological commitment.

At the core of the program is the belief that many businesses will not be willing or able to pursue additional green measures and actions unless they feel it will yield a monetary return for them. Businesses going through the program will be not only greener, it is believed, but also "smarter" in the sense of operating more efficiently, and thus will see their profitability enhanced in important ways. One benefit of the program, Heath believes, is its ability to allow businesses to learn about one another. It has the potential to build networks, he thinks, and to provide important business information about useful services and products available in the area.

One of the businesses to go through the training and certification is Cloudlands (a mountain retreat). Its proprietor, Anne Elliott, found considerable value in the workshops and training, and it helped her identify new things that she could be doing that she hadn't thought of (for example, new ways of reducing energy consumption and ways she might further purchase local goods and products). It led as well to her starting a spin-off business, an Internet site to sell handmade gifts and hampers from the Blue Mountains.

The Blue Mountains has also seen the emergence of impressive grass-roots efforts by citizens to protect and speak out on behalf of their special place on Earth. Elliott has been one of the local leaders and has been a hearty force behind one organization, MAM (Mountains Against McDonald's). Formed to combat plans to build a McDonald's franchise in the mountains, Elliott counts at least five efforts at bringing in these fast-food chain stores that she and her group have been able to repel. She attributes the success to a "vigilant community," one that truly does not want to see the unique flavor and feeling of the mountains and the predominantly small, locally owned shops and restaurants be lost. MAM has waged effective campaigns, with rallies and public events, engaging in what Elliott calls "terror tactics," being relentless and never giving up. In the most recent case, MAM ran an Internet campaign called "SOS," soliciting letters of support from around the world.

In 2003, at least a partial victory was realized by MAM in the passage of the council's Local Environment Plan (LEP), which restricts any new "formula fast food" chains to the Katoomba and Springwood shopping areas. Elliott, who was one of the main campaigners, thinks the LEP did not go far enough: "Over the years thousands of ordinary mountain people have said they want this region protected against any more fast food chains. . . . There is a mandate for prohibition [and] our mountains deserve better" (quoted in Peatling, 2003).

MAM is typical of many local activist groups in Australia, which rarely have more than about ten to twelve active members but which—partly because of their size and their close connections—are able to achieve highly effective outcomes in their local area. Elliott and her colleagues have many ideas about how to strengthen place and build further commitments to the special region that is the Blue Mountains.

Elliott envisions what she calls "front gate meanders," the notion that nuts and fruits from one's property would be collected and wares displayed at the front gates (perhaps with "honesty boxes") as the basis for a walking, strolling community economy. This would be a good way, she thinks, to meet the neighbors, get some exercise, and strengthen the local economy. It would be a particularly Australian contribution to the Slow Food movement.

Other Australian communities have pursued similar defenses against fast food and corporate food in places where they threaten a strong local sense of place. For example, Byron Bay, a charming coastal community in northern New South Wales, is well known for its ban on drive-thru restaurants.

In Sydney, a popular campaign was waged against a McDonald's that opened on historic Oxford Street in charming Newtown. No official council action was ever taken, but failing business as locals boycotted the place eventually caused the store to close its doors. Newtown is a remarkable place for the quality of its historic architecture and the vibrancy of its streetscape. While there are some chain stores, there are a remarkable number of locally owned and locally oriented shops, cafés, and businesses of various kinds.

Artful Cities: Place-building through Public Art

Public art receives significant attention and is given great importance in many Australian cities. Notable are Melbourne and Port Phillip (adjoining Melbourne). These two cities have made substantial financial and public (as well as private) commitments to art and artistic expressions in the public realm, yielding a major positive impact on the distinctiveness of these cities. A comprehensive arts policy and program entails many other things, of course, including support for young artists, programs to nurture art in the schools, and festivals and arts-based celebrations.

The City of Melbourne operates under an Arts Strategy, adopted in 2004, guiding its arts commitments (City of Melbourne, 2004a). The strategy presents a vision of the city as a "crucible for the arts" and makes specific commitments around seven themes. Already, substantial investments in public art can be seen throughout Melbourne. These artworks make a real and lasting contribution to creating a sense of the city and are a positive part of the experience of living or visiting there.

One of the most visually distinctive pieces of art that one encounters in the Docklands (an area of Melbourne discussed later in this chapter) is artist John Kelly's "Cow Up a Tree" (figure 4.12). It grabs your attention and is a highly unusual sight, which is much of the idea behind the public initiative; these are visual surprises that make walking through streets and public spaces pleasant and intriguing. And the stories behind the bold artistic statements help to deepen the appreciation—the "Cow" is something you might want to bring visitors to see; they are not likely to see a cow up a tree anywhere else. Kelly's work is a cast bronze statue, some eight meters high, and was inspired by a famous Australian painter, William Dobell, who was given the task during World War II of creating papier-mâché cows to place around air bases in Australia in an effort to trick Japanese pilots. Kelly had the curious image of what would happen to these cows during a flood—and thus "Cow Up a Tree"!

Figure 4.12 Called "Cow Up a Tree," this public art, located in the Docklands development in Melbourne, is the creation of artist John Kelly, and reflects the importance given to public art in that city. *Photo credit:* Tim Beatley

One role of public art in sustainability is to tell stories about the past that can help us to see our way to the future. In Fremantle, one of the most unusual public sculptures is the long jetty, a project of noted local artist Joan Campbell (figure 4.13). The timber structure lies on Bathers Beach, about where the colony's first wood and stone jetty was built, a major gateway to the new settlement. It is an unusual piece of work that effectively

Figure 4.13 The "Long Jetty" a piece of public art in Fremantle, is the work of the late-artist Joan Campbell, and intended to draw attention to the historic significance of the site of the settlement's first stone jetty. *Photo credit:* Tim Beatley

draws attention to the location and its historic significance (the remnants of the original jetty structure can be seen in the water nearby). The structure is a magnet for small children, who eagerly climb on all parts of it. The side of the jetty is embellished with handmade tiles, designed and made by local schoolchildren and depicting different events in the city's history as well as explaining how the site was sacred for both Aboriginal people (where the river meets the sea) and Europeans (where the first settlers arrived). Maintaining the area as a special public place is therefore of high priority. Not all in the community were happy with this bit of historical art, and the owners of the McDonald's just landward of the beach objected the most. They soon changed their tune, though, as the installation became very popular, further attracting families to the area.

Support for the arts in Fremantle takes many forms. In previous decades, the city provided special space for budding artists on the basis that artists would create their own economy and would contribute to a vibrant arts community as the city tried to rebuild itself from its former industrial base. The city instigated many smaller street festivals, as well as a few major festivals, to bring people into closer contact with their heritage townscape.

In Fremantle, the emphasis on the arts has carried over to what the city buys—it has its own art collection that now amounts to some one thousand pieces, quite impressive for a relatively small city with a population of only about twenty-six thousand people. There is no central art museum where these pieces are displayed; rather, they appear on the walls of the city hall, the library, and other city spaces and buildings.

Fremantle's former community arts officer Phil Thompson is a well-known local playwright and actor who has developed a series of plays based on Fremantle's history and characters. The plays have a strong sense of the physical place, giving the city another way to celebrate itself. Local author Tim Winton has also given the WA coast its special place in literature (Winton, 1993).

In Port Phillip, an Urban Art Strategy has been prepared, similarly making a strong case for the importance of art to a city and identifying a number of specific actions and directions for the future, including the adaption of a 2-percent-for-art requirement for capital works projects, an additional urban art budget, and the creation of the position of urban arts officer, among others (City of Port Phillip, 2002).

The Port Phillip strategy explicitly uses the term "Urban Art," as opposed to "public art," to emphasize "a strong interrelationship between art and the physical nature and cultural fabric of an urban site. Thus, the city of Port Phillip's Urban Art Strategy evolves from the definition of Urban Art as site-related and place-responsive art in the public domain, which enhances the built and natural environments and adds value to the urban character and the cultural identity of a city through the use of a diverse range of art forms and design applications" (City of Port Phillip, 2002, p. 2).

One of the most creative urban arts projects undertaken in Port Phillip is its Margins, Memories and Markers. Supported financially by Vic Health's "Art and Environment Scheme," it involved collecting stories from residents about their histories and recollections and then translating these into public art. The stories, some four hundred in the end, were collected through a series of public workshops, a "targeted memory-gathering" for more marginalized groups in the community. Together these stories "form a valuable and engaging local history of each neighborhood area" (see http://www.portphillip.vic.gov.au/marginsmemories_markers.html). Artist Julie Shiels collected the stories and created six major public installations from the major themes, as well as twenty-eight bronze plaques, which are fairly evenly distributed across the city's neighborhoods. In Shiels's words:

> The stories that are told and represented in the artworks often flow from individual recollections, but by conceptualizing those stories into public monuments, the artists have vested those stories with shared meaning. The artworks mark our memories of place, and so give those places renewed public value. We remember our shared past, not in the form of monuments to famous men and public figures, but in a celebration of the everyday life of the community. (City of Port Phillip, 2003)

One of the more intriguing installations is called "Tommy's Story," a bronze casting of a set of boots and clothes laid on a wall, depicting the story of a man who during the depression would swim to his job at the wharves. All of the collected stories can be found on the Web site (http://www.portphillip.vic.gov.au/marginsmemories_markers.html), which itself contributes to a shared sense of history and community.

An interesting element of Melbourne's public arts programs has been its efforts to bring art to its many laneways and alleys. Its laneways art program sponsors artists to design and install art, usually for a temporary period. The notion is to instill a new appreciation for these spaces, to get more people to visit them, and to challenge conventional thinking about them. Laneways are described as "the hidden treasures of the city," and laneways art is intended to "transform" them into "forums for comment, questioning and enchantment" (City of Melbourne, 2004a).

The artwork produced is bold and eye-catching, to say the least. "Walking on Air," for instance, was an interesting temporary installation by artist Duke Albada. Described as an "interactive installation," the design transformed the center of a laneway called Cohen Place into a moving, gurgling flow of soapy, bubbly water, and pedestrians were encouraged to step into it. The artwork sought to remind observers "that there is more to walking than simply putting one foot in front of the other. In the center of this narrow lane, soap bubbles pop, sway and push their way up and under passing feet. Challenging the notion that having one's feet firmly placed on the ground is always desirable; visitors to this installation will discover a lighter way to travel, one that invites and celebrates play and experimentation" (City of Melbourne, 2004d).

Public art can also apply creative impulses to aspects of the city that might not seem on first blush to be the most obvious places for this. Brisbane's unusual program to promote the painting of otherwise visually

Figure 4.14 In Brisbane, there are some 900 painted signal boxes, such as this one, a result of a city community arts initiative. They add a certain visual liveliness to downtown Brisbane and are an unusual way for citizens and neighborhoods to express their artistic creativity. *Photo credit:* Tim Beatley

bland traffic signal boxes (TSBs) has been widely recognized by visitors and residents alike, becoming one of the more notable artistic and visual elements of the city (figure 4.14). Begun on a pilot basis in 2000, it was prompted by an effort to stop graffiti vandalism of the boxes. In a trial, turning the boxes into community art emerged as the most effective "target hardening strategy" (Hodgson, 2003). Since then, the program has been wildly successful and some nine hundred boxes have been painted. Participating is relatively easy—an individual or group can pick a TSB (or have one assigned) and submit a design, and the city provides the paint, tape, and safety equipment. The organization Artforce, which runs the program, suggests that designs should be "bold, original, exhibit artistic merit and reflect one of the following: the immediate environment; the character or culture of the suburb; the history of the area; community pride; creativity" (Artforce, 2003). Each year, a contest is held to select the best TSB design, with a $1,000 AUD first prize.

All nine hundred of the boxes—those painted to date—have been photographed and can be viewed online (see http://svc189.bne146v.serverweb.com/artforce/painting.asp). Online visitors are encouraged to vote on their favorite five, and the site keeps a running tally. Brisbane's lead has been followed by other cities. In Sydney, there are some similarly painted traffic boxes in Newtown, for example, and other cities have had active programs to distinctively paint other kinds of community objects (such as, in Fremantle, bus stops in nautical themes).

Public Space and Sociability

Fremantle is a city ideally to be savored and enjoyed on foot. The town form is based on a grid street layout, few of the streets lack sidewalks, and the visual and other sensory delights are considerable. Much of the city's uniqueness of place can be seen in its layering of neighborhood details— the sum of its character, if you will, that would simply go unnoticed by passengers in cars. These features are found in the pavement, fences, trees, and streetscapes that can be seen only when walking.

My own modus operandi was to disembark from the bus a considerable distance away from our home in South Fremantle and then to wander home, preferably taking a different route each time. The result was an ability to notice neighborhood details that would otherwise be missed— shades and hues of color on limestone walls, flowering eucalyptus trees, the flutelike sounds of magpies and the sharp acoustics of red wattlebirds, the different colors of fencing along sidewalks, and the many ways in which residents have personalized their homes and yards. It was enjoyable and therapeutic and, perhaps most importantly, produced a depth of feeling for and sense of place that solidified my positive affection for this city.

The living environments in Fremantle have been strongly personalized, with individuals and families making their mostly indelible mark. The extent and nature of these personalized markings vary. On some streets, there are beautiful mosaic walkways lovingly constructed, another spot where the sidewalk has been inscribed with a child's name and birth date, and yet another spot where a specially designed wavy fence screams that this is a kind of different place, *my* place, *my* home. Opportunities for personalizing one's landscapes are important in creating both a sense of place and a sense of personal connection to and commitment about that place. It

Figure 4.15 In Fremantle, residents are encouraged to personalize their sidewalks, and along many streets there is a kind of sidewalk mosaic art such as this. *Photo credit:* Tim Beatley

is actually a matter of policy in Fremantle that residents can do these kinds of things when sidewalks and streets are being put in or upgraded (figure 4.15). Such activities are criticized by some as conveying a messy feel, a sense that these things lead to lower property values and put off those looking to buy a home and join a neighborhood. South Freo, however, shows that this is certainly not the case.

Melbourne also has a definite sense of character and a special sense of place, a function (like Fremantle) of a large number of heritage buildings as well as the Yarra River, the many parks in and around the center of the city, and most especially the grid street pattern. Melbourne officials acknowledge the importance of this original Hoddle grid and has been working to strengthen and expand its pedestrian qualities.

Grids and Greenery, a book produced by the city's Urban Design Division in 1987, remains a key reference. It identifies many elements of the city's distinctive character that can be strengthened and reinforced. The city's distinctive grid street pattern—a slightly tilted two-by-one-kilometer rectangle dating to an 1836 town plan—remains visible and coherent today. The streets and pedestrian spaces within the city center are at the heart of this city's feeling and flavor: "It has a character of regular and spacious main streets, and irregular and narrow lanes and arcades. The main streets give the city center a coherent and grand formality. The little streets, lanes and arcades within this simple grid have the potential to become enormously diverse and exciting places" (City of Melbourne, 1987, p. 11).

Twenty years later, it is clear that this has happened with the laneways of Melbourne, which are now a major feature and tourist attraction with their "diverse and exciting places." This city has done many things to extend its pedestrian realm in recent years, and the story of how it has become one of the most pedestrian-friendly cities in the world is an important one.

In the mid-1980s, with stories in the newspaper about a city in decline, there was a growing view in Melbourne that something needed to be done to stop the outflow of people, to turn the city around, to move beyond a city that was essentially a commuter city with life downtown ending at 5 p.m.

Like many cities, Melbourne began its regeneration by creating opportunities for people to live in the downtown; this step has achieved spectacular growth. However, Melbourne also made a particular effort to focus on the walkability of its urban environment—a key strategy that is now evident in every street and alley.

An important step was to bring in Danish pedestrian and public space guru Jan Gehl, whose extensive recommendations served as an important guide to actions needed. Every year, the city implemented more of the plan, slowly converting each street to a more attractive environment.

Gehl was able to say many things about what needed to be done, things that were difficult politically for city staff to say but that nonethe-

Figure 4.16 Few cities have been as successful at nurturing a pedestrian and café culture as Melbourne. The city has done many things, including new bluestone street pavers, new street furniture and extensive public art, and the creation of new public spaces such as Federation Square. *Photo credit:* Tim Beatley

less needed to be said, such as that the traffic light phases for pedestrians were too short, that traffic congestion can never be solved by speeding up traffic, and that the quality of the sidewalk is more important for the local economy than is the ease of driving through a city. In 1993, Gehl conducted the first public space survey of the city and its streets and squares, recording outdoor seating, usage, and pedestrian numbers and patterns. His report made several recommendations for improving the public realm and public life of the city, and to its credit, Melbourne has implemented many of them (figure 4.16). Melbourne has emerged as a remarkable case study in an emerging pedestrian city, having shown some dramatic, positive change in its pedestrian character and public sphere in the relatively short span of about twenty years.

The creation of an Urban Design Division within the city government is an accomplishment in itself. Enhancing the visibility and importance given to public space, this group has effectively developed, advocated, and implemented the city's comprehensive public space parking. On-staff designers in the division have provided the architectural and aesthetic wherewithal to produce the city's distinctive street furniture and detailing, which accounts for much of the look and feel of this contemporary city.

Gehl refers to this metamorphosis as the "Melbourne miracle" and gives the city much credit for what it has done to bring this about. According to Gehl: "Of all the things a city can do to improve its environment, Melbourne has done almost everything: more residents and students, more 'people' streets, squares, lanes and parks, wider sidewalks, quality materials, active shop frontages, fine furnishings, new street trees and public art programs" (City of Melbourne, 2005).

The city restored an old railroad turning barn along the river and in the process created a new river park and several new pedestrian streets and placed considerable emphasis on redesigning sidewalks, including planting five hundred new street trees each year and placing street furniture and public art. A number of steps have been taken to restore and strengthen the city's traditional grid pattern. One of the most significant was a forty-meter height limit within the city's central retail core. Among other things, this has ensured that the city's public spaces—its sidewalks, parks, and outdoor cafés—receive adequate sunlight. Taller buildings on the hilliest areas of the city have been allowed (and even encouraged), but the city's CBD sits mostly in a bowl where reduced height makes sense. New projects are encouraged to be mixed use, and the city has taken a number of steps to promote a twenty-four-hour city and bring people back into the city to live. In some cases where taller buildings have been permitted, developers have been encouraged to build them set back, with structures up to the street but with higher buildings behind with forty meters in height contained in front.

The city has sought to turn around the empty floors of office spaces through a variety of financial and regulatory incentives to encourage the conversion of offices to residential. Since the 1980s, CBD population has gone from one thousand residents to more than ten thousand today, and it will continue to grow as many new residential developments are planned. The city also converted a property that it owned to residential as a demonstration to help shift perception by the building/development community. This project was extremely successful, tipping the perception in favor of such residential conversions. Most units were sold before the project was completed, a trend that has continued with most new residential projects.

The city has also had a policy of encouraging outdoor cafés and restaurants, leasing these spaces at relatively low rates. The feeling has been that by receiving this break, merchants are expected to invest whatever savings they incur in quality chairs and tables and in creating a quality service and experience for customers. With a few exceptions, this has been the case.

Melbourne is not resting on these accomplishments but appears to be forging forward on several fronts. The new Docklands development, a brownfield redevelopment, will add fifteen thousand people to the city's population. The city is presently extending the CBD grid to reach the Docklands and in many other places is seeking to build new pedestrian connections.

The extensive network of trams, ever present in the center of Melbourne, is also an important aspect of the unique character of this city. The trams, five hundred in all, are of various ages and colors, with vintage trams operating on the circle line, which (as the name implies) circles the CBD. Trams are as central as anything to the history of this city, dating back to 1869, when they were originally horse-drawn. The city never gave up on them, despite the state government's wanting to close them down, as they have been in most cities around the world. Now Melbourne has a transit system that means a person may never need a car in the central and inner areas, and the trams have become an important icon in their own right.

Pedestrian connectedness has been encouraged again through renewed emphasis on and appreciation of the lanes and alleyways between buildings. Throughout the CBD, these areas become vibrant pedestrian spaces, serving as places for new activity, such as outside cafés and small boutiques. In many places, spaces have been taken back from cars and given over to pedestrians.

Gehl's 1993 study of pedestrian spaces and use patterns set an important benchmark against which Melbourne's progress has been judged. Gehl was invited back in 2004 to see how much progress had in fact been made, and his conclusions are striking. He found that by 2004 there were 40 percent more pedestrians on the streets on a typical workday, and twice as many pedestrians in the evening. Foot traffic along such key streets as the Bourke Street Mall and Swanston Street has dramatically risen. The number of café seats, one measure of the draw of a place and its relative level of activity and energy, rose by 275 percent in this period (Gehl, 2004). The city has also improved considerably in economic activity and property values. The city has grown from only 2 outdoor cafés in 1973 to an astounding 356 today, signaling a café culture and public realm more akin to Italy than Australia.

Clearly, the presence of more residents and students living downtown has been a big part of the Melbourne story. The number of downtown flats increased by 3,311 percent between 1982 and 2002, contributing especially to making Melbourne more of a twenty-four-hour city and probably accounting for much of the nighttime pedestrian increases (City of Melbourne, 2005).

Melbourne has gradually been designing back in connections to the Yarra River. This has included impressive pedestrian space and development along the Southbank and especially the new Birrarung Marr Park on the north side of the river. Adjacent to Federation Square, this park features such creative elements as a distinctive pedestrian bridge, bike and pedestrian trails, an interesting musical installation called the Federation Field of Bells (which chimes out music composed especially for it), a children's art center (ArtPlay) created in an old railroad structure, and a speaker's corner. The park takes a more natural, less formal approach to the landscape along the river, including the use of bioswales to collect rainwater and the planting of native trees (as well as the protection of thirty-six heritage-listed elms). Most importantly, the park—whose name means "river of mists" in the language of the Wurundjeri people, who occupied this landscape before European settlement—entices residents and visitors to walk and bike along the river and generally to reconnect to this important natural feature.

Another distinctive pedestrian realm, this one found in Brisbane, is the South Bank Parklands, located along the Brisbane River. Here, a seventeen-hectare pedestrian district has been created with a unique (and rather large) system of human-made lagoons and beaches in the center of the city. A haven for kids, it is a distinctive and highly unusual scene; perhaps a modern incarnation of the Australian tradition of rock pools, the sight of sunbathers and swimmers framed by tall buildings and an urban scene is striking. And it's all part of a larger pedestrian district; there are shops and restaurants nearby as well as an area of outdoor barbecues. The Clem Jones Promenade takes strollers along the river, and a bougainvillea-covered arbour walk runs a full kilometer, the length of South Bank. On weekends, South Bank hosts a thriving market. The pedestrian realm here is vibrant and offers a natural counterpoint to the Queen Street Mall. This highly popular location was built for a world trade fair at a time when Brisbane was just coming out of a period of suburbanization and highly conservative government that frowned on the use of public space by people in groups. The resulting pedestrian celebration that followed the building of South Bank has spread to many other areas of Brisbane.

The presence of a major pedestrian core in most Australian centers is often commented on by visitors. These important spaces include, for instance, the Queen Street Mall in Brisbane, Rundle Street in Adelaide,

Hay Street in Perth, and Martin Place in Sydney. The Queen Street Mall in Brisbane is especially impressive, boasting some seventy thousand visitors a day and an incredible diversity of stores and activities in a highly walkable, highly pleasant outdoor space (including 1,200 shops, restaurants, and movie theaters) as well as a below-grade bus terminal providing easy transit access.

In a nation with most of its population in locations that hug the more hospitable coastline, Australian cities offer many good examples of how to facilitate access to beaches, harbors, and coastal edges. During our time in Sydney, we enjoyed daily visits to the shore near our home on Coogee Beach, within the municipality of Randwick (figure 4.17). It was possible there to travel by foot a great distance north and south, as most of the beaches were connected by trails and pathways. In Coogee, a terrific wooden walkover structure allows pedestrians to travel along the cliff's edge, with spectacular views of the ocean and with the protection of a wild buffer between the edge of development and the sea. This elevated walkover has small, built-in benches for stopping and sitting, and an interesting habitat of windswept vegetation, small waterfalls, rock pools, and other microhabitats of special interest to kids.

In Western Australia, formal planning policy for nearly fifty years has mandated the setting aside of a relatively wide public beach, again allowing pedestrian movement and prohibiting the encroachment of homes and hotels on this recreational and pedestrian swath. A Metropolitan Improvement Fund (land tax) has been mandated for this period that is specifically used for purchasing such land (as well as other parkland and infrastructure easements). Nearly 90 percent of all foreshore in Perth, for example, is now in public ownership.

Australian life is clearly oriented toward being outside, celebrating the climate and natural conditions of this special place on earth. Much of the country is fiercely hot in summer, but residents simply organize and prepare accordingly for the elements.

It should be admitted, however, that Melbourne, and indeed all the major metropolitan areas in Australia, are highly car dependent and exhibit regional growth patterns historically similar to those in the sprawling United States. As Gordon Price, a keen Canadian planning observer, rightly notes about Melbourne: "Melbourne is really two regions: the city of trains and trams and the inner neighborhoods—and then the city of the automobile and the sprawl beyond" (Price, 2007). All other Australian cities could be described similarly. Perhaps significant is that these older, inner areas have no sense of the kind of decline that has been evident in American

Figure 4.17 The Coastal Walk near Coogee Beach in Sydney. Extensive wooden walkover structures and pathways along residents to access dramatic cliff edges and spectacular ocean views. *Photo credit:* Tim Beatley

cities. The challenge for many Australian planners is to take some of the inner area features into the outer suburbs; this is a big challenge, but at least most people can see what they want demonstrated in the older areas.

The Dynamic Heritage of Places

Fremantle has made efforts more recently to give due consideration to the rich Aboriginal culture that existed when the area was settled by Europeans in the early 1800s. The Fremantle story demonstrates the truism that community history is not a static but a dynamic thing, subject to constant restatement and reinterpretation. One place where this dynamic nature has been most evident is in how Fremantle treats its statues and memorials. A dramatic case in point is the controversy over the Maitland Brown Memorial (also known as Explorers Monument), a statue placed in 1913 at a prominent location on the Fremantle Esplanade to commemorate the leader of a search party sent to find a small group of surveyors killed by

Aborigines in the north. Brown successfully retrieved the bodies but also inflicted considerable loss of life on an Aboriginal camp in the process.

The original Maitland Brown Monument speaks in solemn tones about the events that transpired:

THIS MONUMENT WAS ERECTED BY
C J BROCKMAN
AS A FELLOW BUSH WANDERER'S TRIBUTE TO THE MEMORIES OF
PAINTER, HARDING AND GOLDWYER
EARLIEST EXPLORERS AFTER GREY AND GREGORY OF
THIS TERRA INCOGNITA. ATTACKED AT NIGHT BY
TREACHEROUS NATIVES THEY WERE MURDERED
AT BOOLA BOOLA NEAR LA GRANGE BAY
ON THE 13 NOVEMBER 1864. ALSO AS AN APPRECIATIVE
TAKEN OF REMEMBRANCE OF
MAITLAND BROWN
ONE OF THE PIONEER PASTORALISTS AND PREMIER POLITICIANS
OF THIS STATE. INTREPID LEADER OF THE GOVERNMENT
SEARCH AND PUNITIVE PARTY. HIS REMAINS TOGETHER
WITH THE SAD RELICS OF THE ILL
FATED THREE RECOVERED WITH GREAT RISK AND DANGER
FROM LONE WILDS REPOSE UNDER A PUBLIC MONUMENT
IN THE EAST PERTH CEMETERY.
LEST WE FORGET

The original plaque states that Maitland Brown was "attacked at night by treacherous natives." In the late 1980s, Murdoch University historians and local Aboriginal groups successfully lobbied for adding a new plaque, below the original one, offering a much different perspective on the events. The work of the historians uncovered quite a different side to the conflict: the original party of white explorers had been warned off the land by the Aboriginals (the response of the whites was to shoot their rifles at the Aboriginals and to generally ignore the warnings), the party was likely not killed in their sleep (a fairer fight than the white myths had told), and the retaliatory attack on the Aboriginals more punitive and brutal than probably was appreciated. Righting the historical record, and doing it in a visible, public way, seemed an essential part of any true process of reconciliation between white and Aboriginal societies, and Fremantle took a positive step when it finally unveiled the "corrective" plaque in 1994 (figure 4.18). Elders from the aboriginal community where the village attack occurred came to

Figure 4.18 The Maitland Brown Memorial in Fremantle contains the perspective of both original European settlers about a tragic event, but more recently the quite different perspective of Aborigines. *Photo credit:* Tim Beatley

Fremantle for the plaque ceremony, sprinkling dust at the base of the structure. The addendum plaque added the following to the monument:

> THIS PLAQUE WAS ERECTED BY PEOPLE WHO FOUND THE
> MONUMENT BEFORE YOU OFFENSIVE. THE MONUMENT
> DESCRIBES THE EVENTS AT LA GRANGE FROM ONE
> PERSPECTIVE ONLY; THE VIEWPOINT OF THE WHITE 'SETTLERS.'
> NO MENTION IS MADE OF THE RIGHT OF ABORIGINAL PEOPLE
> TO DEFEND THEIR LAND OR OF THE HISTORY OF PROVOCATION
> WHICH LED TO THE EXPLORERS' DEATHS. THE 'PUNITIVE PARTY'
> MENTIONED HERE ENDED IN THE DEATHS OF SOMEWHERE
> AROUND TWENTY ABORIGINAL PEOPLE.
> THE WHITES WERE WELL-ARMED AND EQUIPPED
> AND NONE OF THEIR PARTY WAS KILLED OR WOUNDED.
> THIS PLAQUE IS IN MEMORY OF THE ABORIGINAL PEOPLE
> KILLED AT LA GRANGE. IT ALSO COMMEMORATES ALL OTHER
> ABORIGINAL PEOPLE WHO DIED DURING THE INVASION
> OF THEIR COUNTRY.
> LEST WE FORGET

Such steps are crucial to helping construct more balanced community histories. Indeed, while they often feel like small gestures in the face of the lingering injustices in the way Australia's first peoples have been treated, they are nonetheless positive steps in the direction of community healing and in corrective history.

Much of Australia's settlement history, and the history of its cities and towns, as conveyed in similar fashion in statues, plaques, and official records is similarly slanted. "Founding myths" need rewriting, and in other cities this has happened to a certain degree. The story of John Batman, "founder" of Melbourne, and his "purchase" of land from the Wurundjeri tribe is one of the most egregious stories. Arriving in June 1835, Batman essentially traded a set of relatively valueless objects—"scissors, shirts, tomahawks, knives, blankets, and handkerchiefs"—for about six hundred thousand acres of land. He boasted later, "I am the greatest landowner in the world," even though it appeared to the Aboriginal chiefs present that they were only participating in a "friendship ceremony that would allow Mr. Batman temporary rights to cross through their country" (see http://Melbournewater.com.au).

John Wesley Burtt's famous oil painting of the supposed signing of this "treaty" has become a famous (perhaps infamous?) image, depicting a serene and romanticized notion of European settlement. Sometimes the historical balancing happens in brief though forceful ways, as in protests and media events that tell the fuller story. In the early 1990s, for instance, members of a local Aboriginal group stormed the Victoria Supreme Court building and placed the statue of Batman on trial for war crimes, garnering some public attention to a different side of local history. More recently, there have been efforts to erect a statute to an Aboriginal leader, Chief William Barak, who had been with his father at the Batman treaty signing. With strong support from the local Aboriginal community, the statute will likely became a reality, serving as a useful and highly appropriate counter-balance to Batman's statue and prominent place in Melbourne's history.

Making the Historic Visible and Knowable

To the seasoned eye, there are many historical markers in a city like Fremantle. Allowing historical remnants to remain can indeed actively encourage the historical stories to be told and in the process do much to enhance the special feeling and flavor of a place. In Fremantle, one of the more interesting examples of this can be seen along the verandah at the Esplanade Hotel, a historic landmark in itself. Here, simple wooden benches can be seen that, when the story behind them is understood, reflect a humanity and compassion, a story worth knowing and telling. In this case, a local union leader, Paddy Troy, had the benches built during the depression so that those seeking day labor would have a dignified place to wait. (They are now known as the Paddy Troy benches) (figure 4.19).

The more history and insight one has about a place, the more one is able to look at buildings, streets, and urbanscapes and be able to understand and tell that history, then the more connected and thus the more a part of that community a person will be. These forms of bonds to place are probably underappreciated by most in modern cities. We do not care about places because, in part, we do not understand them in any personally meaningful way. Cities like Fremantle are full of stories and have numerous cues in the cityscape that *could* trigger the retelling of such stories and, in turn, the planting of new seeds of personal meaning.

One example of how this awareness of heritage helps in current policy issues concerns the issue of whaling. In 2007, Japan announced that it would be taking humpback whales from the Southern Ocean, whales that migrate along the Western Australian coast and are greatly loved now as part of people's new awareness of the marine environment. It is also ironic

Figure 4.19 The Troy Paddy Benches, in Fremantle. The presence of these benches outside the Esplanade Hotel, reminds visitors and residents of what it was like during the depression. *Photo credit:* Tim Beatley

that the former whaling community of Fremantle would come out publicly, via a statement by the mayor, in support of the International Whaling Commission's ban on commercial whaling and, in particular, targeting the new policy of the Japanese to take humpback whales.

Illustrating the potential international role of cities, Fremantle's message about whaling was specifically directed at its sister city of Yokosuka in Japan, the country leading the charge to resume commercial whaling. Other cities made similar pleas, though without the whaling past of Fremantle. In Fremantle, whaling began with the forming of the Fremantle Whaling Company in 1886; the whaling tunnel, a dramatic excavation connecting high street to the foreshore, remains a visible connection to this time in history. Japan abandoned its plans to take humpback whales after the international outcry.[6]

A marvelous idea is Fremantle's yearly Heritage Festival. Heritage is a special concern in this town, as we have seen, but what happens here during this roughly week-long program could happen anywhere, with real potential to deepen knowledge and understanding of places and, in turn, personal connectedness. The program includes an extensive lineup of lectures, building tours, and walking tours, many distinctively titled: "The Seaman's Strike of 1925," "Dirt, Disease and Depravity" (a look at the seedier history of the city), and "Warships, Heroes, and Legends." A series of radio interviews about the history of the city is carried on the community radio station. More practical and personal are such workshops as "Researching the History of Your House" and "Aborigine Family History." One can even come and play the Moondyne Joe game or go on torchlight tours of the Fremantle Prison.

Aboriginal history does not loom large in the 2005 Heritage Festival, however. There is an Aboriginal Heritage Walking Tour, but not much else specifically addressing this especially important element of the city's history. The bias is perhaps understandable because visible manifestations of Aboriginal history and culture are largely absent throughout the history. (Much of the program understandably emphasizes tours and talks associated with buildings, streets, museums, cemeteries, and so forth that most represent post-1830 European settlement.)

In Fremantle, the painting of a reconciliation mural has been commissioned near the train station, in Pioneer Park, by local Aboriginal artist Melanie Evans. A beautiful rainbow serpent is the prominent feature, representing "the strength, beauty and creation of the natural features of this country," and the blue and green, the ocean and freshwater, indicate the "differences between people" and the possibilities that they might coexist. Along the bottom of the mural is a history of the Nyoongar people, including time before colonization by Europeans.

The Evans mural is striking, with vivid colors. It catches the eye and draws visitors' attention (figure 4.20). Similar reconciliation artworks and projects can be found in many other cities and towns throughout the country, with likely modest effect. Though they are probably well intentioned, given the continued dismal state of Aboriginal society and peoples, one has to wonder about the ultimate effect. However, in 2006, the Nyoongar people were awarded a native title claim covering the whole of the South West of WA, so perhaps these small steps of appreciation and reconciliation do build up.

How to tell the full story of a place remains an essential challenge everywhere, and especially for places where European colonization has imposed its own singular, hegemonic culture and history, displacing not only the indigenous history but the history of conflict between Europeans and Aborigines.

While not a perfect case, Fremantle has gone through an impressive process of preparing and adopting a "policy for respect, recognition and

Figure 4.20 The "Reconciliation Mural," in Fremantle, is the work of Aboriginal artist Melanie Evans, and depicts visually the long history of that community. *Photo credit:* Tim Beatley

reconciliation with aboriginal people" (City of Fremantle, 2000). Officially adopted as city policy in 2000, it lays out a comprehensive set of actions to be taken to address Aboriginal needs in the community (employment, families, health, education, and housing, for instance), giving new emphasis to education about and visibility of the history and culture of the Nyoongar people. As important as the tangible action is the tone and philosophy of the policy—acknowledging in plainly written words the inequities of the past (and present). The city's policy states, for instance, that the city council "recognizes that the Nyoongar people are the original owners of the Fremantle area."

One key message in the policy plan is an acknowledgement of the relative invisibility of Aboriginal history, traditions, and culture in Fremantle (and most other Australian communities). The plan states the intention to promote Nyoongar culture and history, "including it in public artwork, community art, cultural events, the planned performing arts centre and other public buildings, recreation events, corporate events, signage and naming of streets and parks" (City of Fremantle, 2000, p. 22).

Giving explicit consideration to underrepresented, underappreciated Aboriginal history remains a struggle in many places. It is now common for local councils to employ one or more Aboriginal Heritage officers. In Manley, in the Sydney metro area, such an officer exists. This council is also attempting to restore many of the original/traditional place names there.

Collecting oral histories has become another fairly common strategy for capturing and understanding the history of a place and for uncovering the stories of the people who may have played especially important roles— as well as residents who have lived through significant historical events or periods. In Fremantle, many of these oral histories have been recorded on tape and are now available to be borrowed by patrons from the main library's local history section.

Many Australian towns and cities attempt to take full advantage of the heritage assets of their place. Often, this means redefining liabilities as assets, creatively reenvisioning elements of the built environment as opportunities to nurture an interesting and unusual face for a place. Few examples of this are as clear as the Fremantle Prison. Australia has an ambiguous and conflicted view about its convict past—it is an odd mix of embarrassment and pride, depending on the day of the week and the context in which it comes up. At the Fremantle Prison, visitors can search for ancestors in the convict database, an entertaining and informative process called "find a felon in your family tree" on the prison's Web site.

The Fremantle Prison is now a major regional tourist destination. Within its limestone construction is a beautiful facility. Its dramatic entrance belies the suffering that took place there. Built in 1855 by convict labor, the prison closed its doors in 1991. Touring the prison's extensive underground tunnel system, through which fresh water was provided not only to the prison but eventually to the entire town, is perhaps the most interesting of the new touristic ideas being pursued. Hardy visitors don protective helmets and harnesses, climb down ladders, and float through the tunnels on small rubber boats.

Conclusions and Lessons Learned

In our epoch of massive globalization and spreading sameness, maintaining—indeed strengthening—the unique qualities of local places becomes both harder and ever more urgent. My time living in Australia led me to appreciate the special flavor of Australian towns and cities and to wonder how this was feeling was accomplished. Many remarkable creative endeavors are under way: supporting public art, encouraging people to get outside and in the public realm, identifying and preserving the icons that make a place recognizable, encouraging and empowering citizens to make a place their own (as in Fremantle's policy of encouraging residents to personalize their sidewalks), layering on new artistic expressions, and building new social and community institutions that will bring citizens closer to one another and the environments in which they live, among many others.

There is no single action or policy that will be right for American communities, but Australian cities and towns offer much to be inspired by and quite a menu of new ideas from which to select. Most of the actions and ideas, I would argue, would be immediately applicable to the American realm (where the loss of unique place qualities is happening at an even faster pace!), and this chapter has presented a rich palette of possibilities.

The ambiance and character found in the Australian communities profiled here do not come about by accident. Commitments to the pedestrian realm are needed, for instance, as are investments in public and community art and in programs that strengthen social interaction and deepen knowledge of the community and its history and people. The stories and place-strengthening initiatives described here together point to the many aspects that contribute positively to creating unique, distinctive places. It is about preserving historic buildings, to be sure, but also about much more, including heritage trees, historic parks and spaces, and even very specific urban design elements—all can be imbued with meaning and can contribute to place-making.

As these many community stories show, the process of strengthening a sense of place, a place's character, is exactly that—not a onetime action or decision but an ongoing, dynamic process. Even a community's historic monuments, and its self-understanding of its own history, will need to change over time, further contributing to its unique community DNA and strengthening commitments to place.

These rich Australian stories of place-building and strengthening tell us even more. They show the importance of understanding the intrinsic and necessary connection between sustainability and a green urbanism agenda, on the one hand, and a sense of place and place commitments on the other. The many ways we can recognize and nurture the special qualities of places will in turn help to encourage greater rootedness and the extent to which we actually *care* about the places in which we live. The Australian communities that served as my family's homes—Fremantle, for instance—were certainly not nondescript communities that exuded sameness; rather, they were profoundly endearing and charming places, places that celebrated their special feeling and qualities and, even for brief residents such as we were, produced bonds of place that even now beckon us back. They were also communities that placed a high priority on environment and sustainability. Sustaining and stewarding over our cities and landscapes will require the forging of such bonds of place, such place affections. Without these affections, our levels of care and interest will likely wane, and the chances of achieving anything sustainable are unlikely indeed.

The stories told in this chapter show further the importance of emphasizing the social realm, and of making efforts at building up the social capital of a community, in any vision of green urbanism. There are indeed many things that can be done, many creative steps and initiatives that can be undertaken, to begin to buttress the social realm—from funding community centers to sponsoring block parties and street celebrations to supporting public art. Partly this is about overcoming the usual limited notion of what a city or community can do. Cities like Port Phillip show that in addition to the usual public sector functions and services, actively facilitating social interaction and the formation of friendships and healthy social relations can also be an important local goal.

One especially impressive aspect of Australian life and culture is the importance given to being outside. Unfortunately, much of modern society and life is about being inside and spending much too much time behind computer and television screens. In Australia, important factors are working in favor of outside life, including the climate, but the focus on being outdoors also reflects a priority of life and commitments in the form of infrastructure and urban design. There are many benefits to facilitating a greater outside urban lifestyle (including greater levels of exercise and physical activity, more contact with nature, and more social interaction), and this chapter has provided some terrific examples of planning and design that help to bring this about. Melbourne's accomplishments in creating a more pedestrian-oriented urban center are impressive, and most Australian cities have similar exemplary projects and planning that help to send its population outside and into the civic realm. American cities and culture would do well to emulate the Australians in this regard.

5

Bush Cities
Australia's Urban Ecological Capitals

Where we lived in the Sydney beach community of Coogee Beach, almost every evening around nine or ten o'clock, we would hear the delightful sound of wings flapping, signaling the arrival of a large grey-headed flying fox (*Pteropus poliocephalus*) that would visit the palm tree directly behind our apartment. Normally, she made what seemed an awkward and noisy landing and over the next several hours of nighttime and early morning would come and go from the tree, feeding and occasionally resting with her open wings spread. It was undeniably a highlight of my day and, indeed, of my experience living and working in Sydney. And it was a constant reminder of the wildness of the city, despite its facade of being "tamed"— a tribute to its bush heritage in the midst of a fairly dense population.

There are some five thousand flying foxes roosting in the Sydney botanical gardens, and each evening at dusk they disperse in scattershot fashion, seemingly heading in all directions. This dramatic daily occurrence was greeted with apparent ambivalence by most Sydneysiders. It turns out there are many bats in the Sydney region as well as three significant colonies of grey-headed flying foxes: the Ku-ring-gai colony to the north, the colony at Cabramatta Creek to the west of the CBD, as well as the colony at the Royal Botanic Gardens, where we believe "our bat" went home to roost early every morning (figure 5.1).

There is a wildness to Australian cities that is often lacking in U.S. and European cities. Perhaps because of their youngness (Sydney, though, was founded in 1788) and the immense biodiversity of the continent, the natural elements of these cities are striking and visceral. It is refreshing to see friendly competition among cities about which harbors the most biodiversity. Perhaps (again) because they have so much nature, so much biodi-

Figure 5.1 Sydney is home to several large camps of Gray headed flying foxes, including these found at the Botanical Gardens. *Photo credit:* Tim Beatley

versity, in and around these cities, they tend to devote much time and staff to managing, protecting, and educating about it.

These efforts respond to the deep human need for contact with nature, what Harvard University myrmecologist E. O. Wilson calls "biophilia" (e.g., see Wilson, 1984, 1993). Wilson argues that we are hardwired through thousands of years of co-evolution to need this contact and that such contact can serve as a cornerstone of a healthy, meaningful life. These Australian examples demonstrate the very real possibility and promise of *biophilic cities*, cities that in their physical form facilitate and encourage access to natural environments, that work through parks and landscape management to provide a measure of wildness close to home, and that work to protect, nurture, and restore biodiversity and natural systems within cities.

Bushland Parks

The abundant wildness and biodiversity found in and around Australian cities manifests in different forms. Australia can boast of some truly world-class urban parks. Within the city of Perth, for example, extremely large parks with extensive remnant bushland can be found. Kings Park, less than a kilometer from the Perth CBD, includes some 406 hectares of land, of which 267 (or about two thirds) remains in native bushland. Travel writer Bill Bryson speaks with great affection about Kings Park in his popular book *In A Sunburned Country* (2000). He describes the park as "one of the World's largest and finest parks" and something that "especially sets Perth apart" (p. 276).

Kings Park contains a variety of attractions, as Bryson observes, but its essential natural and wild condition remains evident from when it was established in 1905—well before the idea of native bush rather than European parks had caught on in cities like Melbourne or Sydney. Native bushwalks and trails lead away from more human designed picnic and play areas, and a footbridge at canopy level provides a magical view of the park's flora.

Less frequently discussed by tourists but even more impressive is Bold Park, also a very large block of native bushland in the heart of the city—at 430 hectares, even larger than Kings Park, with most in a natural state (figure 5.2). Both parks harbor an incredible level of biodiversity (including three hundred species of "macrofungi"; see http://www.bgpa.wa.gov.au). These areas have never been cleared or made into botanical gardens full of exotic species; rather, they delight in the local biodiversity, which is among the world's most concentrated in terms of species.

In Brisbane, important parks include the Toohey Forest, the Brisbane Koala Bushlands (an eight-hundred-hectare park supporting a population of three to five thousand koalas), the Chermside Hills Reserves, the Deagon wetlands, and the Karawatha Forest. It is Mt. Coot-tha Forest, a large city park, perhaps the city's diamond, that many visitors and residents alike enjoy. About 1,500 hectares in size, amazingly it is only five kilometers west of downtown Brisbane and provides a spectacular view of the city and area. This park is but a small portion of the larger Brisbane Forest Park—in total consisting of some thirty thousand hectares, again highly accessible to this urban population.

The Nature of Cities

Brisbane purports to be "the most biologically diverse capital city in Australia," and while this is challenged by other cities, the diversity in this city is clearly remarkable: 1,500 plant species, 523 vertebrates, and several

Figure 5.2 Bold Park, in Perth, is a large and relatively wild bushland in the heart of the city. *Photo credit:* Tim Beatley

thousand invertebrates (Brisbane City Council, 2004, p. 1). The Brisbane City Council has, perhaps more than any single local government in Australia, sought to develop a comprehensive biodiversity protection and recovery program (Brisbane City Council, 2004). It includes comprehensive biodiversity mapping, critical land acquisition through its bushland levy, research partnerships, and the incorporation of biodiversity issues into local area plans. Under its Brisbane Habitat program, the city also actively supports many community-based groups (more than one hundred groups and 2,500 volunteers) engaged in on-the-ground habitat restoration.

Brisbane's bushland levy was created in 1991, with start-up funding from the state. It is funded by an annual ratepayers fee of $30 and is by all accounts a very popular program. To date, the city has purchased about 1,900 hectares of land, focusing on those lands in the city with the highest biodiversity. The city has spent about $66 million AUD on acquisition and another $60 million on management of these lands. Plans in the future are to purchase another 880 hectares. The emphasis is now on "consolidate and connect"—to build corridors and build onto existing protected areas. Lord Mayor Campbell Newman declared in 2007 the city's intention of eventually setting aside 40 percent of the city in native habitat (already, it is a high 30 percent; see Brisbane City Council, 2007b).

The extent to which the city's current *City Plan* takes account of biodiversity and builds these issues into its statutory plan for the future is impressive. Specifically, it lists all species of regional or local significance that are threatened. For each listed species in the plan, the city is preparing (or has prepared) a Conservation Action Statement (CAS), which identifies the status and condition of the species, the threats to it, and actions to be taken in the future by the city; it is essentially a recovery plan for each species. The city has now prepared twenty-one CASs for these special species of concern (species identified as "significant" in the city's "Natural Assets Planning Scheme Policy," within its City Plan). These CASs serve as important biological profiles to be used by the council but also by the broader public, including by industry.

Perhaps most impressive has been the recent efforts by Brisbane to design new infrastructure to take better account of and mitigate the impacts on biodiversity. Several new road projects, in particular, have been designed to provide for wildlife movement. A significant case in point is the several million dollars being spent by the city along the Karawatha-Greenbank corridor to install "movement infrastructure," which includes "a fauna bridge, fauna-friendly underpasses and rope crossings (for possums and koalas) to re-instate and enhance wildlife movement" (Brisbane City Council, 2004, p. 6). Brisbane has also entered into an interesting agreement with Powerlink Queensland (a government-owned corporation that owns and operates the state's electricity transmission system) to enhance biodiversity and habitat values along its utility system. Under the Greening the Gaps partnership, Powerlink has agreed to fund revegetation work along key utility and transmission line corridors within Brisbane, enhancing wildlife connectivity and habitat quality there.

Few actions speak more to a city's credentials as a biophilic city than the attention it gives to invertebrate life within its borders. Here Brisbane shines again, having commissioned perhaps the most thorough urban survey of terrestrial invertebrates of any Australian city (and perhaps any city in the world). Published in 2005, the Terrestrial Invertebrate Status Review (TISR) was undertaken by the Queensland Museum's Centre for Biodiversity (see Queensland Centre for Biodiversity, 2005). Using a variety of techniques from pitfall traps to hand-netting to night collecting, inverte-brate life was surveyed at ten bushland sites in the city.

The results of the TISR show a remarkable degree of biodiversity and confirm the city's interest in using these species as bio-indicators of eco-logical and bushland health. Ants, spiders, ground beetles, sucking bugs, butterflies, land snails, dragonflies, and damselfies—all are found in re-markable abundance on these urban habitats. The photographic record of the report tells much of the story, depicting the fascinating variety and beauty of darkling beetles, dung beetles, and the ground beetle, for instance. Particularly interesting are the findings for spiders. There are an astound-ing 568 different species found, including a number of new species never before seen. The diversity of the biology of these spiders, and the com-parative display of their different webs and web shapes, convinces one of the wonder and awe that lurks around every tree and under every stone in these bushland reserves and urban habitat patches in Brisbane.

Exemplary efforts at connecting these urban bushland sites and bring-ing the message of biodiversity conservation to an urban population can be seen in Brisbane's Mountains to Mangroves Corridor. Addressing con-cerns that small bushland sites were becoming biologically isolated, a part-nership was formed between environmental centers and several local councils in 1995 to create the Corridor concept. The Corridor now links the D'Aguilar range and the Brisbane Forest Park with Moreton Bay and the mangrove ecosystem of the Boondall Wetlands, a Ramsar-designated wet-lands site (Ramsar is an international convention on wetlands conserva-tion, see http://www.ramsar.org). The Corridor extends a distance of about thirty kilometers, passes through sixteen neighborhoods in the city, and is, as the Corridor's management plan states, "largely a natural strip through an increasingly urban fabric" (Mountains to Mangrove Committee, 1998). The Corridor initiative has helped to coordinate management activities, has helped to link mentally and programmatically the lands and parks in this stretch of Brisbane not far north of the city's CBD, and has raised the visibility and importance of these natural areas locally. Environmental education is a major focus, with a number of schools sponsoring programs and activities tied to land and ecology of the Corridor and its rich biodi-versity.[1]

One highlight is a biennial celebration, the Mountains to Mangrove Festival, a seventeen-day celebration of this environment through a diverse set of media, including theater performances, nighttime and daytime bush-walks, corridor "cruises" (tours of the region by bus), environmental film nights, sustainability workshops, and bushcare volunteer days, when residents are invited to help plant new forests and to do hands-on restoration, among other activities. There is even an "Opera in the Bush" event. A local species of moth—the giant wood moth (*Endoxyla cinerea*)—is the festival's logo and icon, and a distinctive one indeed. The world's heaviest moth (weighing up to 30 grams), the giant wood moth is found throughout the neighborhoods in and around the Corridor and serves as a fitting symbol of the rich and fascinating nature to be found very close to home.

In Adelaide, similar efforts have been under way to better imagine and understand the city as biodiverse and wild, aided especially by an innovative urban ecology center and effort called BioCity. Headed up by Chris Daniels, a professor of environmental biology, it began with start-up funding from the City of Adelaide and is now housed at the University of Adelaide as a research center. BioCity's mission is unusual and perhaps a model for other cities seeking to better understand their own biodiversity and natural history. The mission is to promote interdisciplinary research on urban nature, to educate on these issues, and to provide advice and guidance to planners and policy makers (e.g., exploring and advocating a variety of urban greening projects, from "bushtops" on downtown buildings to converting city parkland back to native habitats; see BioCity, n.d.).

One of the first and most notable projects of the center was to commission a series of essays and analyses of the nature and biodiversity of the city and how that has changed and is changing over time. The result was an unusually detailed inventory of one city's biological history and heritage. The resulting book, entitled *Adelaide: Nature of a City*, is an effort to take stock of and educate about the unique natural heritage and biodiversity of the city (see Daniels and Tait, 2005).

Daniels, the center's director, has been involved in a number of efforts to reach the public with these stories. He writes a column in the local paper called "Can You Believe It?" about various aspects of mostly unknown or underappreciated aspects of the abundant nature in and around this city, including its twenty species of parrots, its bluetongued and stumpy-tailed lizards, and the Adelaide giant worm (reaching a length of up to two meters!), among others.

The state of South Australia has been operating several important programs for enhancing and restoring biodiversity in the Adelaide metro area. These have included the Urban Forest Biodiversity Program, which has provided small grants and technical assistance for a variety of "collaborative community projects," from establishing school bush gardens to floral and faunal research to native tree planting and habitat restoration around the region. More recently, the SA state government has initiated an Urban Forest–Million Trees initiative, which has now been extended and expanded to the bold goal of planting 3 million trees in the Adelaide metro area by 2014. Similarly focused on biodiversity and habitat restoration through tree planting, carbon sequestration is also an important goal.

Perth is at the center of the only biodiversity "hotspot" in Australia, the South West Australia Bioregion (see http://www.biodiversityhotspots .org). Its diversity is most impressive in plants and reptiles. There are more than 1,200 species of vascular plants in the Perth metro region portion of the Swan Coastal Plain alone. An exotic array of fauna exists as well, including such species as Quenda (or southern brown bandicoot), the Quokka, and the Western swamp tortoise, which are threatened, as well as more common species, such as the grey kangaroo, honey possum, brush tail possum, western brush wallaby, and many others. About three hundred species of birds and sixty-four species of reptiles also occur here.

Perth has a range of biodiversity programs, including the use of 1080 poison to eradicate feral cats, foxes, and pigs, which are destructive to native marsupials. This poison does not harm the native marsupials because they have evolved with a plant that contains natural 1080. Thus, in the Perth hills, native Quendas, Woylies, and Tamars (all small kangaroos that are rare and endangered due to feral animals) are returning. The Woylie is the first species to be removed from the IUCN (International Union for Conservation of Nature) endangered species list.

Invertebrate diversity is not well understood but is thought to be very high in the Perth region. A survey of sites in the late 1990s by the Western Australia Museum "uncovered a startlingly diverse ground fauna." The survey reported: "Numerous species and genera were recorded from the Swan Coastal Plain for the first time, and many undescribed species were collected" (Western Australia Museum, 2000, p. 69).

The Perth region has more terrestrial orchids (those that grow in soil), including one rare underground orchid, than does any other state. These orchids have a fascinating biology. The grand spider orchid (*Caladenia huegelii*), for instance, requires other species to coexist; it needs the pollination of a male wasp of a single native species of thynnid, which is attracted to a pheromone produced by the plant mimicking a female wasp.

It is not hard to see why there is an Australian Orchid Council in Perth, which fights to save every plant. Jim Heath (1999) writes about how Western Power donated $200,000 to the council's campaign to rescue six types of orchids through a scientific program using the Plant Science and Propagation Unit at Kings Park in Perth. This unit isolates the "helper fungus" for each orchid, grows thousands of them, and replants them in Perth bushland along with the fungus. When asked why he does this, Heath says it is not because the ecosystem needs them (they are evolutionary pinnacles, which use the ecosystem at the top of the chain but, like humans, are not really needed to make it work), and it is not because they may have some rare chemical in them (it is easier to make chemicals through artificial means these days). The reason is simpler, he says; we like them, and we ought to because they are a fascinating part of life.

Preserving Systems of Urban Bushlands

European settlement has taken its toll in most areas of Australia, especially on mammals and birds, with significant declines in the first 160 years. Only about half the mammal species that existed during settlement can now be found here, though some are making a comeback. Nevertheless, there is much left to protect, and many Australian cities have made significant strides toward habitat conservation.

Bush Forever is the major public program aimed at protecting and restoring native bushland in the Perth region. In many ways, its current incarnation is the result of several decades of work, under different program names and titles. It began in the 1970s with the mapping of bushland under "System 6," a Commonwealth government initiative. Its immediate predecessor was called Bushplan and, prior to that in the mid-1990s, the Urban Bushland Strategy.

Bush Forever explicitly seeks to identify and protect *regionally significant* bushland in the Swan Coastal Plain. The Darling Plateau to the east represents the point of demarcation, and the metro area boundaries mark the limit to the north and south (figure 5.3). Several key criteria were used in identifying "regionally significant" sites, including, most importantly, representation of ecological communities, diversity, rarity, and maintenance of ecological processes (Western Australia Museum, 2000).

Bushland is not just parkland or open space, and here the Australians have an advantage in language: the word *bush* connotes a discernible meaning to most people living in Australia, though it may conjure a different image depending on where one is living. For the purposes of Bush Forever, bush is defined as "land on which there is vegetation which is either a remainder of the natural vegetation of the land or, if altered, is still representative of the structure and floristics of the natural vegetation, and provides the necessary habitat for fauna" (Western Australia Museum, 2000, p. 8). But the words *bush* and *bushland* elicit a visceral sense of the

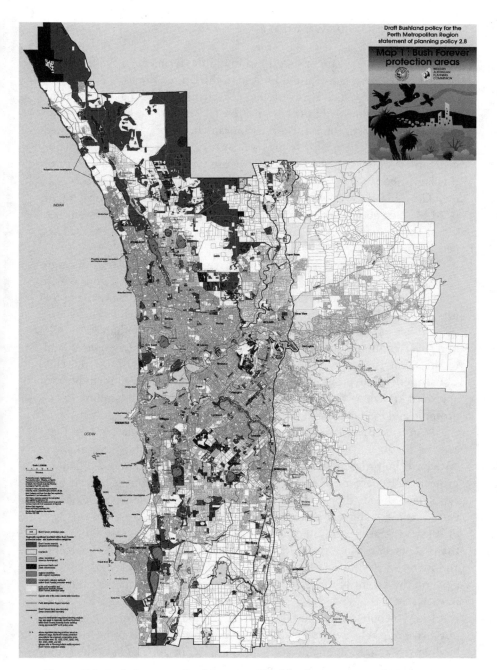

Figure 5.3 Bush Forever is Perth's regional bushland conservation plan. It envisions a regional network of almost 300 bushland sites, together comprising more than 50,000 hectares of protected land. *Image credit:* courtesy of The Western Australian Planning Commission

wild for Australians, one I think is lacking in the terms *open space* (empty space?) and *greenspace* commonly used in the United States.

Under Perth's Bush Forever plan, 287 bushland sites have been identified for protection within the Swan Coastal Plain, most but not all publicly owned. In total, about fifty-one thousand hectares of land are included in this network. The goal is to preserve at least 10 percent of every major vegetation complex in the region (there are twenty-six). The majority of this land, about 65 percent, is already in a protective category, much of it owned by the state Department of Conservation and Land Management (CALM). But about 26 percent of the land is in public ownership but not yet in a conservation status, and about 9 percent, the most controversial aspect of the program, is privately owned.

The state has some capacity to purchase land in this system through a dedicated land tax called the Metropolitan Improvement Fund, which is used to fund land for infrastructure and parks. The fund has existed for fifty years and raises around $45 million each year, so in the past twenty years it has purchased bushland and parkland worth more than $500 million AUD. Estimates are that to fully purchase all the privately owned land in the Bush Forever system would require another $500 million AUD. Consequently, the program sees other strategies as essential, including an approach known as "Negotiated Solutions," to enable local landholders to preserve and manage bush.

Many see Bush Forever as an ambitious, commendable effort at preserving biodiversity in urban and suburban environments. Others have criticized the program, however. Staff note that even the modest goal of protecting 10 percent of each vegetation type will not be met, as several types have already dipped below the 10 percent level in the region. Conservation research suggests, moreover, that to ensure the long-term survival of these vegetative communities will really require preservation of more than 10 percent. More realistically, the goal ought to be 10 to 30 percent, and many in the conservation community believe that this goal will depend on the extent of management, such as weed control, that is exercised in each area.

Many people directly involved in these biodiversity initiatives point out a lack of public awareness of and support for bushland protection and biodiversity conservation. Elected politicians, in turn, do not have the courage to support bolder conservation goals and programs.

While many of the nearly three hundred Bush Forever sites are small (most major bush in the city is already in reserves), there has been an effort to understand their spatial connection and relationship to one another, and to protect and strengthen significant biological linkages where possible. Such linkages are considered critical to preserving long-term genetic diversity and preventing inbreeding as well as being necessary for species with larger ranges, and a key map presents existing and potential linkages in the Perth region. Particular Bush Forever sites, as a result, are seen as especially important as bridges or connections in this linked conservation network.

Biodiversity planning in Perth began with local authorities working in tandem with the state's Bush Forever program, but mostly in a top-down way. However, local governments are increasingly playing a direct role in protecting biodiversity through their own initiatives. To coordinate and facilitate this direct action, the Perth Biodiversity Project (PBP) was begun in 1999. Started through funding from the federal Natural Heritage Trust, the PBP aims to help local government build the capacity to do biodiversity planning by providing technical assistance, information, and education as well as some funding to support these local efforts. PBP has produced a set of local Biodiversity Guidelines that lay out a framework and process for local government in doing this work. Funding of $5 million AUD for local projects has been spent on a variety of on-the-ground projects— revegetation, fencing, management plans, and public education and awareness-raising efforts, to name a few. Most of this money has come from the Commonwealth government, though a small amount has been allotted by the state Department for Planning and Infrastructure (DPI).

A final stage in the local biodiversity planning process envisioned under the PBP is the preparation of a local biodiversity strategy. The Biodiversity Guidelines provide a template or model plan for this strategy. Currently under way is an effort to have the PBP guidelines formally acknowledged by the WA Planning Commission. By doing this, the belief is that the state's Environment Protection Authority (EPA) could forgo requiring an environmental assessment on new subdivisions. This would give the guidelines a big boost, making them much more important and effective and further empowering local decision making.

While it is too early to see the successes of the PBP, there have been some very positive signs. State funds have been used to leverage new local funding for biodiversity. For instance, in the city of Wanneroo, one of two pilot communities, the PBP has allowed them to push (successfully) for a larger land/park management budget to support their biodiversity efforts.

Wanneroo is in the process of establishing biodiversity goals and targets under Milestone 2. This local council has more publicly owned bushland than any other in the Perth region, nearly 1,400 hectares in total.

What the biodiversity qualities of this land are, and how they might be managed to protect and enhance biodiversity, has been a significant focus already in the locality, predating funding under the PBP. By 2003, they had completed a comprehensive inventory and assessment of their publicly owned bushland sites (some owned outright by the city, but much of it "crown land"—that is, Commonwealth land managed and cared for by the city). There are ninety-four sites of publicly owned bushland within the city. Once assessed, these natural areas were prioritized, taking into account such factors as size, vegetation condition, viability, and extent of important ecological linkages provided. Lands ranked as category 1, highest priority, have been the focus of much of the city's recent maintenance and restoration funds. The Koondoola Regional Bushland Preserve is one result of this exercise (figure 5.4).[2]

Among other things, the prioritization study in Wanneroo has helped steer the work of the city's Bushcare Team, which has focused restoration work on nineteen of the top-ranked sites (as of 2004–2005). Weed control is a major part of this work, and a major threat to biodiversity on these city lands, as elsewhere in Australia.

Knowledge of what actually exists on public land in the city is surprisingly sparse and is a major motivation for conducting the assessment. A city memo states it frankly: "Prior to the 2003 Bushland Assessment being undertaken, the city was unaware of which natural areas it was responsible for managing, or the biodiversity values of these areas" (City of Wanneroo, 2005, p. 1). Much was learned in this assessment process, and at least one new floral species was discovered.

It is now recognized that the outlying localities in the Perth region probably offer the greatest potential to protect existing biodiversity. Thus the PBP has decided to focus its limited funds there (on the ten "outer metro" councils, including the cities of Mandurah and Swan).

The next phase of biodiversity planning under Bush Forever is the Swan BioPlan, which will essentially extend Bush Forever to the north and south, to encompass the rest of the coastal plain as well as a portion of the scarp plateau. It will cover a decidedly more rural environment well outside of the urban area and should be able to achieve around 30 percent land protection.

The Urban Bushland Council (UBC) is a coalition of about fifty local bushland groups in the Perth region and actively lobbies on behalf of bushland conservation. They applaud the effort of Bush Forever and the PBP but are critical of steps toward implementation. They believe that the goals are modest (10 percent, but 30 percent if lands covered by the PBP are in-

Figure 5.4 Koondoola Bushland Preserve, shown here, is one of the sites in the Bush Forever system. This amazingly wild park is nestled close to an extensive area of suburban development. *Photo credit:* Tim Beatley

cluded) and minimal and that remaining natural bushland should be considered off-limits to new development, either by private developers and landowners or by government agencies. They disagree most vehemently with the view that the state's Department of Planning and Infrastructure should or must "negotiate" about the use of these lands. They believe there is a tendency to look at these conservation lands through a planning lens—development and conservation are *both* to be accommodated, somehow. As Mary Gray, president of the UBC, notes: "Bushland should be seen as important resources to protect, not just as suburbs waiting to happen" (Gray, personal interview, 2005).

Perth is a boomtown migrant city, so many who live there have no sense that they have come to a city with special flora and fauna or landscape qualities. They bring their own perceptions from their own lands, and it takes time before the special features of Perth become part of their consciousness. For example, the UBC made an effort to promote the use of local plants in a new development, and the local council had adopted a policy in favor of native plants. Yet the developer of this project circulated a petition to allow residents to continue the use of nonnatives.

Not only is there a low awareness of local plant diversity, but there are also active perceptual obstacles at work. There is a sense that to use native will mean a "scrubby garden or yard" and a diminishing of beauty and color. And there remains an almost adversarial relationship with the land and environment, what Mary Gray calls a "colonial land development ethic," that views bushland as essentially empty and vacant, as land to be captured and commandeered. Working alongside this is a fear of the dangers of the bush, that there are snakes and insects and other animals that will harm you, and so these are places to avoid.

Several recent examples show a lack of conviction about protecting biodiversity. At Burns Beach, a new suburb was planned where several recommended Bush Forever sites were threatened. DPI negotiated a compromise between development and conservation, but this compromise is seen by bush protection supporters like Mary Gray as capitulation, as giving in—evidence that the government is not serious about protection but sees the Bush Forever sites as more malleable and open to give-and-take in the course of working through the demands of landowners and others in the community. No development should have been allowed on this site because it is the location of a rare dune ecosystem.

Bushcare and the Grassroots Engagement of Urban Biodiversity

Councils visited by the author have extensive networks of volunteer groups, with citizens often devoting considerable personal time and energy to pulling out invasives, planting natives, fencing, making paths, and doing the many other laborious tasks associated with repairing and caring for bushlands. Local councils also actively promote and manage these "bushcare" groups within their jurisdictions—volunteers from the community that donate their time, often on weekends or evenings, to help with revegetation and habitat restoration work.

The number of local bushcare groups varies, but multiple distinct groups often do this work in a single council's jurisdiction, usually assisted and coordinated by council staff. The number of bushcare groups and the extent of activity depend, of course, on the size of the council and the extent of undeveloped and natural land remaining.

Finding ways to actively involve citizens in the task of caring for and repairing nature in cities is a key part of the mission of growing biophilic cities. Professor Andrew Light considers this focus part and parcel of an urban environmental ethic, part of what it should mean to be an ecological citizen of a particular city or place (Light, 2003). And much progress in activating people to be involved can be made. Again, in Australia, much importance is given to these urban bushcare groups. In Brisbane, there are now 120 bushcare groups, involving more than 2,500 active volunteers (as of December 2005). Known as the Brisbane Habitat Program, these groups are supported as a matter of official city policy through commitment of resources and staff. They produce many benefits beyond the ecological restoration results themselves, of course. Ku-ring-gai Council (in Sydney), in their description of their Bushcare Volunteer program, notes: "In addition to the environmental and educational benefits, joining Bushcare is an opportunity to make friends, become a part of a social group that shares the same concerns and to change community perception about bushland" (Ku-ring-gai Council, n.d).

In Gosford, in the Sydney metro area, there are fifty-five bushcare groups operating, involving some five hundred active volunteers. Here it has been estimated that bushcare volunteers donated more than thirty-three thousand hours of on-site work between 2000 and 2004 (Gosford City Council, 2004, p. 137). This is a remarkable commitment of citizen energies. In Hornsby Council (Sydney), there are more than nine hundred bushcare volunteers; in Ku-ring-gai Council (Sydney), some seven hundred volunteers. In Baulkham Hills, in the Sydney metro area as well, there are twenty-seven different bushcare groups operating. Especially in NSW, one or several council staff—typically known as bushcare officers or environmental officers—coordinate and assist these groups.

Local council bushcare staff are also active in helping citizens in bush restoration efforts in and around their own homes. Under Ku-ring-gai's Backyard Buddies initiative, staff will visit homes to provide planting and regeneration advice. An even more radical notion is being implemented in this jurisdiction. Council staff have been attempting to interest homeowners in restoring native fauna, in particular in breeding and releasing blue-tongue lizards. Most interesting, homeowners' swimming pools are being reenvisioned as new homes for native aquatic species. Peter Clarke, of Ku-ring-gai Council, recently reported on this experience in the Ku-ring-gai *Bushcare News*:

> Elvis Claus has successfully turned his "boring" suburban pool into a magnificent native pond teeming with rainbows and gudgeons. The really exciting part of this is that the fish have bred themselves and we

have used the population in Elvis's pool to populate other ponds in Ku-ring-gai. We now have another pool being converted into a pond in Lindfield and if this trend continues I hope that Ku-ring-gai one day will be known as the Kasmir of the south. (Clarke, 2006, p. 4)

The council is also breeding and distributing the species Pacific blue-eyes, a native fish that is especially effective at controlling mosquito larvae (which, in turn, is perhaps part of the solution to getting kids and families outside).

Bushcare in many ways is an urban extension of the Landcare program, a movement begun more than twenty years ago with more of a rural and farming focus. There are now more than five thousand Landcare groups around Australia; like Bushcare, they are community-based ventures, often a result of extensive community partnerships among farmers, local councils, and the business sector (e.g., Alcoa, in the case of the Avon Landcare group in Western Australia). Like Bushcare, much gets done on the ground, through volunteer labor that results in extensive habitat restoration work (fencing, revegetation works, planting of trees and shrubs to counter dryland saltwater intrusion). The philosophy and movement, which originated in Australia, is being picked up and applied in many other places around the world, from Alaska to Uganda to New Zealand. Landcare's urban counterpart, Bushcare, which plays such an important part of the biophilic cities (such as Brisbane and Sydney) has equal potential for such replication.

Another interesting voluntary effort at protecting and restoring biodiversity is the Land for Wildlife program. Working now in every Australian state, the program depends on the voluntary enthusiasm of landowners who have an interest in wildlife and want to know what they can do to restore and enhance wildlife habitat. Participation begins with a field assessment of the land and suggestions, usually from a state conservation biologist, of actions that can be taken. Full or interim registration occurs depending on what needs to be done. Landowners also receive assistance in accessing financial programs that may help to fund land restoration work. In WA, Land for Wildlife is a very active program, and although WA is an extremely large state, almost 1,300 properties have been registered, covering 934,159 hectares of land.

Land for Wildlife in WA educates interested landowners and helps to keep up their enthusiasm and extend their knowledge through a periodic newsletter called *Western Wildlife* and specific topics such as "Wildlife Notes." The program is found mostly in agricultural areas, but the model could easily be extended into more urban areas.

Restoring Green in the City

Many local councils have undertaken habitat restoration and urban greening projects of various sizes and scopes. Some that are small in size have nonetheless shown tremendous potential to make a tangible difference in the quality of these urban environments. A notable case in point is the Whites Creek Wetland in the Annandale neighborhood of Leichhardt Council region, in the Sydney metropolitan area. Here a community project has led to a retrofitting of an ecological channel or canal, incorporating a small cleansing urban wetland.

The creek project has serves as a staging ground for the city's "Leichhardt Flows Into the Sea" watershed walking tour. Participants from the community learn about urban watersheds and watershed management and the particular attributes and problems of Whites Creek. The creek, 2.5 kilometers long, drains a highly impervious urban neighborhood, and the creek flows mostly through a concrete canal. Though a small urban wetland, its construction was no small matter, necessitating the removal of some 850 metric tonnes of contaminated soil and fill materials (figure 5.5). Construction began in 2002.

The project contains a number of educational elements. Local elementary schools have been involved, for instance, by making and hanging on school walls two large wetland murals that depict the life found in the wetlands and are intended to show the close environmental connection between the schools and the watershed. As another example, Leichhardt High School has formed a Streamwatch Group focused around the wetland and has implemented volunteer planting days and biological monitoring activities.

Originally proposed by the local chapter of Friends of the Earth, this new urban wetland was funded (mostly) through a grant from the NSW EPA Stormwater Trust. The goal behind the wetland was not only to help in a small way to improve water quality but also to educate and engage the community. According to a background report: "By capturing the imagination of the local community and helping them engage with the wetland as a pocket of urban habitat, we hope to foster a sense of care and raised consciousness about the treatment of urban stormwater" (Friends of the Earth, n.d.). The idea was the brainchild of Ted Floyd, a local resident and member of Friends of Earth, who also agitated strongly for it. Floyd views the wetland as a huge success, connecting residents to nature and each other (see Village Voice, 2008). The lush site has brought the natural world back to this setting.

Figure 5.5 Whites Creek Wetland, shown here, is a small urban wetland restoration project, in Leichhardt Council, in the Sydney metro area. This project has shown significant water quality benefits and also injected an impressive green amenity for residents of the neighborhood. *Photo credit:* Tim Beatley

Camden, another local council in the Sydney metropolitan region, has developed a comprehensive "Natural Assets Policy." The stated objectives of this policy are to "facilitate ecologically sustainable development through the substantial retention and long-term management of natural assets," and to "[ensure] that the impacts of future land uses are considered in a cumulative and total catchments management context" (Camden Council, 2003). "Natural assets" are defined as "the stock of soil, freshwater, clean air and vegetation and other resources that underpins survival, health and prosperity of human communities."

Based in part on the no-net-loss standard for wetlands predominant in the United States, this local policy establishes detailed standards for the types of environmental lands that can and cannot be altered in this jurisdiction. For those categories where some alteration is permitted—generally after demonstrating to the council that the destruction or alteration cannot be avoided and where the impacts are minimized to the extent possible—detailed land protection and conservation "off-set" requirements are laid-out. Possibly the most useful lesson from this example, the council has prepared a comprehensive, jurisdiction-wide natural assets map—in essence, a picture of what important natural assets exist and a vision of a future network of assets that the council wants to maintain and extend. This map has become an important framework for reviewing all projects and proposals in the locality. The map includes important bushland corridors, wetlands and riparian areas, and other ecologically sensitive land. Extensive development guidelines are also included as a part of the asset (mandating buffers, protection of mature trees, and so forth). "Ecologically significant land" (as distinguished from "environmentally sensitive lands") is considered protected and off-limits from development under the Camden policy and includes endangered ecological communities, under the NSW Threatened Species Conservation Act.

Ku-ring-gai Council, on the northern side of the Sydney metropolitan area, is bracketed by three national parks, with a relatively high percentage of its council area still contained in natural land. For Ku-ring-gai, the important concept has been what they call BioLinkages, the notion of working toward urban conservation that links together their natural resources—the national parks but also the urban tree canopy, its bushland trails and parks, and riparian areas. The BioLinkages approach is given meaning through the combined implementation and coordination of a number of its specific council programs, including its (fairly stringent) Riparian Policy, its bushcare program, and its Tree Nurturers program, among others. These discrete initiatives are viewed as feeding into the BioLinkages concept. Through its bushcare effort (purported to be the first bushcare program in Australia, started in 1991), hundreds of volunteers work to restore habitat on some 160 sites within the council. The Tree Nurturers program enlists citizens to help plant and then care for trees, and the council has been doing other things to enhance and protect trees, including an innovative "aerial bundle cabling" program "to bundle all power cables into one insulated bundled cable" with streets ranked and prioritized for this based on certain criteria. (Ku-ring-gai Council, n.d.).

Other cities have taken similar efforts to regreening the gray and concrete elements of their cities. Fairfield, another Sydney suburb, has made impressive efforts at restoring natural streams. The history of Fairfield's stream restoration effort dates back to the early 1990s. The notion of converting some of the city's concrete channels back to natural streams really started with the Australian Conservation Foundation, who first lobbied the council to do something about the area's degraded natural assets. A spectacular transformation has occurred, changing Clear Paddock Creek from a concrete channel to an ecologically important creek system (see figure 5.6 for before and after photos). So far, only a five-hundred-meter stretch of the creek has been completed, while the city monitors the first segment and looks for funding to complete the full two and one half kilometers of the restoration project. Funding has been a major obstacle, as the complete project has been estimated to cost $9 million AUD.

The project has been a great success to date. The restoration work has yielded new riparian habitat (a "hive of activity" biologically, in the words of Stephen Frost, the project manager; Frost, personal interview, 2005). In terms of vegetation growth, biological functioning, and aesthetic qualities, the restoration has achieved its goals, and those neighbors originally skeptical of the project now support it. Initially, community members posed obstacles because they sensed that when the plan was presented to them it was a fait accompli, with little advance consultation. As a result, the city staff literally tore up the original plans and began a much more intensive neighborhood consultation, and they were eventually able to overcome this initial perception of a top-down approach.

Some neighbors worried about what a restored stream would mean, including fears that it would stimulate antisocial behaviors, exacerbate flooding, and attract vermin, rats, mosquitoes, and other undesirable elements. For some, the concrete channels had actually become a positive thing—its human-made look created a perception of its being neat, tidy, clean, and safe. Others remembered how the natural streams used to be and viewed

Figures 5.6 (a) and (b) Before and After Fairfield Restoration. The City of Fairfield has been gradually converting segments of Clear Paddock Creek, from concrete chanels (before) back to a more natural and ecologically functioning creek. The visual and ecological results have been dramatic. *Photo credits:* Courtesy Fairfield City Council, NSW, Australia

restoring the creek quite positively. Still others living in the neighborhood had simply not recognized that the concrete channels meant that there was a stream or creek there. It just had not registered as a remnant natural feature or natural system.

Another measure of the project's success is its catalytic effect in helping to push along other watershed projects in the city, including those upstream. Other lessons include the need to include a multidisciplinary team, including those artists who were, among other things, especially effective at interfacing with the general public about the project.

In 2006, a $500 million NSW state fund was allocated (over five years) for innovations in local urban sustainability. These projects include restoring wetlands, regenerating bushland, turning stormwater drains into natural creeks, and reducing the ecological footprint of urban centers. The size of this new fund demonstrates how successful and how popular so many of these greening projects have been in the past.

Teaching about Place and Nature

The importance of educating about place and nature, and of rekindling an interest and fascination with the natural world, is a critical lesson from my time in Australia. And I learned about and visited a number of encouraging efforts around the country to do just this. It is a problem Australian and Americans share, to be sure. For several years, I have administered a "What is this?" slide show and quiz of sorts, asking my students to identify common species of local flora and fauna. I have been astounded and discouraged that few of them are able to recognize or identify even very common species of birds (e.g., mockingbirds), trees (sycamores, poplars), and invertebrates (even our state insect, the Eastern tiger swallowtail, goes unrecognized by most students).

Mike Archer, dean of sciences at the University of New South Wales in Australia, similarly bemoans this lack of knowledge about native species. With coauthor Bob Beale, he has written the provocative book *Going Native*, suggesting a host of unusual and creative ways to rebuild this knowledge and reconnect Australians to their incredible native biodiversity. They speak of designs to "reintegrate" people and nature, such as neighbors joining lots together to create natural habitats. Perhaps the most intriguing idea, and a charge to architects, is to design homes that convert urban wildlife from a nuisance to an opportunity to learn and reconnect:

> Another option we suggest is to share homes themselves with wildlife. People often complain about possums in the roof doing unseen "things", yet at the same time they complain about their square-eyed children spending hours in front of the television watching junk. Why not construct houses so that they actively accommodate native animals such as possums, bats and native bees? Imagine a house—as suggested by biologist Nick Mooney—constructed with a central well from ceiling to floor that had large one-way glass windows enclosing a space with artistically distributed vegetation (nourished by skylights in the roof and soft lights at night) as well as logs. In this in-house refuge,

possums could make nests, mate, raise babies, feed, feud and provide hours of fascinating evening viewing for the human family. Even watching parrots feed in native trees on the outside of a large picture window is a visual and aural treat to start off the working day (Archer and Beale, 2004, pp. 334–35).

In several parts of Australia, there are initiatives designed to encourage residents to be more attentive to the nature around them and to the seasonal rhythms and changes occurring. Alan Reid, a naturalist with the Gould League of Victoria (a one-hundred-year-old natural history organization), is frequently credited with stimulating this idea, and he now runs a program called Timelines Australia that produces a periodic newsletter (*Timelines News*) and a variety of useful natural history materials:

> At the heart of the Timelines Project is the recording of personal observations. It is a process of developing empathy, involvement and engagement with nature. It is a means by which we develop observation and identification skills, learn to record data and process this information into a scheme of things.
>
> We are personally connected to our subject matter through our observations and their place in the scheme of things. We connect with place . . . we connect with the essence of the local detail. . . . Such observations engender an appreciation of regional differences and the essential heartlands of the "sense of place" (Reid, n.d.).

The natural history or local ecology movement is as old as white settlement in Australia (and even older, of course, because Aborigines studied ecology for thirty thousand years). Joseph Banks was the botanist on James Cook's historic voyage to Australia, and his observations began a deep fascination for the flora and fauna of this ancient continent. Following the natural history tradition of Gilbert White, who in the 1780s studied his garden and the surrounding fields and forest in his native Hamsphire, there has been a long tradition of people who have recorded the natural cycles of bird, animal, and plant life in and around Australia's cities. The Gould League is one of those groups, and many of the volunteer bush conservation groups described earlier are also part of this tradition.

Another interesting biodiversity awareness–raising tool used in the northern suburbs of Sydney is a wildlife survey. Sent to households on the central coast in Gosford and Wyong Shire councils, the survey contained questions about what wildlife they have seen in and around their house and also asked questions about needed wildlife protection steps and policy. Some eleven thousand surveys were returned. The results show that residents both are interested in wildlife issues and know something about them. In the Gosford responses, not surprisingly, common animals are most frequently identified as being seen—Kookaburras, sulphur-crested cockatoos, bluetongued lizards, and willie wagtails. The survey generated enthusiasm and allowed for some productive follow-up (e.g., the council received some 1,600 requests for advice about native-friendly gardening) (see the full results at http://www.gosford.nsw.gov.au).

The Naturewatch Diary in Port Stephens and Newcastle is a collaborative effort based on Timeline Project Australia: "The main objective of the diary is to give the community the opportunity and encouragement to record their observations of nature on a day to day basis and to build this into an annual accumulation of information about seasonality of our local environment" (Port Stephens and Newcastle Councils, n.d., p. 125).

The Central Coast Nature Watch Diary project is a collaboration between the councils of Gosford, Wyong Shire, and Lake Maequarie and the National Parks and Wildlife Service. There is a downloadable diary as well as a template that participants can use to record their observation about animals, weather, and seasonal changes (see http://www.wyongsc.nsw.gov.au/environment/cc_nature_watch.html). Hints are provided about researching observations, and at the beginning of each month things to "look out for," or pay attention to, are provided.

Another important idea is the notion of seasonal calendars adapted to particular parts of Australia. It idea grew from the recognition that the Northern Hemisphere's four-season calendar does not fit the Australian context well and that Aborigines had such calendars that helped alert them to when to collect particular foods.

In Perth, the plight of the Western swamp tortoise is of special concern to local conservationists. It is considered by some to be the world's most threatened tortoise, and a number of key sites in the suburbs are now being intensively managed with the release of zoo-bred tortoises. A new suburb called The Vale (by Multiplex) in this area has special classes for residents to ensure that they assist with wetland management and planting of relevant native species in their own gardens. This area drains into one of the few wetlands containing the rare tortoise, so residents are encouraged not to use fertilizer and pesticide in their gardens and to plant only native gardens In the Perth area, the Aboriginal calendar had six seasons, and each is associated with particular flowering plants. Vale is trying to show how the plantings in the area—in both public spaces and private gardens—can be linked into these cycles so that native insects and birds will be provided with year-round habitat.

In some areas in Australia, guidebooks have been prepared to assist in this "re-seasoning" effort. In Tomaree Peninsula (Port Stephens, Nelson Bay Area), two hours north of Sydney, there is a fantastic example in the form of a book called *Bushmates: A Guide to the Wildlife*, the result of the author Michael Smith's sixteen years of observing all things natural in that part of the world. Available for purchase at the Port Stephens visitor's center and a few other places, it is an absolutely marvelous and accessible description of what residents there should be looking out for, organized by month and week. When do local orchids flower? When might I see puff ball fungus? When do Willie Wagtails nest? How does a pygmy possum's tail change from summer to winter? (The answer: it stores fat in the tail, and the tail becomes fatter as winter approaches!) What will the night sky look like in January? In July? In November? Simple drawings, photos, and diagrams embellish and stimulate the reader to learn more of this special place on earth. It also includes instructions for making a crux-clock (for telling time from the Southern Cross), an astrolobe (for measuring the altitude of stars), and a planosphere (a celestial map), as well as a review of the region's vegetation and geology, a discussion of wild food ("bush tucker"), and maps of the best places to see birds and wildlife.

Books like this one encourage us to look around, to step outside of our narrow, self-absorbed routines to notice and understand the natural world of which we are inherently a part. My wish would be to see books like this, compact and all of one hundred pages, handed to all newly arrived residents as they're moving in, with the encouragement to explore their "communities" and "neighborhoods" in their fullest meaning.

How to most effectively reach citizens about this nature around them and when might the best teachable moments be for imparting place-knowledge remain open questions. The Watershed Center in the Newtown neighborhood of inner Sydney has been working with local real estate agents there to connect with residents both as they move in and as they move out, when opportunities to influence decisions about recycling and waste management, for instance, are especially good. This "welcome to the neighborhood" initiative, it seems to me, holds great possibilities for expanding broader education about place, environment, and watershed. Could the standard information conveyed to new residents as they move into a new house or apartment be as much about the unique flora and fauna they might encounter, perhaps including some of the kinds of material found in the *Bushmates* guide?

Using Food to Connect Citizens to the Native Environment

Food has emerged as another possible avenue for learning about and reconnecting to native environments, both within and outside cities in Australia. There is a growing movement in Australia to recognize and cultivate bushfoods used by Australian Aborigines that generally were never taken seriously as a food source by early settlers. Many ecotourist trips (e.g., Margaret River in WA) now feature bush tucker (wild food) as part of their process of explaining how people in the area survived for millennia. Introducing native Australia foods into mainstream food systems remains a challenge, however. Juleigh Robins has applied her cooking knowledge and experience as restaurateur and caterer to developing recipes for many of these bushfoods. She has published a terrific book of recipes, *Wild Lime: Cooking from the Bushfood Garden* (Allen & Unwin, 1996). Here she explains not only how to cook but also how to grow and store these foods. Lemon aspen (having very little similarity to either lemon or aspen trees as known in Europe or North America) becomes lemon aspen mayonnaise, shortbread, or ice cream. Kakadu plums become plum sauce and plumglaze, while lemon myrtle becomes vinegar, fishcakes, and sorbet. Cumbungi, warrigal greens, murnong, quandong, wattle seeds, and kurrajong suggest an exotic, *alternative* place-based cornucopia of foods and flavors that both add diversity of experience and tie us to the natural history and sustaining abundance of the bush.

Robins explains her own motivations for using bushfoods and the benefits for her of learning about the plants and foods growing *where she lives*: "Being involved with bushfoods has really opened my eyes, and my family's, to the way we relate to our landscape. Despite being born in Australia, I was largely unaware of my own land. Here we are, surrounded by coasts, forests and plains that once supported large tribes of people and nurtured them, and yet, I was still ignorant of the food potential of many of our native plants" (Robins, 1996, p. vii).

Predictably, native fruits are especially suited to the dry, marginal environments in which they grow. These are, for the most part, hearty plants highly tolerant of the harsh Australian growing conditions. As Australia faces continual limits in water supply and a changing climate, they seem an appropriate response. Often these bushfoods provide remarkable levels of nutrition. The quandong (also known as the desert peach or native peach), for instance, has about twice the vitamin C of an orange.

As with many of the names that European settlers gave to the things they encountered, the names given to native fruits and bushfoods had few similarities to their namesakes. The desert peach has little similarity to peaches as we know them in the United States. Juleigh Robins describes its taste as "closer to that of an apricot crossed with rhubarb with a slight touch of cinnamon" (Robins, 1996, p. 19). The bush cucumber looks more like a tiny melon; wild lime does resemble a lime, but a tiny version of it; and lady apples only slightly resemble apples from the old world and contain in the center a large, single seed (Robins, 1996). Perhaps these names were given by foreigners in a very foreign land, seeking to create some connection to their homelands. Such names perhaps provided some degree of reassurance in a lonely and difficult time but arguably were (and are) distracting—minimizing the uniqueness and differentness of this new (to them) land and environment. For that reason, the Aboriginal names of these bush foods will probably be the long-term names provided as these foods become more commercial (a process that is accelerating; see http://www.newcrops.uq.edu.au).

A Bushland Education in the City

The United Nations declared the decade 2005–2015 as the Decade of Education for Sustainability. In response, the Australian federal government created the Sustainable Schools Initiative with $2 million in funds, and all states committed to providing matching funds. The project aims to equip students so that "when they leave school they should have an understanding of, and concern for, stewardship of the natural environment, and the knowledge and skills to contribute to ecologically sustainable development" (http://www.environment.gov.au/education/aussi/about.html).

The program was trialed with 320 schools in Victoria and NSW and then spread to all states, with more than double this number now involved. Schools vary in how they are responding to this agenda, but all are including ways to better manage energy, water, and waste in school buildings; how to improve school canteens; and how to get involved in local conservation work. In early results, one school found how to save 40 percent of its water use, another emphasized litter reduction strategies so that scavenging nonnative birds were replaced by native butcherbirds and rosellas, and another used a local Aboriginal elder to help design a heritage walk in the school grounds.

The Western Australian initiative is called Aussi-WA and includes thirty-three schools. Their whole-school approach "embedding sustainability within the culture of the school community" is based on twelve areas, from air to water, and includes Indigenous Culture and Purchasing modules. Their Web site (http://www.sustainableschools.wa.edu.au) contains case studies from many of the schools to illustrate each of the modules or activity areas. At South Fremantle High School, a partnership among parents, community, the local council, and the school has produced a plan for the school to become the first Australian high school to be carbon neutral. This involves energy efficiency, renewables, and offsets through tree planting including high schools in the wheatbelt (http://www .southfremantleshs.det.wa.edu.au).

Local schools are one place where education about local flora and fauna should occur, preferably at a young age. As mentioned earlier, there has been a large tradition of such work in schools by groups such as the Gould League. Although there are many places where environmental education is only minimal, most primary and secondary schools have curricula and special programs to involve their children in their local environment.

One program, Ribbons of Blue, was started in Perth but has spread now across the whole of Australia and to a number of other countries. The program gets local students to collect water samples from local creeks and to analyze them for nutrients, salt, and aquatic life; then, through computer links, a whole catchment of schools compile their results into a watershed action plan for regenerating the water systems in their area. Schools present their plans to local councils and then get involved in the regeneration process, which usually involves helping to replant areas or to build wetlands that can receive stormwater. Teachers receive training and help with equipment. The Ribbons of Blue network has hundreds of active teachers involved in an Internet-based sharing of experiences.

One of the teachers who began Ribbons of Blue, Keith Brown, has continued his work at Coogee Primary School (in the Perth metro area) on a range of innovative environmental programs, including a bush regeneration project that was so successful the adjoining landowner (the WA Water Corporation) has contracted the school to regenerate their bush areas. The Coogee School Nursery now earns money that goes to school programs.

Greening Australia has taken some creative steps to promote biodiversity and place-based education. It unveiled its "Grow Us a Home" Web site, aimed at school kids ages five to nine. It presents easy-to-understand, map-based information about the two main land features in the Perth area, the Swan Coastal Plan and the Darling Range, and the biodiversity likely to be found there. Greening Australia also conducts place-oriented teacher training. According to Greening Australia, the Web site has the potential to reach some 140,000 Perth area students (Greening Australia, 2005). It also contributes to the Curriculum Councils' Curricular Framework for Social and Civic Responsibility and Environmental Responsibility.

Few schools are doing as much as the Noranda Primary School in Bayswater Council in northern Perth to teach about bush values and to integrate this directly into the learning environment. Behind the school's complex of small buildings is remarkably intact remnant forested bush (figure 5.7). There are spots of scarring and degradation, including a place where a horse track existed where now the soil is too hard for much to grow, but mostly the area is home to an abundant and diverse flora and fauna—grass trees, red gums, and even orchids are there, including at least one rare orchid species. The areas have been fenced (to prevent kids from riding their bikes throughout) but have small gates in several places to allow access for students and residents of the surrounding neighborhood.

Figure 5.7 The Noranda Primary School, in Perth, managed to save and restore an adjacent native bushland site. Students from the school visit the bushland daily, use it as a laboratory for many school subjects, and actively care for and steward over the site. *Photo credit:* Courtesy Noranda Primary School, Perth

The most important activity utilizing this special bush is the school's Bush Wardens program. Students who become Bush Wardens participate in after-school bush learning and work activities, where they do many different things, from weed removal and bush regeneration work to seed collection and plant propagation. A management plan has been prepared for the school's bushlands, and the Bush Wardens help implement many of the actions specified in this plan. There are presently thirty to forty students involved in Bush Wardens, and as the name implies, participation involves the development of a sense of ownership about and care for these special lands. The Bush Warden students show a certain pride about their knowledge of flora and fauna and tend to convey this to other students in the school.

Students in all grades in Noranda get exposed to knowledge about the bush at some point during the year. A consultant was hired several years ago to prepare a curricular resource manual, entitled *Our Bushland Classroom*, which provides detailed instructional materials and ideas for all grades (1 through 7). The result of a collaboration between the Bayswater Council and the local catchment authority, the manual provides materials that have helped convey this important natural history to the students.

Schools like Noranda give hope that the next generation of Australians will be educated about, connected to, and emotionally concerned about their native bushlands and biodiversity. But just as important will be to find creative and effective means to reach adults (a potentially more difficult task). One exemplary effort has to do with an immensely underappreciated but essential element of the bush: fungi.

The Perth Urban Bushland Fungi project received funding from Lottery West (providing almost $400,000 AUD in grant funds). Under the project, funds have been available to provide a salary for a mycologist (a person who studies fungi) and an education officer, based out of the WA herbarium. The goals of this project are both scientific and educational. It is very much a volunteer-based project, and much of the work is done by people who spend many hours helping to catalog fungi and do the other things needed to maintain and expand the fungi database.

It is somewhat shocking that current knowledge of fungi species is so limited. There are an estimated 250,000 species native to WA, but only an estimated 5 to 10 percent have been discovered and named, according to Neale Bougher, the project's mycologist. Land management agencies—CALM being the main one in WA—have not been very concerned with fungi, even though an understanding of them is likely essential to effective long-term landscape regeneration (due to the close link between plants and their ability to access nutrients via fungi in this highly leached environment). Their unique involvement in the life cycle of orchids is just one example. Another problem is that there are just no mycologists on staff in these key agencies. "We just don't employ them," says Bougher, who himself finds his employment tenuous. "And so we're losing these remnant fungi" (Bougher, personal interview, 2005).

"Out of sight, out of mind" is a clear problem when it comes to appreciating fungi, and especially so given that most are microscopic. The fungus season in Perth is a relatively short one, essentially June and July. During this time, shortly after the first rains fall, fungi start to emerge on the surface.

Roz Hart leads the educational component of the project, which involves a project Web site and the convening of both workshops (six hours long) and fungi walks or "forays" (lasting about two hours). She has been involved in conducting forays through the WA Naturalist Club since the late 1990s, and they seem to be growing in popularity. Roz has had to turn interested people away, as the forays can only reasonably accommodate about thirty people. Feedback is positive, moreover, and the forays appear to have a major impact on peoples' perception of nature and the places in which they live.

Participants in the forays and walks also help to collect specimens, and there is also much work in drying and cataloging specimens following foraying weekends. Nearly a thousand specimens have been collected through the forays under this project so far.

Other elements of the educational campaign have included a radio show (WA-wide), the Web site, and the production of an online field book, which already contains forty-five species. The latter, which organizes and presents common fungi species, with photographs, is especially useful to promoting local knowledge about fungi.

Fungal inventories have been conducted in only a few parks and bushland sites in Perth, Bold, and Kings parks. Knowledge of fungal species present in most bushland locations, however, is very limited and is likely to be one of the expanding agendas of bushland conservation in the Perth area.

Bush Restoration and Social Capital Building

APACE is an unusual community-based nonprofit in North Fremantle. Formed in 1983, it specializes in the propagation of and education about flora native to the Perth region of Western Australia. With offices located in a heritage cottage (and encompassing the surrounding property) provided essentially cost-free from the Fremantle Council and the WA planning council, the organization performs a number of important community functions. It operates a fairly large community revegetation nursery that grows and sells, both wholesale and directly to community residents, some three hundred different species of native plants (about 20 percent of the native flora in the Perth region). Over the years, APACE has learned how to collect local seed and how to successfully grow these native species, something others—including most commercial nurseries—have been unable or unwilling to do. The nursery has been quite successful and forms the largest part of what APACE now does. Each year, it sells about four hundred thousand native plants grown from the nursery. The one-hectare property contains the house (which includes a resource library, or "knowledge center," about native plants and other appropriate technologies) and extensive plant-growing sheds. Volunteers and some paid workers (several of whom are severely disabled) do much of the work.

One interesting element of APACE is its community seed bank (figure 5.8). Funded by the National Heritage Trust and officially known as the Swan Regional Seed Bank, it contains facilities and fairly specialized equipment, such as a seed-sorting machine and a refrigerated locker for storing the seeds. APACE is frequently hired by councils to collect local seed stocks on sites about to be lost to development projects. The refrigerator contains bins bearing the names of councils, with vacuum-packed containers of seeds inside, all numerically coded. As with any bank, the donors receive a yearly statement of which seed stock they have on deposit. Individuals and groups in the community are also able to collect and store their seeds in this facility, and APACE runs introductory seed collection courses to help in this endeavor.

APACE, moreover, has developed "soil type plant catalogs" for different parts of the Perth region that show what species of plants are found in which soil and geological assemblage and which will likely do well, simplifying the task for councils and individuals wanting to use native plants.

APACE's agenda has a clear community education element. It offers courses on bush regeneration and, as mentioned, seed collecting. On site, as well, are community gardens where local residents grow organic food (about twenty plots are available). There is a community building and classroom available for community use. They have a rammed earth building for display, PV panels on their roof, and a conservation garden with interpretive signs.

Figure 5.8
The APACE Seed Bank, in Fremantle. Here a community seed bank has been established in which citizens and volunteers collect, catalog and store seeds from native plants and that are later used for revegetation projects.
Photo credit: Tim Beatley

APACE also works extensively with local schools, providing bushland appreciation and plant identification courses. These classes typically begin by taking the students out into the bush and end with students involved in an actual replanting project.

A key idea behind the community nursery and seed bank is the importance of "local provenance" species. While the same species of plant may grow and exist in other parts of WA or even elsewhere in Australia, the belief is that there may likely be special adaptations of that species to the unique local soils, plant communities, and climate. It is believed that local provenance plants—that is, plants that grow and derive from local stock—are more likely to thrive and survive. Of course, in some cases, seed collection is also about using a resource that might be expensive to purchase commercially or even may not be available. Moreover, there is much power of "provenance" to begin to bind us to place. The recognition of provenance, and the act of collecting (growing) and replanting local provenance stock, is an act of connecting to specific places.

As impressive as the nursery's annual production is, APACE's greatest contribution is likely to be the extent to which it has changed the entire revegetation industry, not only by creating awareness about the need to use native plants but also by providing the practical means to do so. For example, they invented a bush regeneration tool called a Peter Lever (a crowbar-like device used for digging out invasive weeds). As a consequence, revegetation is now almost universally occurring on public lands, such as schools and parks, and even individual residences commonly use native plants, often local provenance plants, where in the past that would not have been the case.

Despite these successes, APACE has not been without its challenges. Remarkably, in 2001, the state government threatened to sell one of the parcels that makes up the APACE site. The government was looking at the land essentially as a short-term source of economic gain, and it took an APACE public campaign to beat back the effort. As Tony Freeman, the coordinator of APACE, notes, the community aspect of the site and organization and the diversity of services and benefits provided to the community were probably the things that saved it. Support was garnered from across government, business, and the community, reflecting the good work APACE has done for many years.

Conclusions and Lessons Learned

Many Americans know about Australia through Steve Irwin, "The Crocodile Hunter," who sadly was killed in 2006 by a stingray. Many people see the crocodiles, sharks, snakes, and spiders of Australia as objects of fear, but to Steve Irwin they were "beautiful." Living for a time in Australia (mostly in Australian cities), one rarely sees such animals other than in zoos. But one does have a strong sense of the flora and fauna of this country. It seeps into every suburb and central city in ways that seem much more obvious than American cities. Is this just an accident, or is it planned and encouraged? My experience suggests that it is encouraged and will only increase, not decrease. It has become part of the culture to appreciate the native bush and to try to make it as much a part of the city as possible. There are many lessons that can be learned for American cities.

At least for an outsider, nature in Australia seems ubiquitous, exotic, around every urban corner and "in your face," a visceral part of urban life, and one that suggests how special living in Australia can be. Australian cities show us that it is possible indeed to live a life of nature, to live and work in a city but to also have direct contact with nature and have great physical access to the primordial bush. There are, to be sure, plenty of places in urban and suburban Australia that exhibit little natural life, but I have been more taken by what is there.

It is also a matter of what can be done to protect, restore, and nurture this nature, and as the stories in this chapter have shown there are some terrific positive examples. In many cases, it is about establishing parks and setting aside bushland preserves within reach of urbanites (such as Perth's Bush Forever program) but also about the smaller ways that nature and development in the city can coexist, even where the city can help regenerate the ecology, as with many bush regeneration projects. It is about incorporating nature and biodiversity into the planning process and system, giving it explicit attention in urban decision making.

I am convinced of the truth of what E. O. Wilson referred to as *biophilia*—our innate need for contact with nature—and see in Australian cities the possibility of a biophilic urbanism. It is not a perfect model, of course, and much urban nature has been lost and remains threatened in Australian cities, but there is growing consensus in Australian urban circles that nature in cities is not a luxury, not optional, but is as essential as cultural amenities, offices and apartments, transit, and soccer pitches.

As my experience with grey-headed flying foxes in Sydney attests, there is still much work that must take place in every city (in Australia as well as the United States) to reconnect urban populations to nature and to educate and build awareness about this biodiversity around us. In my time in Australia, I've uncovered some terrific examples of ideas and strategies aimed at overcoming this disconnect. These have included wildlife diaries, bushland guides and workshops, fungi forays, school-based natural heritage efforts, and bushcare and other hands-on learning opportunities, among others. One of my pet ideas has been the need to find creative ways to reach new homeowners and renters as they move into a new neighborhood. I have proposed elsewhere the concept of an *ecological owner's manual*, which new residents might receive as they move in and which might challenge them to see their new home in the broadest possible sense (as a watershed, as common habitat shared with many other species, as a part of an interconnected landscape and urban or suburban environment). Some the closest examples of what I have in mind have been unearthed in my Australian travels (e.g., the Bushmates guide, the Welcome to the Watershed initiative and materials), and they should provide some very useful guidance and prototypes of what could be done in American communities.

It is a real challenge to create ways to entice urbanites to more actively engage with the nature around them; to learn to recognize common species of trees, birds, plants, and butterflies; and to develop a deeper understanding of the geology and ecological systems that support them. Many marvelous ideas about how to do this can be found in Australian communities, from attending a fungi foray to keeping a wildlife watch diary to even reconceptualizing your backyard swimming pool as an aquatic habitat!

We must also begin to rethink schools as opportunities to teach about natural heritage and urban biodiversity, and such examples as the Noranda Primary School in Perth provide much inspiration. It requires reforming curricula and also suggests that we conceptualize what a school needs in order to undertake the mission of teaching. The equipment of a school, as the Noranda example argues for, should be productively expanded: it should be not just basketball courts and conventional playground equipment but also perhaps a functioning bushland (or wetland or stream or prairie).

I have been particularly taken by the notion of direct participation and engagement by the urban population in restoring and managing urban nature. Typically, under the rubric of local Bushcare programs (though they go by different names in different cities), cities like Brisbane have seen the direct involvement of a remarkable number of its citizens. The size of these programs, and the extent of participation, is truly impressive. The benefits of this engagement, furthermore, are many, some direct and some more indirect, but at a deep level they speak to what it means to be a citizen of a modern city in an age in which urban nature (all nature) is in a state of distress and under pressure. Philosopher Andrew Light would identify such bushcare programs as examples of ecological citizenship that in addition to the obvious value of restoring urban nature, help to cultivate stronger participatory and democratic skills and sensibilities as well as a closeness with and care for nature in cities. Urban bushcare is a grassroots democratic movement that could and should be replicated in American cities.

Finally, the bushcare and other examples in this chapter suggest the importance of a kind of *ecological social capital*. Many of the usual elements of social capital—personal relationships, clubs, organizations and social networks, community institutions, and more—in the Australian cities that I've been studying have a nature or ecological dimension. They serve not only a social function but also an ecological and biophilic function and indeed suggest the potential of merging together these ideas. A volunteer-staffed community seed bank, for instance (of the APACE sort), is both an element of the city's environmental management capacity or capability and a part of the community's broader social capital. These Australian examples show that it is possible to build and grow these together and show how important ecological social capital is to achieving the vision of green urbanism.

6

The Importance of Regional and State Planning

While U.S. cities and metropolitan areas continue to grapple with an ineffective or even absent regional planning framework, the situation is quite different in Australia. Relatively strong regional planning exists, and regional plans have been prepared in each of this country's major urban areas. States take the lead, and it certainly helps that Australian states are large and thus that major urban centers in Australia do not cross multiple state boundaries as a consequence. While the specifics are different from place to place, these Australian regional plans set impressive visions for more sustainable and compact growth patterns and are tackling head-on the unsustainable sprawl that characterizes much of the recent past there and that requires looking beyond the state and local levels. Statewide sustainability strategies are also now common. Western Australia and South Australia, for instance, have developed impressive state plans and planning requirements centered on sustainability, further reinforcing the goals of regional plans.

What follows below is an effort to describe these regional and state planning efforts, providing detailed examples of how commitments and creative planning and implementation tools at these levels can greatly help to shape a more livable, sustainable future. While the story is not a perfect one, and the full measures of success will be years in coming, these emerging stories of how visions of regional growth and state leadership can be based on sustainability provide inspiration for an American audience with a similar governance structure.

Regional Plans

Australia's metropolitan areas are guided by visionary and ambitious regional plans—a distinctive and exemplary feature of the Australian sustainability scene. While not always fully or effectively implemented, they are, on the whole, compelling in their scope and coverage and represent tremendous efforts at mapping out more sustainable patterns of regional development and growth. What follows are detailed descriptions of these regional plans and their key planning and sustainability elements.

The South East Queensland (SEQ) Regional Plan

Few parts of Australia have incurred as much population growth and as much development pressure in recent years as Queensland. Much of this growth has been centered around Brisbane, the main city, and along the Gold Coast and Sunshine Coast. The greater Brisbane metropolitan area—known as South East Queensland (SEQ)—adds about fifty thousand new residents each year and is projected to grow by about a million over the time frame of its regional plan (to 2026, or approximately twenty years).

Brisbane has had a reputation for not planning this area, but eventually the demands grew for a better framework to show where to develop and where not to, as well as better infrastructure. After extensive public consultation, the final SEQ plan was released by the Queensland government on June 30, 2005, and an updated and amended final version was released the following June (2006). This plan was well received by developers and by the public as it provided a clear statutory base for regional planning and was associated with an infrastructure plan as well.

All of Australia's regional plans call for substantial new growth to occur in the form of infill and in already developed locations, and Brisbane's plan is one of the most ambitious in this regard. In the Brisbane Plan—the SEQ Regional Plan—the target is to accommodate 40 percent of the area's growth through infill (areas within the "Urban Footprint") to 2016 and then 50 percent to 2026.

The SEQ plan has several key elements that are entirely new for planning in this region: (1) an effort to sharply delineate where urban growth can and cannot occur in the future, (2) designation of areas to be protected (a Regional Landscape and Rural Production Area), and (3) dedication of a network of "Regional Activity Centers" connected by public transit and within which higher-density mixed-use developments will occur. The plan maps an area called the Urban Footprint, representing those areas in the region where existing and future urban growth is to be encouraged (figure 6.1). "Investigative Areas"—areas generally contiguous to the urban footprint—have also been delineated; they are essentially areas of urban reserve that could accommodate growth in the future, if needed. This plan, moreover, specifically assigns new dwelling targets—total and infill

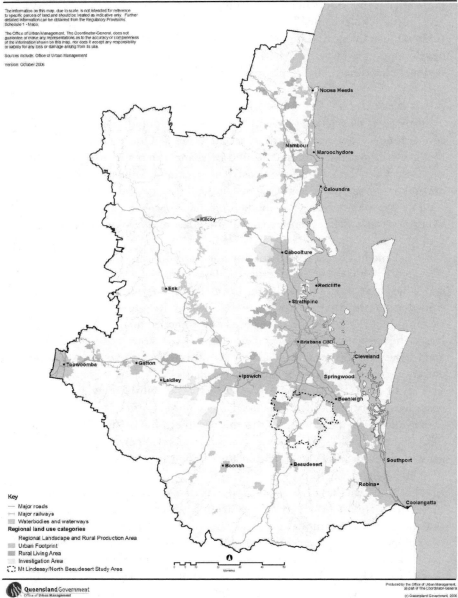

Figure 6.1 The South East Queensland (SEQ) Regional Plan Map.
© State of Queensland (Department of Infrastructure and Planning).

dwellings—to all local government areas in SEQ and sets a minimum density target of fifteen dwellings per hectare for new residential development.

Interestingly, the draft SEQ plan actually includes a set of "Draft Regulatory Provisions," which place fairly stringent restrictions, for instance, on the subdivision of land within the delineated Regional Landscape and Rural Production Area, specifically to no smaller than 100 hectares in size (about 250 acres) (Queensland Government, Office of Urban Management, 2005).

Extensive mapping and analysis have gone into delineating the Regional Landscape and Rural Production Area, which includes forested lands, crop and grazing lands, and water and groundwater resources. The nature conservation element is also considerable, and a key map in the plan delineates core Biodiversity Protection Areas (including those of local, regional, and state significance) and Bioregional Wildlife Corridors. Other elements of landscape and nature conservation include World Heritage sites, (i.e., the Central Eastern Rainforest Reserves), coastal lands, twenty-nine Bioregional Wildlife Corridors, and significant biodiversity areas, including areas of important koala habitat.

Economic development is also a key element of the SEQ plan in an attempt to ensure there is a reasonable distribution of jobs and to minimize the growth in transport. An emphasis is placed on building a "strong, resilient and diversified economy," with a series of economic principles and strategies presented in the plan as well as a visual expression of these through an "economic activity" map (which, for example, identifies the location of existing knowledge hubs, high-quality agricultural land, and commercial areas; Queensland Government, Office of Urban Management, 2005, p. 46). The SEQ Regional Plan is a statutory plan and, under Queensland's Integrated Planning Act, takes precedence over all other plans and decisions. "If there is an inconsistency between the SEQ Regional Plan and any other relevant plan, policy of code relating to the SEQ, the SEQ Regional Plan prevails" (Brisbane City Council, 2007a, p. 54).

Indeed, much of the implementation of the regional plan happens through local councils, which are required to prepare and submit for state approval a "Local Growth Management Strategy" (LGMS), indicating how they intend to accommodate the growth in the areas assigned. These local strategies, including for the city of Brisbane, were to be submitted by June 2007 (and, in fact, most councils have now complied). To help localities identify suitable sites to accommodate additional urban density and growth in their communities, the Queensland government commissioned the University of Queensland to prepare an "Urban Housing Capacity Template" (Queensland Government, 2006). This report "presents a methodology to identify how much additional housing could be accommodated in selected locations and within specific timeframes" (p. 3).

While each LMGS is somewhat different, they all provide much more detailed plans and strategies for how and where the development targets set out in the regional plan will occur. A review of the draft LGMSs suggests that they are impressive efforts at fleshing out where and how future development and growth will occur to 2026, as well as creative efforts to map out a future vision for city development that builds on unique place qualities, protects and restores biodiversity, and leads to more sustainable neighborhoods and urban form. The city of Brisbane's LGMS is called "CityShape" and specifies in great detail where and how its more than one hundred thousand new dwelling units will be accommodated (Brisbane City Council, 2007b). A high percentage (75 percent) of this development will occur in infill and redevelopment areas, specifically in Regional Activity Centres and designated Growth Corridors (transport-intensive corridors where major busways and railway lines are found).

Brisbane's LGMS envisions a city of connected, walkable centers flanked by large blocks of protected green land and habitat to the east and west, with "ecological corridors" between them. The Brisbane LGMS sets an aspirational goal of protecting 40 percent of the city's land area in native, natural habitat, with the need to secure and set aside new open land mostly within ecological corridors. The Brisbane plan envisions a "canopy of shade" across the city, achieved through new tree planting and building design, and a "city of walks" (Brisbane City Council, 2007b, p. 36). The Brisbane strategy, as with most, also contains within it a detailed "Development Sequencing Strategy," by which a preferred timing and phasing of development (area by area) is laid out (in three time periods specifically, up to 2026; p. 51).

While the content, form, and structure of other LGMSs in the region are quite similar, they do vary in content depending on local circumstances and values. Redland Shire, located adjacent to Moreton Bay and to the east of Brisbane, is home to important koala habitat, and so this issue is addressed in their LGMS. Redland Shire proposes, for instance, protection of koala habitat areas as well as koala corridors that will connect "patches of koala habitat" to a regional network of conservation areas (Redland Shire Council, 2007, p. 59). As a further example, the LGMS prepared for Gold Coast reflects its special circumstance of seventy kilometers of ocean and beach shoreline (in terms of recreation, tourism, and hazard mitigation; see Gold Coast City, 2007). Each individual locality is able to address special and unique needs, and important local goals, while at the same time respecting and implementing regional targets and goals.

Infrastructure investments will be one important key to implementing the plan. In total, about $66 billion AUD in infrastructure investment, through 2026, will be needed to carry out the plan. The infrastructure plan includes two new rail projects—one to the Sunshine Coast and one to Springfield, which will be important catalysts in concentrating development in centers along the corridors. Regional planning is always controversial as most local governments prefer to be independent, but they realize that most infrastructure is regional and requires population and employment that is consistent with it. Setting aside land as "never to be developed" rural or bushland is also controversial locally, and sometimes local councils like regional plans because it gives them cover—they can say, "The state made us do this." A clause in the planning act allows landowners to submit claims for compensation if they feel a regulatory action or down-zoning has injured them. Whereas most other cities have had such regional plans before, Brisbane and SEQ have not, so this regional plan was historic for the area and was well received by the public, who were keen to see sprawl controlled and better infrastructure provided. The Queensland government says the plan will protect some 80 percent of the land (and habitat) in the region from urbanization pressures.

There is an extensive mapping of biologically significant lands in the plan area through the SEQ Regional Nature Conservation Strategy, which was based on a common framework for assessment. Will the plan protect biodiversity and ensure that these important habitat areas are protected? The answer is not clear, as the regional plan and biodiversity strategy depend on local nature conservation strategies to identify priorities and management strategies. Most of the key habitat or sensitive lands are private property (large public parks and protected areas are a much smaller percentage in SEQ compared with Sydney, for instance) and will require changes in land management practices as well as, in many cases (such as key habitat areas), substantial public buying as has occurred in Perth and parts of the city of Brisbane. A mechanism for this is not yet obvious. However, the first steps—a regional plan with clear statutory demarcation of land that should and should not be urban and an infrastructure plan to make the urban part work—are now in place. Also, as of January 2007, there is a total clearing ban in place across Queensland, which means landowners now have an incentive to manage the land for conservation because no further agricultural potential remains.

Adelaide Metro Regional Plan

The Adelaide regional plan, called "The Planning Strategy for Metropolitan Adelaide," follows closely from the South Australia Strategic Plan and was released in final form in August 2006, with a strong set of directions consistent with its past planning history.

The Adelaide metro region plan begins its discussion of strategic framework with a prominent statement of the importance of sustainability: "Our ability to make Adelaide sustainable and prosperous in the future depends largely on development decisions made now and how we provide access to and manage the resources Adelaide relies upon from both within and beyond the urban area" (Planning SA, 2006, p. 8). The plan also makes explicit reference to the National Strategy for Ecologically Sustainable Development (1992) and utilizes its main principles as the plan's guiding principles (see p. 9). The plan states an intention to "improve the integration of ecologically sensitive design principles into housing development" (Planning SA, 2006, p. 96).

Like the other regional plans, the Adelaide plan seeks to bring about greater urban containment and has to this end delineated a clear "urban boundary" as well as landscape and environmental protections. It incorporates the region's network of open space—called MOSS, or Metropolitan Open Space System. Some preexisting conservation elements are given prominence. Protection is given to the western face of the Mt. Lofty ranges through the Hills Face Zone (Planning SA, 2004).

Section 2.5 of chapter 2 of the Adelaide plan, one of its meatier components, is entitled "Attaining Sustainability" and includes extensive and detailed discussion of water, energy, biodiversity, coastal environment, and waste. The analysis and concepts contained there are far-reaching, advocating a whole-of-water-cycle-approach, promoting renewable energy (especially solar), and protecting biodiversity, building on and coordinating with the state's progressive Nature Links initiative.

The plan maps, not always elaborated on in the plan text, together paint a picture of an ecologically sophisticated view of the city and region. Map 4 of the plan presents an unusual accounting of the metro area's water cycle: where water comes from and where it goes (stormwater, wastewater), by subwatershed. An ecosystem assets map presents a succinct impression of where the region is—main conservation lands and green spaces—and also identifies areas for future revegetation (figure 6.2).

As with the Brisbane SEQ plan, implementation responsibilities apply to both local authorities and state agencies; thus a Strategic Infrastructure Plan for South Australia and a Residential Metropolitan Development

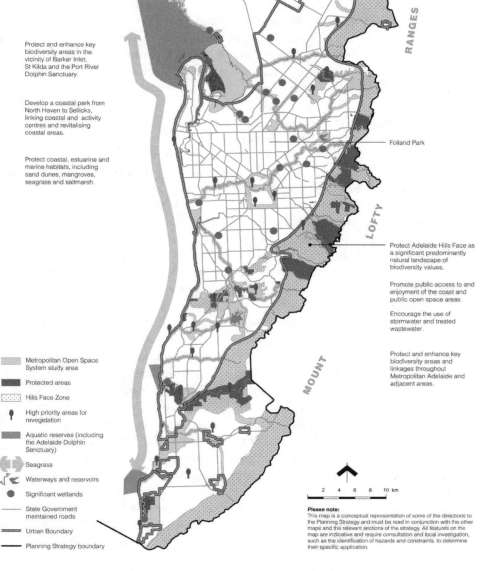

Protect and enhance key
biodiversity areas in the
vicinity of Barker Inlet,
St Kilda and the Port River
Dolphin Sanctuary.

Develop a coastal park from
North Haven to Sellicks,
linking coastal and activity
centres and revitalising
coastal areas.

Protect coastal, estuarine and
marine habitats, including
sand dunes, mangroves,
seagrass and saltmarsh.

RANGES

Folland Park

LOFTY

Protect Adelaide Hills Face as
a significant predominantly
natural landscape of
biodiversity values.

Promote public access to and
enjoyment of the coast and
public open space areas.

Encourage the use of
stormwater and treated
wastewater.

Protect and enhance key
biodiversity areas and
linkages throughout
Metropolitan Adelaide and
adjacent areas.

MOUNT

Metropolitan Open Space
System study area

Protected areas

Hills Face Zone

High priority areas for
revegetation

Aquatic reserves (including
the Adelaide Dolphin
Sanctuary)

Seagrass

Waterways and reservoirs

Significant wetlands

State Government
maintained roads

Urban Boundary

Planning Strategy boundary

2 4 6 8 10 km

Please note:
This map is a conceptual representation of some of the directions to
the Planning Strategy and must be read in conjunction with the other
maps and the relevant sections of the strategy. All features on the
map are indicative and require consultation and local investigation,
such as the identification of hazards and constraints, to determine
their specific application.

Figure 6.2 Adelaide Ecosystem Assets Map. *Image credit.*Planning SA, Government of South Australia

Program provide the infrastructure and establish land release and development targets for the region.

The plan also presents a very detailed "sequencing" plan, essentially a timeline for when particular residential areas will receive public services. Adelaide has very slow population and economic growth and thus has not set out an ambitious public transport plan as in other Australian cities, though it has begun to rebuild its light rail. Adelaide's main contribution (as discussed in chapter 2) is its renewable energy and carbon-neutral strategies, which are reflected in this regional plan but were developed through separate processes.

Melbourne 2030

Melbourne was the first city in Australia in the current era of regional plan development to enter into a new strategic planning process. Its "Melbourne 2030" plan came out in 2000, and since then the city has produced a series of detailed follow-up plans. The Melbourne regional plan, like all of the Australian metropolitan plans, puts forth a spatial vision of the future and is intended to guide future investments and state and local use of development decisions. It takes as its starting point the need to accommodate significant population growth—up to a million new residents by 2030.

The several key conceptual elements to the plan include an urban growth boundary, the protection of "green wedges," and the steering of future growth into a set of "activity centers," based along transit corridors. In delineating the region's growth boundary, a series of "growth areas" were identified, mostly at the edge or periphery of the metropolitan area. These are natural, contiguous extensions of existing urban areas. These greenfield sites will certainly accommodate significant growth, but Melbourne's regional plan, like the others in Australia's major cities, is impressive for the extent to which it aspires to accommodate much of its growth in already urbanized areas, and mostly within activity centers (figure 6.3) (Victoria Department of Sustainability and Environment, 2004a). In the case of Melbourne 2030, about 70 percent of the area's future growth is to happen on nongreenfield sites—that is, either within designated urban activity centers or through "dispersed urban and non-urban development," with "non-urban" including sites in and around small townships (Victoria Department of Sustainability and Environment, 2002a Melbourne 2030: Planning for Sustainable Growth, 2004c, see http://www.dse.vic.gov.au/melbourne 2030online/)

Strengthening and intensifying "activity centers" is a key planning feature in Melbourne 2030 (box 6.1). The plan designates about a thousand

Activity Centres and Principal Public Transport Network Plan, 2003

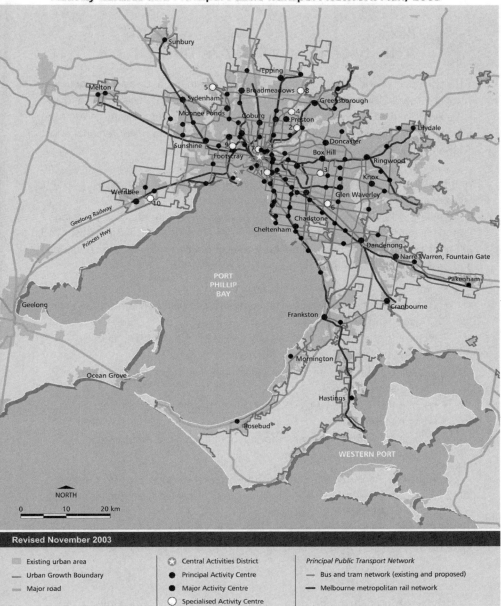

Figure 6.3 Melbourne 2030 Urban Growth map. *Image credit:* © Department of Sustainability and Environment, Victoria, Australia.

Box 6.1
Activity Centers: What Are They?

Activity centers provide the focus for services, employment, and social interaction in cities and towns. They are the places where people shop, work, meet, relax, and live. Usually well served by public transport, they range in size and intensity of use from local neighborhood strip centers to traditional universities and major regional malls. They are not just shopping centres; they are multifunctional.

Activity centers attract high numbers of people and generate a significant volume of trips in metropolitan Melbourne. Because of the vital role played by activity centers in everyday urban life, their planning is always important.

Since the 1950s, activity center policy has been a feature of urban planning in Victoria. Essentially, this is a matter of clustering—rather than dispersing—uses and activities to derive social, environmental, and economic benefits for the community and business generally. These benefits include the following:

- providing a strong basis for economic growth
- creating opportunities for the more efficient and balanced concentration of goods and services
- increasing the potential for the exchange of ideas and other synergies among businesses and for new job creation
- providing an important focus for communities by increasing opportunities for social interaction
- making the most of the community's investment in physical and social infrastructure
- providing greater opportunities for integrating land use and transport, particularly public transport and walking.

Stand-alone single uses do not constitute activity centers; nor do industrial estates. In fact, Melbourne 2030 seeks to restrict out-of-center development and contains separate policies for industrial land.

Source: Victoria Department of Infrastructure, 2004a.

---

activity centers throughout the region, classified into five types: Central Activities District, Principal Activity Centres, Major Activity Centres, Specialized Activity Centres, and Neighborhood Activity Centres. The vast majority (about nine hundred) are neighborhood centers. This classification moves from the largest centers of activity (Central Activities District—

Figure 6.4 Melbourne city center. Melbourne 2030 calls for guiding most future growth in the region into activity centers such as this, where it can be best accommodated and can contribute positively to the creation of transit-friendly, walkable living environments. *Photo credit:* Tim Beatley

essentially downtown Melbourne, with the largest concentration of retail, amenities, government, and education) to neighborhood centers (with generally less than ten thousand square meters of retail but that represent smaller but important community focal points, close to schools, police stations, and neighborhood-level activities and services). Melbourne 2030, then, envisions a vibrant and comprehensive network of these activity centers "of varying size and function that are linked with a strategic public transport network" (Victoria Department of Infrastructure, 2004, p. 5) (figure 6.4).

In 2005, a set of "Activity Centre Design Guidelines" were prepared to provide advice to councils and developers about how to achieve activity centers. Activity centers are intended to be the "focal points" around which population, infrastructure, and civic and commercial activity will occur (Victoria Department of Sustainability and Environment, 2005a). The aims of the activity centers are shown in box 6.2. The design guidelines attempt to answer the key question: "So how should different activities be integrated into a coherent, compact, walkable centre" (Victoria Department of

Box 6.2
Melbourne 2030 Activity Centre Design Guidelines

Aims for Activity Centres Design

1. Develop a good-quality public environment
    Ensure public spaces within individual developments and throughout activity centres are comfortable, engaging environments.

2. Promote street-based patterns of connection
    Directly link developments within activity centres and with their surrounding neighbourhoods using a fine-grained street system that accommodates diverse modes of travel.

3. Improve community safety
    Promote the natural surveillance of public space and street edge activity. This can be achieved by ensuring buildings address the street and contain active uses on the ground floor. Clearly define public and private space.

4. Encourage a mix of uses
    Optimise the diversity of uses in activity centres where the mix promotes vitality, extends the hours of activity and intensifies the use of existing infrastructure.

5. Improve pedestrian and cycling amenity
    Encourage an increase in pedestrian and cycling traffic by maximizing the convenience, safety and appeal of these modes of travel.

6. Promote a public transport focus
    Better integrate public transport with activity centres by increasing community comfort, safety and accessibility.

7. Increase accessibility and integration
    Ensure activity centres are a focus for the entire community, are accessible to all, and are physically integrated with the surrounding neighbourhood.

8. Encourage environmental sustainability
    Promote the efficient reuse of existing assets, prolong the life cycle of structures, ensure energy efficiency, and water and resource conservation and encourage appropriate orientation and use of materials.

Source: Victoria Department of Sustainability and Environment, 2005a.

Sustainability and Environment, 2005a, p. 4). The guidelines provide a series of specific design suggestions and visual examples organized around eight design elements (urban structure, stations and interchanges, street design, public spaces, building design, malls and large stores, higher-density housing, and car parking). Local councils must now work to modify their plans to reflect and be consistent with the metro plan.

As with other metropolitan strategic plans, the Melbourne 2030 plan identifies a number of specific actions to be taken by various state offices and agencies, policies to steer business growth and development to activity centers, proposed changes in the state's planning framework and guidance, and proposals to "lead by example." The state government's Transit Cities program has been the largest and most significant effort in the latter category and has aimed to design and redevelop the space around a number of targeted rail stations in the region.

The infrastructure portion of the Melbourne 2030 plan was added in late 2006. It contained $10 billion of support for transport infrastructure, although little of this was directed to providing new electric rail to the suburbs and hence has been criticized as inadequate (among other elements, the plan includes some investments to address freeway congestion and to expand and improve bus service; see Department of Infrastructure, 2006).

Twelve large green wedges have been identified in the wedges implementation plan; these include important agricultural areas as well as natural and ecological areas of importance. The green wedges, beyond the urban growth boundary, are intended to be off-limits to new urbanization, and the 2030 plan envisions a variety of actions aimed at strengthening their protection, including tightening development controls (amending Ministerial Direction 6, rural residential development) and developing an individual action plan for each of the different wedges (Victoria Department of Infrastructure, 2004b).

The Docklands project, eventually to be home to twenty thousand new residents and forty thousand new jobs, is being heralded as Australia's "largest urban waterfront renewal project," and incorporating green and sustainable elements has been a priority from the beginning. Specifically, VicUrban, Victoria's urban development agency, has prepared comprehensive sustainability standards, published in its *Melbourne Docklands Ecologically Sustainable Development (ESD) Guide* (VicUrban, 2006). This document identifies the project's main sustainability goals as well as a detailed set of criteria and goals that all new commercial and residential development in the project must meet. Some standards are mandatory (incorporating recycling facilities, for instance), while for others developers have flexibility. All projects must meet at least a minimum number of points from the list (to meet the lower of three levels of achievement, the ESD Certificate of Achievement). Designing projects to achieve higher point totals is encouraged through the awarding of higher-level certificates (in this way, it is similar to the U.S. Green Building Council's LEED rating system), with the "Award of Excellence" as the highest level of green distinction. The extent of points awarded to buildings depends on the degree to which the criteria are satisfied: the more natural lighting incorporated into residential and commercial units, for instance, the higher the points given (e.g., if more than 60 percent of the living space is provided with natural light, 3 points are awarded; if more than 90 percent, 6 points).

These ESD standards and guidance do appear to have injected an impressive degree of sustainable design into the development of the Docklands, in addition to the other basic aspects of this project that make it sustainable: its walkable and transit-accessible location, its compactness and density, and its recycling of urban brownfields land (figure 6.5).

Melbourne has drawn significant opposition to the 2030 plan from such groups as Save Our Suburbs, which sees any increase in consolidation (urban infill and densification), even if focused on subcenters, as a threat. They often argue that the amenities of existing suburban neighborhoods are in jeopardy from increased traffic and congestion, loss of greenspace and views, and negative impacts on property values, among others, and they express concerns about government imposing its planning will against the wishes of neighborhoods. Much of this fear of redevelopment was seen by Peter Newman (2005) as baseless and comes from a series of other fears. This debate is well known in the United States, though in Australia it appears to be moving more obviously toward the need to control sprawl and promote redevelopment inward—Melbourne shows perhaps the most political opposition to this.

Sydney Metropolitan Strategy

Sydney is perhaps the metropolitan region most known and most associated with Australia by non-Australians. Its beautiful harbor, opera house, and water's edge skyline are well-known. Its population is expected to grow by 1.1 million people (putting its estimated 2031 population at 5.3 million), still relatively small by megacity global standards.

Figure 6.5 The Docklands is a major redevelopment area in Melbourne. All development and building there must adhere to a comprehensive set of green guidelines. *Photo credit:* Tim Beatley

Sydney is the financial center of Australia and has always had a history of entrepreneurs whose activities have been hard to contain in government plans. For twenty years, there was a deliberate policy not to have a regional plan but to allow the market more freedom to choose where and how to build. However, by the late 1990s, transport—both public and private—was crowded, and problems with water, power, and the provision of human services meant that the city was clamoring for a plan. The community was eager for a plan that would also protect the rapidly disappearing bush on the urban fringe. A "Campaign for Sydney" run by the *Sydney Morning Herald* received ten thousand letters and articles pushing for a renewed commitment to planning in the city (see Newman, Newman, and Whitehead, 2006).

The regional vision titled *City of Cities: A Plan for Sydney's Future* was published in late 2005. As with the other metropolitan strategies, it contains a number of constituent parts. The plan emphasizes strengthening the centers that already exist and envisioning Sydney as a series of compact, transit-connected urban centers. Specifically, five "regional" centers and twenty-two "strategic" centers are identified. The strategy presents the typology of centers and provides specific 2031 capacity targets for each.

The strategy states succinctly the important role of centers:

> Through new development these centres provide for increased social interaction and enhanced services. Busy and lively centres provide communities with a sense of identity and assist some people to overcome a sense of isolation. They can facilitate upgrades of services due to higher potential returns from growing use.
>
> Centres encourage diversity. Successful centres provide a range of cultural, community and educational services as well as business and retail activities. As well as the other actions to encourage greater activity in centres additional residential development is also encouraged. (Department of Planning, 2005b, p. 96)

These centers will be areas where population density will increase and much of the future growth in jobs will occur. Considerable activity by councils and developers is occurring around the planned new stations. The plan also envisions future development and growth along corridors between major centers. The first and only one designated, with others to follow, is the Sydney city to Parramatta corridor.

The regional plan supports containing growth and protecting rural and resource land, thus containing the city's "urban footprint," and states its intention not to release new land for urban development in the future unless it meets "the Government's sustainability criteria," which require most infrastructure to be present or to be provided by the developer. Seventy percent of all urban growth will be directed to the centers, and only 30 percent to the urban fringe.

Strengthening the level of transit service to and from these urban centers is a key element in the metropolitan strategy; to go with this, a new urban rail system stretching from the northwest through the city center to the southwest will provide the framework for city growth. This new rail system, projected to cost $8 billion, would link new growth areas to jobs as well as provide the incentive for new centers to be built.

Transit to the new areas was originally going to be just by bus, but part of the Campaign for Sydney focused on the need to link the new areas into the rail system. This intent was finally announced after a new rail conception (the Global Arc rail) was developed (Newman, 2006).

Implementation measures include an expanded Stronger Cities Initiative, in which the state has provided funding to localities for center-strengthening infrastructure and projects, major new regional transit investments, and the mandating of the Local Environment Plans (discussed in chapter 4) that must now reflect and accommodate the jobs and population targets contained in the strategy.

Although accounting for only 30 percent of future development in the region, new land release areas in the southwest and northwest of Sydney are immense—fourteen to fifteen thousand hectares for the southwest site and about ten thousand hectares in the northwest. These areas will accommodate phased future growth over about a thirty-year period and eventually will accommodate some two hundred thousand new residents.

A Growth Centers Commission (GCC) has been established to raise funds from a levy, and the state government, to build infrastructure (including the new rail line) early in the land development cycle. The GCC will also buy biodiversity lands. In the northwest site, about five thousand (of sixteen thousand) hectares will be set aside as conservation/natural land. These are partly existing remnants of Cumberland Plain woodland and some riparian land. The delineation of these areas resulted from a National Parks and Wildlife methodology that shows these areas to be extremely biodiverse. These will be protected conservation lands, much of it revegetated. Some (the key parts) will be purchased, and some will remain in private ownership with restrictions on the development allowed.

A major concern (and possible failing of the plan) is housing affordability. The use of government housing to influence affordability is no longer considered feasible as it is only a small part of the housing market. More will likely need to be done to ensure affordable housing. The team does believe though that the planning system can help by ensuring that multifamily, higher-density housing is provided as this will help affordability because a range of smaller units can be provided at half the cost of detached homes.

Overall, the targeted density of the plan is not bad—fifteen units per hectare overall (minimum)—but this will probably be much higher around centers and train/transit stations. About 80 percent of jobs will also be provided through a full range of office, commercial, and even industrial land that will be accommodated in the areas.

Other green/sustainable elements included in the new land release areas follow:

- They will have to meet BASIX (see chapter 2).
- Water recycling at 100 percent will be mandatory.
- Centers will be very walkable, with a grid street pattern leading to the suburbs.

- All major infrastructure will be provided beforehand so that early settlers will have schools, transit, and so forth nearby.

Future plans will need to be consistent with the structure plan, and this and other criteria will be contained in a SEPP (State Environmental Planning Policy), a statutory development order that developers must follow.

The 70/30 consolidation/greenfield split is higher than in other Australian cities, and some wonder why they cannot do more in the existing city. The target was based on actual performance over the last decade. The government planners seem to feel constrained by several factors, including the beliefs that greenfield restrictions/limits on development have served to fuel high housing prices, that there is an "Australian dream" (single-family detached house with garden, garage, and pool), and that it would be unrealistic to ignore these conditions.

The NSW Minister for Planning announced, with the backdrop of the Sydney Olympic Parks' water recycling facility, that all Western Sydney homes will "have access to recycled water for non-drinking purposes" (NSW Government, 2005). Engineers have now been appointed to do the studies for this system, beginning in the new areas, and the new GCC will oversee the investments in such innovations along with roads, schools, and so forth.

Sydney's environment is one of the most spectacular in the world, with its beautiful harbor, beaches, and rocky headlands. Its suburbs are also set among many inlets and rocky gullies that give each one a special identify and a special set of bush or waterfront that is integrated into the management of suburban life. Nurturing these special qualities remains a challenge.

The Sydney urban area is set in the Cumberland Plain, which stretches west to the Blue Mountains (a World Heritage area) and is constrained north and south by rocky hills that have been set aside as national parks for a long time (the Royal National Park was the second national park in the world, after Yellowstone National Park). Thus the city has few directions to spread other than into the Cumberland Plain, which is crisscrossed by creeks and wetlands. In recent years, these areas have been found to have very high biodiversity. The Sydney Basin has been declared to be the fifth most biodiverse region in Australia (and the others are mostly wilderness areas). There are 267 species of plants and animals within the Sydney region that are listed as threatened, with land clearing being the key threat. Thus a biodiversity plan was needed as part of the city's future planning.

Biodiversity and open space in the Sydney Regional Plan have been addressed through detailed studies that found all remaining areas of high-quality habitat on the Cumberland Plain and tied in some form or other to set them aside. One key new park is the Western Parklands, land acquired by the state government over about thirty years, much of it for infrastructure corridors, that has now been pieced together into a substantial parkland area. The Western Parklands—about 5,500 hectares in size—is a north-south linear park, connecting the North West and South West land release areas. The parks will offer various amenities, including various recreational facilities; the main habitat restoration work is happening in a riparian corridor. Work on bush regeneration is being done by Greening Australia, using mostly volunteers from the community, so it has the nice effect of helping to build community at the same time (as discussed in chapter 5).

The biodiversity mapping process that provides the basis for these decisions was conducted using the Conservation Significance Assessment Methodology developed by the Department of Environment and Conservation. Management consists of a series of tools, the first of which is used to designate an area as having priority for biodiversity protection in the LEP. By doing this, the land must then be purchased by the State whenever the landowner wishes to sell it. Some of the levy raised by the GCC is set aside to purchase key biodiversity areas. If, however, landowners are prepared to hold onto the land and guarantee protection of the biodiversity values, then they receive assistance for this after a biodiversity certification process. In most cases, this means people can continue to live on the land, although it cannot be subdivided or cleared and there are restrictions on dogs and cats, for example. Some cleared land also needs to be revegetated and rehabilitated.

Where possible, these areas are set aside in corridors and contiguous parcels of land to improve management of biodiversity values. Many of these areas have "Friends" groups, which provide the volunteer help to assist in management. It is a key goal of the Sydney plan to ensure that biodiversity is strengthened while development continues in the Cumberland Plain. Indeed, the development process is deliberately being used to help create possibilities for biodiversity improvements. It is hoped they can get this right.

Perth's "Network City" Plan

The Perth Regional Plan, dubbed "Network City," is notable for the prominence it gives to the environment. It specifically cites the WA Sustainability Strategy, "Hope for the Future" (see the discussion later in this chapter about that strategy), and contains some environmental objectives not typically found in a regional plan. Consider strategy 5-9, for instance:

"Reduce the ecological footprint of Perth, Mandurah and Murray." Prominent attention is given to ecological footprints, with an entire page comparing the per capita footprints of Australia and other nations.

This most recent regional spatial planning in Perth was generated by an interesting and, for Australia, unique participative process. Called "Dialogue with the City," the process was intended to engage and consult the public about what sort of future vision they would like to see for their city. Among the steps in this process were a random sample survey sent to eight thousand residents, preparation and distribution of a series of issue papers, an interactive Web site, extensive media coverage that included weekly newspaper articles and television coverage (including a one-hour prime time documentary), a school competition, and various "listening and learning" sessions to reach groups whose voices might otherwise by missed (Hartz-Karp and Newman, 2006). The culmination was a major interactive community event focused around four potential broad-scale growth scenarios for the future of the Perth and Peel regions (figure 6.6).

At the day-long forum, participants (about a hundred people were crammed into the Fremantle Passenger Terminal building) were grouped in tables of ten people inputting responses directly into a computer (with trained facilitators and assistants). The participants were made up of one third experts, one third groups and stakeholders, and one third citizens selected at random from the electoral roll (the latter group is found to be very significant for providing the common good perspective rather than specific lobbies of special interest groups). The morning involved discussions about participants' "hopes for the future, what they would like to keep and to change, the value of different potential scenarios and finally, which scenario they would prefer to evolve" (Harts-Karp and Newman, 2006). Box 6.3 presents the vision priorities generated from these discussions.

Hartz-Karp and Newman (2006) describe this process further:

> Using GIS, participants were asked to place chips or icons representing future housing and density on a map, giving tangible expression to how the particular growth scenario chosen would be implemented.
>
> Chips or icons representing the housing densities, industry and commercial areas required by 2030 had to be placed on a map. Trade-offs could be made between different housing densities and different urban forms. Decisions where not to grow were marked on the map. Transport linkages were made. Many inserted an urban boundary.

Each table had to completely agree on the assignment before chips could be peeled off and applied. At the end of the exercise, participants

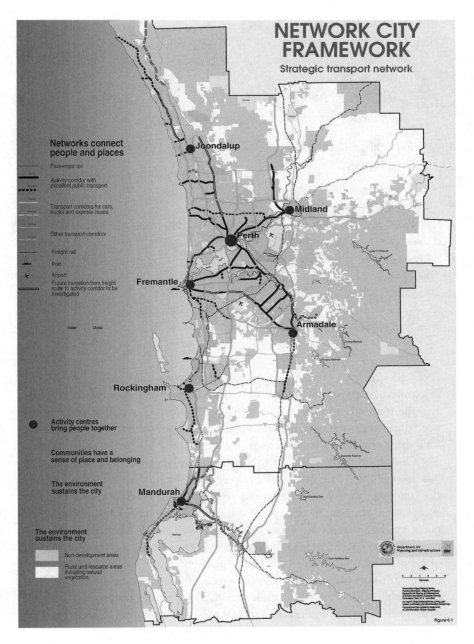

Figure 6.6 Perth Network City Map. *Image credit:* courtesy of the Western Australian Planning Commission

Box 6.3
Vision Priorities from Dialogue for the City
(in order of priority)

1. Strong local communities (city of villages)
2. Clean, green city
3. Urban growth boundary
4. Connected, multicentered city
5. Reduced car dependence—better public transport, especially rail, better local bike/walk, and integrated land use
6. Housing diversity (more options)
7. Access to city services for all

Source: Western Australia Department of Planning and Infrastructure, 2003.

received a copy of the map generated by their table (as well as an overall integrative map), a unique approach to nurturing ownership of the process and the planning outcome. Beyond the forum, much additional work has been done in engaging and listening to stakeholders and the community. A final draft of the plan was released in 2005.

One interesting result of the broad-based approach to planning that has been adopted in Perth was a campaign run by the local newspaper after the release of the "Perth: Network City" report. The newspaper wanted to create a sensation by insisting that if the report was opting for a more compact city, then that would mean building flats in people's backyards and removing open space for development. However, the reaction from hundreds of people who had attended the Dialogue event swamped the talk-back and letters columns, so the campaign collapsed. Obviously, a far more sophisticated urban citizenry could understand how planning was able to focus density to create viable centers and transit while retaining other parts of the city for less intensive activity, including bushland.

The use of these unique community engagement techniques reflects a strong belief by the minister of planning and infrastructure Allanah MacTiernan that good planning decisions—decisions that provide for the broader community good—will have to overcome the predominant NIMBY (not in my backyard) dynamic. The use of a broad community engagement approach seemed to be the only way to overcome this. Dr. Janette Hartz-Karp—a community engagement consultant—was hired to spearhead these efforts, and she has brought to bear a range of new techniques and methodologies in WA planning. More than forty different deliberative democracy projects have been taken on covering a range of planning issues, including truck noise, highway planning, density issues, water supply options, and locational decisions (see http://www.21st centurydialogue.com).

In WA, more compact, walkable, mixed-use developments have been encouraged through the preparation of an optional code called "livable neighborhoods" (based on New Urbanism), adopted by the WA Planning Commission. Developers have the option of using this code or adhering to the commission's "conventional policies" (Government of Western Australia, 2000). In recent years, this has become the norm for all developments, especially after the Network City strategy was released. More detailed follow-up in terms of population and employment targets and an infrastructure plan have yet to be done. In 2005 and 2006, Perth was rather run off its feet with development pressure following an economic growth spurt of 10 percent in each year. The planning system was able to live off the strategic directions that had been set and tried to direct growth into centers and corridors, including much greater densities. This appears to have been only partly successful, although no one is saying the plan was not needed.

Conclusions about Regional Plans

Strong regional plans exist not merely in one Australia city but throughout the country, in each major metropolitan area. While the full implementation of these plans has yet to occur and represents a significant challenge, the scope and quality of these plans are exemplary and bode well for their ability to guide future growth and urban change. These plans also represent a wealth of good ideas about process, methodology, and the many specific substantive notions of what constitutes, or might constitute, a sustainable region and regional pattern of growth.

All of these regional plans, more so than U.S. regional plans, explicitly address and incorporate sustainability. In the SEQ Regional Plan, for instance, a set of "Sustainability Indicators" is incorporated as a key element of its monitoring framework. Reference to sustainability appears in various places throughout the document. It figures prominently in the plan's stated regional vision, and it is presented as the major goal of its regional growth management strategy (see pages 9 and 16, for instance, Queensland Government, Office of Urban Management, 2005). A set of "Principles for a Sub-Tropical Environment" is also included, which discusses the need to recognize subregions and their special topography and climate, promoting diversity in type, scale, and so forth, and the need to design with "appropriate climate-based orientation in mind," including to "allow for the penetration of breeze, sunlight and the natural environment." (Queensland Government, Office of Urban Management, 2005, p. 41).

The Sydney Metropolitan Strategy is distinguished by its sustainability framework as well. It set out five aims: to enhance livability, strengthen economic competitiveness, ensure fairness, protect the environment, and improve governance. As each strategy is unveiled for centers and corridors, housing, transport, biodiversity, and parks, it runs through a checklist of the five aims to ensure that *all* are met on *each* of the strategies. This approach emphasizes the synergism of sustainability and is a model for how planning and sustainability are now inseparable. It is neither an economic plan with the environmental and social tacked on nor an environmental plan with the cities tacked on. All are part of a long-term approach that improves the whole city, and the factors depend on one another. Such a framework is conceptually very satisfying but also highly practical as it shows, for example, how biodiversity and environmental improvement will at the same time improve the economy while economic development (new jobs in the new economy) is necessary to ensure that environmental improvement can occur.

In New South Wales, two part-time sustainability commissioners were employed to help generate this framework and to provide advice on how to apply it in the strategy. Once the strategy was released, the positions were dropped. Although Sydney's ongoing commitment to sustainability can be questioned, it has the framework in place and continues to develop specific programs to apply it.

State Sustainability Plans

At the state government level in Australia, sustainability has emerged, to a remarkable degree, as a central organizing concept and a primary goal. It is reflected in state-level plans and decision making, and each state visited by the author had prepared a state sustainability plan or strategy (as well as other related plans and strategies with a sustainability emphasis). It is remarkable, moreover, how strident and strong the language is of current premiers in Australian states. They profess, for the most part, clear and unambiguous commitments to the values of sustainability, and they often campaign strongly on those commitments. These state plans and their implementation measures are especially promising models for U.S. states and are described in detail below.

Victoria

Victoria began making commitments to sustainability in 1999. It created a Department of Sustainability and Environment (which includes planning) and another agency called Sustainability Victoria, which works on energy efficiency, renewables, clean industry, waste, and recycling.

Premier Steve Bracks, in his preface to the 2005 Environmental Sustainability Framework, mentions Victoria's "huge" environmental footprint and his intensions of making the state a world leader in the environment. Said Bracks: "If everyone in the world lived like Victorians, we would require four planets. I am making environmental sustainability a priority for our government" (Victoria Department of Sustainability and Environment, 2005b, p. 6).

In Victoria, a special independent position called the commissioner for environmental sustainability exists. Created in 2003 by an act of state parliament with a similar title, the position of commissioner is intended to serve as "an environmental guardian for Victoria—an independent voice that advocates, audits and reports on environmental sustainability" (Commissioner for Environmental Sustainability, 2004, p. 5). The commissioner's office is required to perform four specific functions: developing a State of the Environment report for the state; performing an annual audit of state department environmental management systems, preparing a study of the effectiveness of education programs for sustainability, and advising the minister on sustainability matters. One stated goal of Dr. Ian McPhail, the first person to hold this position, has been to raise the profile of sustainability in Victoria.

Many of these functions are still in the research and development stage, but the commissioner's office released, in 2005, its strategic audit of departmental environmental management systems ("Local Environmental Performance"). The report shows that Victorian agencies are now all performing against a set of environmental indicators (energy, paper, waste, transport, and greenhouse gases) with an assessment process in place. Unfortunately, it also shows they have a lot of work to do and are in fact lagging behind best practice in Australia. (One hesitates to think what the performance would be like in U.S. agencies, where such assessments and requirements are rare.)

Progress by state agencies in implementing their work is assessed each year by the commissioner for environmental sustainability in his annual report. This report provides a nice summary of the range of actions currently being taken by Victorian government departments (Commissioner for Environmental Sustainability, 2005), and along with the audit itself, the commissioner's office provides an extensive set of recommendations aimed at helping departments improve their performance.

Other reports by the Commissioner for Environmental Sustainability include "Government Procurement and Environmental Sustainability," "Commonwealth Games Report Card" (its goal was becoming carbon neutral, generating low waste, and becoming water wise), and the "State of Environment Report-Framework," which provides the basis for this much larger project (see further below). In addition, "Understanding Environmental Performance" examines how Victorian agencies compare in their environmental performance with others across Australia, and "Creating a City That Works" provides an approach to addressing transport funding in Melbourne to ensure that sustainable modes are not neglected.

These many positive steps reflect explicit state policy, adopted in 2002, that the ten principal state agencies be required to adopt a formal environmental management system (consistent with ISO 14001). Only "office-based" impacts are addressed (energy, water consumption, waste generated per square meter of office space, and transport), but these are not insignificant, as the commissioner's audit reports show (e.g., see Commissioner for Environmental Sustainability, 2007).

The Victoria government adopted an ambitious Environmental Sustainability Framework in April 2005. Essentially a strategic plan, it provides a comprehensive accounting of where the state currently is and in turn sets goals and interim targets. Acknowledging (and describing) that much has already been done by the state (box 6.4), the plan states: "We now need to take a more comprehensive and coordinated approach to achieving sustainability" (Department of Sustainability and Environment, 2005, p. 16). Three broad directions are identified in the framework: maintaining and restoring natural assets, using resources more efficiently, and reducing everyday environmental impacts. These are to be measured against "a comprehensive set of 13 environmental quality objectives" and a series of more specific targets that incorporate commitments made in other, more specific state plans (e.g., the state greenhouse strategy, the state water strategy).

More generally, Victoria prides itself in "leading by example." It has adopted minimum green power usage targets as well as targets for reducing greenhouse gas emissions (10 percent by 2006, initially), and has already planted some 250,000 trees to offset the greenhouse emissions associated with its eight thousand state government vehicles. It underwrites 50 percent of the cost of solar features on elements of public facilities or buildings.

As discussed in chapter 2, a number of dramatic green buildings can be found throughout Australia, and these are often the result of green building commitments made by state and local governments. In Victoria, the state's green procurement and sustainability orientation has led recently to an unusual new home for the Department of Primary Industries. The new Queenscliff Centre (located in an outer suburb of Geelong, Melbourne) seems almost to have grown from the very ground it sits on, following closely the contour of the shoreline and with a green meadow for a rooftop. The building employs a number of green ideas, including rainwater tanks (used for watering the roof and for extinguishing local bushfires) and on-site stormwater collection (through a wetland system that also provides wildlife habitat). More fundamentally, the structure's design takes advantage of the site and the climate, especially utilizing thermal mass:

> The Centre has been designed in a unique way—almost from the inside out. The concrete structure is exposed on the inside and timber cladding insulates from the outside, maximising the benefits of thermal mass. Its walls and ceiling absorb heat in summer and naturally warm its interiors in winter. Its grass covered roof also helps in this process.
>
> By altering the traditional shape of a building, the Centre's walls are inclined and as a result become solar controllers. . . . On a summer's day when the sun is hot and higher in the sky, the building is protected from overheating. Operable windows react to the internal environment, and open, allowing warm air to escape and cool night air to circulate within the building. (http://www.arup.com)

The Queenscliff Centre was awarded a six-star rating, which represents world best practice, and when built was the first six-star eco-building in Australia (figure 6.7). Another feature is that the building actually had to clean up a contaminated rubbish dump in order to be built and has planted sixty thousand native plants in a model salt marsh native garden. It has therefore contributed to the ecological regeneration of the region.

South Australia

The new Australian Labor Party (ALP) government of 2003 immediately set up an Office of Sustainability and began to coordinate a range of activities across government agencies through the minister for the environment. Rather than making a separate sustainability strategy, as in WA

Figure 6.7 The Queenscliff Center, near Melbourne, provides space for the Victoria Department of Primary Industries. The building includes a number of green features, including this dramatic green rooftop, and reflects the State of Victoria's commitment to sustainability. *Project by:* Lyons. *Photo credit:* John Gollings

(discussed later in this chapter), they worked closely with the Department of the Premier and Cabinet on a State Strategic Plan, which includes a substantial commitment to sustainability and integrates economic, environmental, and social goals.

The Office of Sustainability focused on triple bottom line reporting processes and measuring progress toward sustainability, sustainability assessment in government decisions, a greenhouse strategy, local government sustainability, and sustained business development, as well as the many innovations discussed earlier around Sustainable Adelaide and the Green city project (see chapter 2 for a more detailed discussion of Adelaide and its green efforts).

Since then, the SA government won re-election with a greater commitment to sustainability. They have now created a minister for sustainability and climate change, who is also the premier, and thus sustainability

Box 6.4
Victoria's Sustainability Accomplishments

- Thirteen new marine national parks and eleven marine sanctuaries
- Approximately 3.75 million hectares of parks and reserves (17 percent of the state)
- State green power purchasing of renewable energy increased to 10 percent
- Five-star energy standard for all new homes; Victoria's water-efficiency standards for all new homes
- First Victorian environmentally sustainable suburb: Aurora and Epping North
- Led development of wind energy across the state (five hundred megawatts in development) with a goal of 10 percent renewables
- Greenhouse reduction plan: "Greenhouse Challenge for Energy"
- Sustainability covenants—first ones signed with private sector and Environment Protection Authority
- Sustainability fund—created and funded through a levy on landfill waste
- The Global Reporting Initiative's Centre for Public Sector Sustainability Reporting in Melbourne; creation of sustainability index for cited companies

(with a big emphasis on climate change and water) is now based in the Department of the Premier and Cabinet.

SA announced at the state election in March 2006 that it will legislate to require a 60 percent reduction in greenhouse gases by 2050. The legislation was introduced to Parliament in December 2006. In order to facilitate this, Premier Mike Rann has announced a chair of a new Climate Change and Business Sustainability Task Force.

In the past few years, SA has introduced several wind farms, and they now obtain 15 percent of their electricity from the wind. Their goal is to reach 20 percent by 2014.

The initial chair of SA's Sustainability Committee was the globally famous Tim Flannery from the SA museum, whose books on human ecology—including his latest on climate change, *The Weather Makers*—are best sellers. He has been pleased to see sustainability raised to such a high level in his home state, although as one who sees the long view, he remains very skeptical about our ability as a species to make the necessary adaptations in time to avert disaster. In 2007, Flannery was named Australian of the Year and spent his time talking across the country about the need to respond to climate change. This kind of work, along with the preliminary policy work occurring in states like SA, was one reason Australia placed climate change at the top of its agenda in the 2007 federal election, ultimately leading to the ALP government's decision to sign the Kyoto Agreement.

Australian Capital Territory (Canberra)

The Australian Capital Territory (ACT) government also established an Office of Sustainability within their chief minister's jurisdiction. They have produced a strategy called "People, Place, Prosperity: A Policy for Sustainability in the ACT," containing a set of principles and committing the ACT government to embedding sustainability in decision making, promoting sustainability to the wider community, developing partnerships for sustainability with the ACT community, and developing indicators for annual reporting. A Sustainability Advisory Committee was established, with a large community and business contingent represented. At the last election, in early 2006, they committed to sustainability legislation based on these principles from their strategy. Although there is no doubt that they have a strong sustainability framework in place, little progress on this seems to have occurred since this commitment was made. The person who was in charge of this process, Peter Otteson, who was closely involved with the Sydney Green Games, has described these initial efforts by ACT as the first steps in a "long journey" in the direction of sustainability (Australian Capital Territory, 2003, 2004).

Western Australia

Although only a small state in population terms (2 million), WA covers an area the size of Western Europe, with a booming economy based around minerals, agriculture, and the city of Perth (where 1.8 million people live). WA has perhaps taken the sustainability concept further than any other state government—and perhaps of any government—though its implementation may be lagging on many fronts.

In early 2001, the ALP government was elected in a landslide after changing their environmental policy to stop the logging of all old growth forest—a long-standing issue in WA, which has in its South West region towering forests of Karri and Jarrah eucalypts (some of which are among the tallest in the world). The populace's mood to be more conservation minded was taken to the ballot box in no uncertain terms, and the ALP unexpectedly won many seats where the forests were a major factor.

The ALP government was also committed to developing a state sustainability strategy, which began the process of a state coming to terms with this concept and indeed bringing the idea into state politics, where it then spread to the other Australian states.

The state sustainability strategy was developed over two and a half years and covers forty-two areas of government activity. It developed eleven principles of sustainability (box 6.5). As the notion of sustainability was new to government, an emphasis was given to developing background papers that set out best practice from around the world on sustainable procurement, sustainability assessment, indigenous sustainability, and case studies from local firms, agencies, community groups, and local governments that were already doing innovative things on sustainability. The Web site containing these background papers (http://www.sustainability.dpc.wa.gov.au) received eight thousand hits per day (half of them from the United States) in the 2001–2003 period as the strategy was being developed.

Bjorn Stigson, president of the World Business Council for Sustainable Development, visited WA in 2002 at the height of the public discussions on the draft strategy. He said: "I am impressed by the work that you and the government of Western Australia have been doing to create a sustainable development for your State. I have not come across any similar extensive process as that you are going through anywhere else in the world" (WA Department of the Premier and Cabinet, 2003, p. 1).

The final state sustainability strategy, entitled "Hope for the Future," was launched with a flourish in September 2003 at an international conference involving twenty other state governments from around the world. It was at the time the first state government to have created such an overall assessment of what sustainability meant for each area of government—and it probably remains the most comprehensive.

The process of formulating the concept was highly participatory, with more than 150 public workshops and seminars.

> At every meeting in the city, and in other regions, the notion of sustainability has intrigued people and demanded responses that went beyond their commonly held views. At all meetings, the notion led to people discussing what the legacy of current development plans were, and hence people engaged easily in issues of ethics and values. This appears one of the most significant characteristics of sustainability, that it encourages and enables values-based discussion on future issues rather than just expert opinion. (Newman, 2006, p. 277)

One potentially very important result of the WA Sustainability Strategy has been to provide space and legitimacy for a variety of professions working in sustainability. In WA, the clearest expression of this has been

Box 6.5
Sustainability Strategy in Western Australia—
Vision Statement

The Western Australian State Sustainability Strategy is the first comprehensive strategy at a state level to examine what sustainability can mean across 42 areas of government responsibility. It is based on 11 Principles:

FOUNDATION PRINCIPLES

- LONG TERM ECONOMIC GAIN
  Sustainability recognises the long term needs of future generations (as well as the short term) for economic health, diversity, innovation and productivity of the earth.

- ACCESS, EQUITY AND HUMAN RIGHTS
  Sustainability recognises that everyone should have their interests recognised and share in the fruits of development, that an environment needs to be created where all people can express their full potential and lead productive lives, and that dangerous gaps in sufficiency, safety and opportunity endanger the earth.

- BIODIVERSITY AND ECOLOGICAL INTEGRITY
  Sustainability recognises that all life has intrinsic value, is interconnected and that biodiversity and ecological integrity are part of the irreplaceable life support systems upon which the earth depends.

- SETTLEMENT EFFICIENCY AND QUALITY OF LIFE
  Sustainability recognises that settlements need to reduce their ecological footprint (i.e. less material and energy demands and reductions in waste), whilst they simultaneously improve their quality of life (health, housing, employment, community . . .).

- COMMUNITY, REGIONS, 'SENSE OF PLACE' AND HERITAGE
  Sustainability recognises the reality and diversity of community and regions for the management of the earth, and the critical importance of 'sense of place' and heritage (buildings, townscapes, landscapes and culture) in any plans for the future.

- NET BENEFIT FROM DEVELOPMENT
  Sustainability means that all development and particularly development involving extraction of non-renewable resources should strive to provide net environmental, social and economic benefit for future generations.

- COMMON GOOD
  Sustainability recognises that planning for the common good requires equitable distribution of public resources (like air, water, open space) so that ecosystem functions are maintained and a shared resource is available to all.

PROCESS PRINCIPLES

- INTEGRATION
  Sustainability requires that economic, social and environmental factors be integrated by applying all the principles of sustainability at once, and seeking mutually supportive benefits with minimal trade offs.

- ACCOUNTABILITY, TRANSPARENCY AND ENGAGEMENT
  Sustainability recognises that people should have access to information on sustainability issues, that institutions should have triple bottom line accountability on an annual basis, that regular sustainability audits of programs and policies should be conducted, and that public engagement lies at the heart of all sustainability principles.

- PRECAUTION
  Sustainability requires caution, avoiding poorly understood risks of serious or irreversible damage to environmental, social and economic capital, designing for surprise and managing for adaptation.

- HOPE, VISION, SYMBOLIC AND ITERATIVE CHANGE
  Sustainability recognises that applying these sustainability principles as part of a broad strategic vision for the earth can generate hope in the future, and thus it will involve symbolic change that is part of many successive steps over generations.

Source: Newman, 2006.

through the creation of the Sustainability Practitioners Association (SPA). Their motto is "Making a Living from Making a Difference."

Networking has been a key function of SPA, which organizes social events and in a sense acts as a support group, saying to its members that they are not alone in their commitments and passions and that sustainability is indeed a legitimate professional path. Members of the group come from diverse backgrounds and job settings. Craig Salt, cofounder and first president of SPA, has developed a sustainability consultancy that works for big companies who are trying to come to terms with the new ideas of sustainability. He comes to this role with a background in mining (he was part of the Argyle project discussed later in this chapter).

Changing the way state government works and moving state agencies and departments in the direction of sustainability are key goals of the Western Australian plan. And much good practice and work has occurred. The Water Corporation in Western Australia is perhaps the government agency most committed to sustainability. It has undertaken a number of initiatives to embed sustainability across all of its activities and business decisions. It has commitments to being carbon neutral based on its power options and plantations that are part of its wastewater-polishing process from country towns (box 6.6). It also is heavily committed to educating about water conservation and promoting behavioral changes. It has attempted to reach the WA public in some interesting ways, with a number of subsidies to promote water-saving appliances, rainwater tanks, and graywater recycling. Through its Waterwise program, the water conservation message in gardens has been conveyed through schools and garden centers with a strong emphasis on planting low-water native plants.

To receive the Waterwise certificate, the three hundred participating schools must put into practice a water education policy (most on an ongoing basis), incorporate water into their curricula, and take part in the annual National Water Week. The Water Corporation provides help in the form of educational materials and lots of ideas for activities and field trips.

In an essay about the state's Sustainability Strategy, Newman (2005) suggests that sustainability has begun to create change in WA in important ways through changes in language, thinking, and culture. People have begun speaking about and understanding projects and programs through a sustainability lens, with the *language* now becoming commonly adopted in local and state government (e.g., "sustainability officers" in local councils). The broader changes in *thinking* are important to note in WA, Newman believes: "The Sustainability strategy has gone beyond the mere redefinition of words, to the level of changing how policy-oriented people think about development and the future" (Newman, 2005, p. 278).

The WA strategy's goal of effecting cultural change is its most ambitious and to date is the place where the least progress has probably been made. According to Newman: "After a two-year intensive engagement, the WA Sustainability Strategy has, it appears, at least created change at the first two levels [language and thinking]. . . . However, it has yet to reach the broader community" (Newman, 2005, p. 283). My own sense is that

Box 6.6
WA Water Corporation:
A Model of Sustainable Management?

The WA Water Corporation has taken a number of steps to reduce its considerable level of energy consumption (due to pumping water over thousands of kilometers), with substantial reductions in greenhouse gases already being found. By its own calculations, these initiatives have already resulted in a 14 percent reduction in greenhouse emissions over its projected "business as unusual" scenario (Humphries et al., 2005).

An important step was signing on to the Australian Greenhouse challenge, a program run by the federal government's Australian Greenhouse Office. Among the key initiatives has been the formation of an Energy Management Unit within the corporation; significant energy retrofitting of its headquarters building (now a 3.5-star building under the Australian Building Greenhouse rating program); the capturing and burning of biogas at its wastewater treatment plants; a "greener motoring program," whereby the corporation is replacing more fuel consumptive vehicles in its fleet with more efficient vehicles (moving from six- to eight-cylinder vehicles); and sequestering carbon through the "men of trees" carbon-neutral program (planting certain number of trees per vehicle).

In late 2006, the Water Corporation turned on its new 45 Gl Desalination Plant. This plant is one of the biggest in the world and is partly a response to the drying climate in the South West of WA. The desalination plant is being powered by a new wind farm to the north of Perth.

One of the corporation's most interesting initiatives has been the application of wastewater effluent on woodlots, with the largest example in Albany in the South West of the state. Here, 450 hectares of Tasmanian blue gums are irrigated with wastewater, promoting tree growth and carbon sequestration. Most country towns offer similar prospects for sequestering carbon from their wastewater effluent. Now the Water Corporation is seeking to pull all of its initiatives together into a goal of carbon neutrality by 2015. The company's board of directors has agreed to this action, and a detailed strategy is being developed to show how it can be done.

there is considerable movement at that cultural level as well in WA, though it may be just too early to see clear results.

Western Australia has a draft Sustainability Act that will embed sustainable principles throughout government and that, if enacted, will be a significant legacy for WA and other states seeking to deal with sustainability in government. However, there seems to be little movement on delivering this act.

In WA, a Sustainability Roundtable (SRT) was created to advise and guide sustainability in the state. This group of sixteen members consists of members of the state's environmental community and also representatives from larger state agencies and from some of the state's larger industries (e.g., mining). The SRT is committed to developing a household sustainability program called Living Smart (discussed in chapter 2), which would bring householders into close contact with how they can reduce energy, water, waste, and travel and create more biodiversity and less impact from their gardens. This program, which was trialed in 2008 (with twenty thousand households), will significantly link sustainability into the culture of West Australians.

In terms of government culture, a Sustainability Code of Conduct has been created that sets minimum ways in which state agencies must take sustainability into account. Developed within the Department of the Premier and Cabinet, it requires each state agency to prepare an annual "Sustainability Action Plan"; these plans then serve as the basis for CEO performance agreements with the premier's office as well as for being audited. No process for formally conducting these audits appears to have been developed yet.

A series of other important state strategies have been developed in WA, stimulated at least in part by the state sustainability strategy or at least developing in parallel while referencing and connecting with the state strategy. A greenhouse strategy has been prepared, and state salinity and regional sustainability strategies are the next step in fleshing out what the state strategy means on the ground. Some $100,000 was allocated to develop a pilot regional sustainability strategy for the Pilbara region in the north of the state (Newman et al., 2006). No action on taking these regional sustainability strategies further has been apparent.

A "Sustainability Scorecard" has been developed in order to bring sustainability more clearly into the WA planning system. This is being trialed in the Armadale region (see http://www.ara.wa.gov.au) and should become standard practice. A sustainability assessment approach has been adopted by the Department of Sport and Recreation as it examines the provision of community facilities.

The WA strategy has clearly taken a partnership approach, one very significant part of which has been bringing the nongovernmental organization sector together into a unique "WA Collaboration," funded by the Lotteries Commission. This collaboration is based on key groups from social justice, the unions, the churches, the conservation movement, and multi-cultural interests. The collaboration initially ran parallel workshops to provide input to the strategy and continues to represent sustainability interests to the government.

While it remains too early to fully assess the success of the WA approach, the program has undeniably had some positive outcomes. Much has already happened, and in a short period of time, to begin to turn that slow-moving (unsustainable) ocean liner of government around. Sustainability has been and is clearly still being institutionalized into state government. A Sustainability Directorate has been created in the Department of Planning and Infrastructure to promote and guide sustainability in that critical agency. There have been considerable amounts of on-the-ground programs as well, many of which are well documented in the first year's *Hope for the Future Progress Report*.

In Newman's view, the WA strategy is indeed a "hopeful" process, and this he believes is a significant aspect of the plan's success. The message needs to be hopeful. He describes the strategy document as "inspirational" and embodying a "politics of hope" (Newman, 2005, p. 284).

The WA strategy also speaks to the very important role that universities can play as partners in such endeavors. Without the contributions of Murdoch University, much of what has occurred might not have been possible. Peter Newman, the author of the report, brought with him to government fifty students who worked on these background papers and the case studies.

One of the clearest results from the new emphasis on sustainability can be seen in the coastal management area, in particular the new sustainable development management regime put into place for the Ningaloo Reef area (as discussed in chapter 3).

The state strategy has already influenced several prominent planning decisions, showing how the plan and its philosophy are modifying some of the background assumptions and framework in which planning and development occurs. The Moore River Estuary, seventy-five kilometers north of Perth, is the best recent example (figure 6.8). Here a local organization, Friends of the Moore River Estuary, had been campaigning for several years against a proposed development to the south of the town of Guilderton, just on the other side of the Moore River. The development would have resulted in some five thousand new housing units and more than 13,500 new residents and would have necessitated the clearing of some 550 hectares of land. The proposal seemed inappropriate in just about every sense but was still moving forward, having been officially endorsed in the

Figure 6.8 The Moore River, north of Perth, has been the site of a major development-conservation battle. The Western Australia Planning Commission decided against allowing substantial new development here in large part because of the state's Sustainability Plan that calls for minimizing urban sprawl and its environmental impacts. *Photo credit:* Tim Beatley

State's Gingin Coast Structure Plan, developed under the previous, conservative state government.

In March 2005, in response to local concerns, the WA Planning Commission issued a proposal to modify the Gingin plan, essentially nullifying the Moore River development plan. The planning modification stated that "there are a number of aspects of the proposed urban development . . . that are considered to be contrary to the State Strategy's sustainability principles, such as the scale, purpose and location" of the urban expansion (Western Australian Planning Commission, 2005, p. 1). The proposed project fails a test of ecological sustainability given the extent of the land clearance and destruction of native vegetation that would be required, and in other respects it would generate many of the usual problems of sprawl (though that word is not actually used in the planning commission's statement) and "car-dependence." Less damaging alternatives were also considered to be available. The level of urban growth, it was believed, could be accommodated by expanding existing towns, such as Lancelin, and by thinking more carefully about how growth in Guilderton might be sensitively accommodated : "The scale of urban expansion . . . is considered to be contrary to environmental sustainability principles because of the need to clear large tracts of land prior to development, destroying native vegetation" (Western Australian Planning Commission, 2005, p. 2).

This issue has now gone into a significant legal process because it challenges much of how Perth has developed in the past and is obviously going to cost some developers a lot of money and pain as they change to more sustainable development practices.

The Labor government came to power in WA with an explicit commitment to sustainability. In Premier Geoff Gallop's own words: "The transition to a sustainable future is a long-term agenda that requires rethinking the way we live, use resources, govern and do business" (Gallop, 2003, p. 28).

The promise and potential of the Western Australia Sustainability Strategy has been to move all sectors of society—government, businesses, civil society—in the direction of sustainability. And this has happened to a remarkable degree and continues. One test of "Hope for the Future" is how it influences even the most (on the face of it) unsustainable of corporate and business activities. In some ways, it is hard to imagine how a state that depends so heavily on resource extraction could ever be considered "sustainable." The challenges to envisioning a state sustainability strategy here, and to bringing it to meaningful fruition, are extreme. Western Australia, for many of these reasons, remains paradoxical. It has innovated some of the most imaginative and proactive conservation efforts anywhere and has put into place many impressive urban sustainability measures. Yet, at its core, the state's economy remains strongly dependent on nonsustainable extraction and expropriation, such as mining. The seriousness of these contradictions would likely stifle many working on sustainability issues, but it seems to have had the opposite result in Western Australia as the state explores what sustainability indeed means in a resource-extractive culture and economy.

About fifty years ago, iron ore was discovered in the Pilbara region, in the north of WA, and it has grown to a $5 billion a year industry, largely fueled by demand for steel in China, Korea, and Japan. WA represents 18 percent of world iron ore supply and is said to have at least six hundred years of iron ore available (perhaps more sustainable than a lot of agriculture or industry). The state is also a significant exporter of aluminum, nickel, gold, and natural gas. These resources represent 30 percent of the

WA state product, contributing more than $4 billion in sales annually. Nearly $2 billion comes back to the state in royalties (which is about 12 percent of state revenues). Thus it is not easy to disregard this industry when considering a state sustainability strategy.

In 2005 and 2006, the WA economy began a "resource boom" as China and India dramatically increased their need for iron ore (the Pilbara is doubling output in five years) and Japan, China, and the United States turned to WA for more natural gas. Part of the boom's result was an unexpected growth in WA government royalties, which were used to pay off debt, including all debt associated with Perth's new rail system (which included the $1.6 billion Southern Rail even before it was completed). Other funds in this government windfall were used to purchase several large pastoral stations across the state, which had huge conservation benefits— less spectacular than the forests but very important for biodiversity and endangered species. Hence, there are some sustainability gains associated with this side of the resource sector. However, the true sustainability perspective of WA resource industries is a more subtle concept.

The Minerals Industry Council of Australia has outlined this concept as "enduring value." The idea is that development provides an opportunity to leave a legacy in a region that can last several generations. This can be in establishing biodiversity conservation programs or providing life skills and employability skills for people who do not have such skills or providing infrastructure that can be used for generations.

Enduring value as a concept was originally developed by the Argyle diamond mine in the remote Kimberley region of WA. Argyle Diamonds is a wholly owned subsidiary of the global mining company Rio Tinto. Under the leadership of its managing director, Brendan Hammond, it began exploring what sustainability could mean for the company when it was threatened with closure in the late 1990s. They decided it must mean eco-technologies, such as renewable power and water-saving technology; better rehabilitation of their land (including the use of local "bushtucker" plants); and, most of all, training of local indigenous people to work in the mine so they had life skills and employability for several generations. All of this was done.

Argyle confronted a number of significant issues when it decided to take on this latter area of training and employment of indigenous people. The Kimberley area is 40 percent Indigenous, and a long history of abuse and exploitation by miners and pastoralists in the region had left a legacy of suspicion and mistrust. Most of the local indigenous people could not read or write and had police records.

Argyle committed to training through selecting people to help who had shown their skills at driving trucks; as respect, confidence, and trust grew, other skills were introduced. High salaries were accompanied by high expectations for being drug and alcohol free and for keeping punctually to the "ten-day-on/ten-day-off" routine. Special consideration was made for indigenous funerals (usually several days long) and for customary law business (often several weeks).

Since starting in 1998 with no indigenous workforce, Argyle moved quickly to 27 percent by 2006, with a goal of 40 percent. They also moved from 11 percent to 42 percent local workforce, thus significantly reducing their fly-in/fly-out requirements and bringing substantial economic benefits to the region. The skill levels of their new workforce have become dramatically dominated by indigenous people, whose hand-eye coordination skills (from their hunter-gatherer heritage) have adapted spectacularly to the mining industry.

Perhaps one of the most significant elements of enduring value that has been created in the region has been the reconciliation and mutual respect that has been built up between white and black elements in the region. Argyle does much for indigenous art and culture in the Kimberley (Kimberley Aboriginal artists like Rover Thomas are now famous for their striking dot paintings) as well as in direct employment of indigenous people. Argyle faced a crisis in 2006 as it confronted the question of whether to close down or instead follow the diamond pipe underground at significantly greater cost. They concluded that a profitable operation could happen only if they were given a reduction in their royalty payments. Regional and indigenous interests joined forces to lobby the government to ensure that another twenty years of operations could proceed—an unheard-of coalition of interests that saw the long-term value of Argyle to their region. The state government agreed.

Argyle's commitment to sustainability through developing enduring value assets in the region has been a beacon in the Australian mining industry. Cynical observers predicted that the company could not last in the marketplace, that their profits and share price would go down unless they focused more on the single bottom line. However, over the period 1998 to 2005, Argyle's shareholder value went from $200 million to $2 billion—a tenfold increase. Like most aspects of sustainability, the blockage is not financial; it is in the mind.

There was much discussion of the notion of creating "enduring assets" after the Argyle success, and this idea has now become mainstream thinking in the Australian minerals industry. Nothing as spectacular as Argyle has followed, though the bar has now been set quite high (Newman, Stayton-Hicks, and Hammond, 2006).

Conclusions and Lessons Learned

The existence of strong regional planning is one of the clearest differences between Australian and U.S. cities. Only a few metropolitan areas in the United States (Portland, Oregon, in particular) have been able to undertake effective regional planning, yet it is commonly viewed as something U.S. cities need and desire. In this sense, the Australian experience with regional planning is of special interest and is potentially quite valuable as an instructive model. Not just one city or metropolitan area but all of Australia's major urban centers have gone through an extensive regional planning process and have produced impressive regional plans. Each of these plans represents a valuable source of both inspiration and practical insights about such things as strategy for citizen involvement (e.g., Perth's Dialogue with the City) and ideas and conceptual elements of a regional plan (e.g., activity centers, green wedges, and transit corridors).

Taken together, these regional plans are impressive in their scope and content. The targets they endorse for accommodating future urban growth within urbanized areas are ambitious (e.g., the goal of 70 percent in the case of both Melbourne and Sydney; 50 percent for Brisbane and the SEQ Regional Plan), and worthy of emulation by U.S. cities. Impressive as well is the remarkable degree to which sustainability is explicitly incorporated into these plans.

The United States has a limited history of effective regional planning. The Australian experience is both inspiring and enviable, but many in the United States may view it as unrealistic. Much of the Australian success can explained by the generally stronger planning role played by Australian states, and by the relatively large size of Australian states, which in effect contain entire metropolitan boundaries and growth patterns within a single state's borders. American metropolitan areas are far more fragmented jurisdictionally, with growth and development often crossing multiple state boundaries. Yet the Australian approach of a coherent (and comprehensive) regional growth vision and plan, with strong sustainability elements, is possible and not far-fetched, especially given the other Australian-American similarities. And while it may be more difficult to accomplish given U.S. state boundaries, much of what Australian cities are doing could be successfully emulated. American state governments could take the lead, as Australian states do, in convening public discourse and visioning about future metro growth and development as well as in preparing compelling and inspiring regional plans. Local governments could be required to ensure that their plans conform to and help implement these regional schemes, and states could provide financial incentives, technical assistance, and major infrastructure investments (as the Australian states do) in ways that help to advance and implement these plans. While a challenge certainly, partnerships between states to develop Australian-style metro area plans could also be forged.

The Australians show convincingly that much on the sustainability front can and must occur through state government leadership. Only a few American states to date (notably California) have been as ambitious or comprehensive in incorporating sustainability as a core feature in their planning and governance. The basic similarities between the governance structures in Australia and the United States—and, namely, the importance given to state governments in each system—means that these outstanding examples of Australian state sustainability plans and programs are very relevant to the U.S. scene. What state governments have been able to accomplish in the realm of sustainability provides many good ideas about how to—and a very convincing argument that state governments can indeed do much to—shape the debate and stimulate forward movement. To an impressive degree, then, Australian state governments have developed strong sustainability strategies (WA's is perhaps the most impressive in coverage and scope), have set specific and often ambitious state environmental and sustainability goals and targets, and have already employed a dizzying array of tools and policies to help implement these plans. State sustainability efforts in Australia entail a mix of mandates and state regulations (e.g., NSW's BASIX green building requirements), funding of pioneering initiatives and projects (e.g., South Australia's solar schools initiative), and leading by example (e.g., the Queenscliff Centre's green offices).

These state sustainability efforts, moreover, show the importance of reaching out to enlist, on behalf of an agenda of sustainability, the full and diverse portfolio of agencies and offices, many of which may not immediately see the value or connection to sustainability. And this is being done through some creative ways (e.g., WA's requirement that each state agency prepare a yearly sustainability action plan). Changing the values and culture of some state agencies will definitely be difficult, but these are good initial steps—and good, pragmatic ideas about how to overcome disinterest and inertia within state government.

Perhaps even more important than the specific content, programs, or mechanisms contained in each state sustainability strategy is the value statement each strategy makes. These plans have helped to raise the visibility and priority given to sustainability and have helped to readjust the relative importance given to environment and sustainability matters on the ground. The Moore River decision, based on the goals and content of the WA sustainability plan, is just one example of how the decision making (and political context) has changed as a function of the adoption of the plan (although it also true that the creation of the plan itself reflects the growing political and popular importance given to these issues).

I am especially convinced that state government, and the elements of a state sustainability strategy, can be helpful in beginning a shift that can nudge the larger culture in a more sustainable direction. States are often in a position to do this (certainly in the United States) in ways that individual cities or localities may find difficult.

7

Learning from Australia

Some Final Thoughts on the Value of Comparative Green Urbanism

Australia is a truly amazing country, with spectacular landscapes, exotic biodiversity, and astounding beauty and spirit. It is a unique and special place in the world with a rich Aboriginal history and culture and immense natural resources and antiquity. These things I very much looked forward to experiencing firsthand but generally expected in advance. It was a special and welcome surprise, however, that Australian cities and towns had so much to offer. And although one can see much sprawl and the kind of mindless cityscape and fast food stores of many U.S. communities, there is so much that is distinctive and special in Australian cities as well as many stories and positive examples that tell of an emerging and promising green urbanism.

With any comparative planning research project, including this one, there are several key benefits to be gained from looking closely at practices in other places. A first benefit is often just inspiration: gaining a sense of enthusiasm and optimism that what is being done in one place can in fact be done in one's home country and community. This benefit was delivered in droves, made more the potent because of the parallel circumstances and similar political and cultural contexts that Australia and the United States share. Inspiration involves at least part hope, and it is difficult to be truly inspired by a project, program, or urban environment if it seems as though the social, cultural, and political circumstances by which it came about are so different, so foreign, as to seem impossible to replicate. I have been inspired, for instance, by the state sustainability strategies and regional plans I have analyzed in part because of their admirable ambitions and content but also because there is the clear potential to apply these ideas back home in the United States. They are not hard to imagine happening with wide appeal, and at least one city (Portland, Oregon) in the United States has already done this.

A second benefit is perhaps a bit more pragmatic. This kind of comparative study often yields important and useful ideas and practices to help in tackling particular problems. I often found myself saying, at times out loud, "Wow, I hadn't thought of that before." While it sometimes feels as though there is nothing original in the world and that we are often re-creating the wheel, it is remarkable how often time spent in other countries (or states, regions, or localities) looking at practices there yields much in the way of new thinking and practical insights about how to create more livable and sustainable communities.

That said, certain themes or broader planning and policy patterns stand out from looking at these Australian cities and communities. The extent to which sustainability has been embraced, and incorporated into state, regional, and local plans is impressive. Many specific actions have been taken, and decisions made in response, but as much as anything the result has been a gradual move of the entire culture in the direction of sustainability. Sustainability, sustainable and green building, sustainable lifestyles—these concepts are commonly understood and increasingly internalized on the part of Australian citizens and leaders alike. Sometimes in the United States, we feel as though these concepts and ways of thinking, which are seen by so many writers and academics as the next great paradigm, will remain forever in academia and libraries.

While Australian society and culture are highly consumptive to be sure, there has been greater tangible movement in the direction of committing to sustainability and acting on those commitments. Australian state governments and local councils, for instance, have shown a willingness to mandate green building and design, when the approach in the United States has been the somewhat more timid approach of incentives, though that is changing. In New South Wales, the BASIX green building standards that have been mandatory since 2005 are already revolutionizing the building trades in that part of the world, and the cumulative results in terms of reducing energy consumption and greenhouse gas emissions are potentially great indeed. The seriousness of our times—global warming, declining supplies of oil, droughts and looming, unprecedented serious water shortages—all suggest, of course, that the time for small actions, and small incentives-based approaches to curtailing resource consumption, with their modest accomplishments, is over. Australia is on the front line when it comes to experiencing the early effects of climate change. Some would say that innovations and regulations about how we use energy, water, and land are no longer optional in Australia but requisite given the new environmental and climate realities.

The urban experiences reported on here challenge us to think about cities in new and different ways. These exemplary Australia cases and stories provide some tremendously helpful ways of envisioning cities. Adelaide's efforts, for instance, at recasting itself as a green city—and more recently as a solar city—are an example. This city provides a profoundly new way to look at buildings and streetscapes: seeing an urban district as a solar power–generating station is unusual indeed. The installation of solar mallee trees recognizes the potential of sidewalks, streetlights, building facades, and the details and fabric of urban centers as possible partial solutions to energy and climate change. Adelaide's example should be applied wherever we can in U.S. cities, reenvisioning the cityscape as a venue for the generation of sustainable and renewable energy, and not simply as a resource and energy drain. This is a new and important way of understanding cities and urban life.

Australian cities also help us to begin to overcome the bifurcation between nature and urbanity. They show that green urbanism can and must include access to nature and even may enable cities to assist in regenerating ecological systems. While not a perfect story, Australian cities give us some glimpse of what a true urban wildness might look and feel like. Cities like Brisbane and Perth are close to being biophilic cities, cities with immense nature and biodiversity and at least beginning to show that one can live an urban life close to the natural world. As a result of the relative youth of these cities, and the recent nature of urban development, Australian cities and metropolitan regions are blessed with incredible amounts of wild nature that is remarkably close to where thousands of people are living. In such cities as Perth, Sydney, and Brisbane, wild nature seems so close at hand, and as cities they have taken important steps to recognize this nature and wildness, to steward over it, to restore and nurture it, and through programs like Bushcare, to engage citizens directly in the tasks of tending to urban nature.

Many of the cities and projects examined in this book, moreover, recognize the new realities of needing to address multiple social and environmental problems simultaneously. Solving one problem, addressing one issue at a time, is simply not enough; it is wasteful and inefficient, and the magnitude of our contemporary problems increasingly requires more holistic solutions. So the planting of mallee tree farms in the Perth bioregion, for instance, has the potential to generate new jobs and rural income, to sequester carbon, to generate a renewable energy and fuel source, and to restore rural landscape damages that have resulted from historic and unsustainable farming practices.

An important message from these exemplary Australian cities is the need to understand the green urban agenda in a more integrative and holistic way. Sustainability and green cities in these best-case examples are not seen as a narrow compartment of isolated policy areas but, rather, as one that carries over and has important implications for many other things. It is also notable how in many Australian cities this commitment to sustainability is finding creative application in parallel policy and management sectors. In transport, commitments to sustainability are resulting in the development of new green vehicle technologies (e.g., the hydrogen fuel cell bus in Perth and the solar electric bus in Adelaide), new extensive electric rail systems (e.g., in Perth), and new operational strategies (e.g., Melbourne's green tram depot). Sustainability in these progressive Australian communities is not viewed as a standalone or isolated value or commitment but, rather, as one that productively spills over into other areas, and in some very interesting ways.

There is the need to think both in terms of technical innovations and solutions and behavioral and social changes. No single action or silver bullet exists, for instance, in dealing with the problems of drought and serious water shortages. Many promising technologies have been discussed here, including water reuse and reclamation plants, but just as important are the things that can and must be done to reduce the overconsumption and wasteful use of water. The Australian stories show the power and necessity of combining these approaches into viable, holistic strategies—we will need technologies like the WRAM system demonstrated in the Olympic Park in Sydney but also the educational and behavioral approaches of programs like Waterwise in WA.

Australian cities also lead the way with countless creative ideas and new ways of thinking about place and community. Many of these ideas are foreign yet compelling to Americans, such as the notions that every local council ought to run its own native plants nursery, that toy libraries and community centers could facilitate community sharing and at the same time reduce resource consumption, and that neighborhoods could reconceptualize themselves as "sustainable streets" and take collective steps to reduce their impact on the world.

My travels and research in Australia have reaffirmed the primacy of place in any program of green urbanism. Commitment to and care for place will need to be an essential cornerstone for any effective sustainability initiative. It is unlikely that we will care enough about making the changes needed—technological or behavioral—unless we viscerally and deeply care about the landscapes and communities in which we live. This commitment to place was evident in many cities and communities in Australia.

There is a harmony and synergism between the goals of protecting uniqueness of place and sustainability. We visited and lived in many places during our time in Australia that were notable for their special feelings and qualities. Fremantle in Western Australia and Newtown and Coogee Beach in Sydney were places we grew to admire and appreciate and for which we developed a deep affection. Many of these Australian cities and communities demonstrate well the need to take creative steps to protect and nurture the unique sense of place, the history, the human and natural stories that deepen our understanding, connection, and commitment to places, the distinctive landscapes and immense beauty of these places, and their biodiversity and wondrous natural heritage.

The value of this kind of comparative research also involves the benefits of spending time in another country. When learning about planning and environment through travel and research abroad, one returns to see one's home place in new and helpful ways. The experiences, insights, and discoveries experienced while traveling affect one's life in often profound ways. In my own case, I came back with new sensibilities about place, history, and the importance of personal contact with nature. And my personal lifestyle, the extent and nature of my community service, and my teaching priorities, among others, have all changed and deepened in valuable ways.

Such experiences help one to see one's own home anew. Exposure to the plight of Australian Aborigines—their deplorable treatment at the hands of Europeans and the continuing legacy of social and economic discrimination and disadvantage—have made me begin to confront the history of native peoples in my own country, state, and community. Aboriginal culture and heritage have much to offer all Australians, and especially their caring relationship to a land the Europeans found harsh and unforgiving holds promise as a more appropriate and sustainable vantage point on this unique continent. My family and I have become deeply moved by Aboriginal art, by its unusual beauty and spirit, its connections to land and place, and the deep historical time it reflects. I returned to my home city of Charlottesville, Virginia, wondering why the history of its native peoples—the Monacan nation—is given little or no attention while statutes of presidents and other heroes of European decent (men mostly) are celebrated. I came to realize the need for a more balanced and accurate history of this place, a more inclusive history that seeks to understand and fully appreciate the culture, society, and people who inhabited my home for ten thousand years prior to European settlement. It took the vantage point of a continent thousands of miles away to stimulate this thinking in me.

Similarly, exposure to the unfamiliar climate, topography, landscapes, and biodiversity of another place stimulates questions about one's own home. The plants and trees, the birds one sees, the smells, even the color of the sky, provoke comparisons, queries, and ultimately new home sensibilities. I have become interested in fungi after learning about their importance to plants and trees in the nutrient-poor soils of Western Australia and experiencing the "fungi forays" and other programs under way for educating about fungi. I find now that I am constantly looking underfoot, searching out (and photographing) organisms that I would otherwise have missed or thought unimportant. Intimately learning about a new place, what makes it feel different or special, invariably provides insights about the place one has left, and the reasons, sometimes unclear, for why one looks forward to an eventual return. Australia has helped me to become a more caring, curious, and rooted citizen in my own home place here in Virginia.

Afterword

Peter Newman

I have read *Green Urbanism Down Under: Learning from Sustainable Communities in Australia* with great interest. It is a remarkable set of stories that has deepened my reflections on our Australian cities and their struggle to be more sustainable.

As the reader may have gathered, there are parts where I have intervened to provide some context or additional detail, but the flow of the text is Tim's and his first and most vivid impressions are what shine through.

It helps to see one's own cities through the eyes of a visitor. There is a freshness, and perhaps a welcoming forgiveness for some things that we wouldn't otherwise quite so easily forgive. Perhaps, then, I could say at the outset that there are some things that aren't quite as rosy as they may have seemed from Tim's account. From the inside, they are more complex. But it would be a pity to spoil a good story!

It almost goes without saying that this is not the whole story on Australia's sustainability innovations. There are other stories, of course, but these are the ones that Tim encountered. Following is a list of things I feel should be added to fill out the green urbanism story from down under.

1. *Technology and cleaner production.*

The general impression of Australia from afar is that we provide resources for the world and buy our technology in. There is a lot of truth in that, but we also do add our bit on technology and in recent times we have done quite a lot in eco-technology as the sustainability revolution has influenced everyone, including our engineers and scientists. Here are a few brief stories.

The **Sydney Olympics** were the first green Olympics, and all subsequent games—including the Melbourne Commonwealth Games—have tried to demonstrate the latest developments in sustainable building. The Sydney Games are described by Tim in terms of the wastewater systems, but it was also a regenerative project as the site became the largest single land renewal project in Australia with expertise and technologies being developed for bioremediating toxic soil to a habitat suitable for native forests and even endangered wetland species. The Olympics event was car-free and hugely popular as a result, which has long-term consequences in showing people that they can live without a car. Expertise from these Olympics has been used in subsequent green games and now in Beijing. The new Olympic swimming center is an Australian innovation with low-energy requirements as the building's skin breathes and reacts to light, helping to collect heat for the pools.

Renewable energy is abundant in Australia, and despite the lack of large-scale programs to assist it, there has been significant development of Australian technology, including the world's most efficient photovoltaic cells (20 percent); new wind power technologies, especially the control systems that integrate it into grids; groundwater heat exchangers developed to heat buildings; a wave power technology that is on trial; and an Australian ceramic fuel cell that is doing well in the competition for a new small-scale electricity source.

Cleaner production innovations are occurring in every industry. BP Australia reduced greenhouse gases in its refineries by the Kyoto requirements in just five years. A new industrial paint system has been sold to DuPont that is cleaner, greener, and more durable. The use of a very light magnesium metal is increasing, and an Australian technology has made its refining much cleaner and cheaper. And an Australian mining technology has been combined with the best chemical engineering to create a solid waste recycling system in Sydney that creates electricity (without incineration), compost, and a stream of materials ready for recycling; the system has now been purchased for use in northern England.

2. *Settlements in the outback.*

Australia is mostly "outback," although not many people live there. Being off the grid means that settlements have to be supplied with energy, water, communications, and waste systems that are small scale and self-sufficient. Australian ingenuity has created a range of new small-scale systems, including small wind-powered desalination systems, combined solar-diesel power, and solar telephone systems; permaculture (a great Australian invention for small, diverse, synergistic farming systems) is being used to transform landscaping. These systems are now moving back into cities as small-scale localized technology becomes more relevant.

3. *The water crisis.*

The year 2006 in Australia was a watershed literally as the north had more rain than it has ever had and southern areas had the worst drought on record, which has largely continued. The drought was predicted as part of climate change modeling, but it is still scary when dams run dry in most cities. Water theft began to occur from irrigators and people with tanks, and at the same time innovators began to have their products applied as well as a range of demand management tools. In Hervey Bay, the water provider was able to reduce demand for supplies by one third with, among other things, a new leak detection system. Irrigators are reducing losses by 50 percent in places. Water efficiency devices and appliances are becoming standard, and new technologies for recycling stormwater and wastewater are being fitted rapidly. As soon as they are used, the world is waiting to take them on as well, so the water crisis is becoming an opportunity for Australian eco-innovation.

Australians are also known for their drinking and their fine wines. Perth's Swan Brewery has done an eco-audit to show how it can become a model of cleaner production. It found, for example, that it could save fifty thousand kiloliters of water a year by diverting the water it uses in washing cans into its cooling tower. Banrock Station winery has been able to reclaim a degraded wetland and farm area into a thriving winery with a wetland of international significance. A proportion of each bottle of wine sold now goes into wetland conservation projects in ten countries.

4. *Getting on with it.*

Another trait of Australians is the notion of just getting on with it. One who did that was Ian Kiernan, who was a round-the-world yachtsman. He decided to help clean up litter in water systems after seeing rubbish in the world's oceans. Now we have a national Clean Up Day, when thousands of volunteers help collect rubbish from unusual places, especially in creeks and beaches. The idea has now spread to the United Kingdom.

Surprisingly, I found quite a few things I didn't know from Tim's stories—some even from my hometown—like the fungi story. There is a lesson there: we think we know our own city, yet there may be extraordinary things happening and great experiences to be part of if only we were more curious.

As a student of the United States and a resident of Australia, I would like to make some concluding remarks about what Tim's book could mean for Americans.

1. *Australian cities can be a good place for Americans to visit.*

Our cities may move you the way they moved Tim and the way I find myself moved whenever I visit U.S. cities. We are kindred spirits on many things. We are part of the New World, freed up to create a new way of living and governing that built on the Old World but gave us a freedom to try things out. We share this desire to be risk takers, to try for innovation. In Australia, this can be even more risqué and honest than in the United States because we don't try to hide too much. The way that I am received in the United States as something of a special kind of new species—the Aussie—is the way we tend to see American visitors, especially those that have come to learn. So do come and check our cities out for yourselves.

2. *Australian cities do have a special kind of natural environment.*

The U.S. landscape is spectacular in so many places, and although we have a few standouts, we are mostly a more subtle kind of landscape. The bush, however, is very diverse, and it seeps into our cities. The trees, the grasses, the "black boys," and the wildflowers are not like any others in Europe or the United States, and the bird life is ever present. I do miss that when I leave, and I was pleased to see how deeply it affected Tim. His story of the fruit bat in Sydney was remarkable. It is, of course, a rich natural heritage, and it is one that each generation of Australians has learned to love—right from the beginning. It is also one that hundreds of groups from across the country are seeking to retain and rebuild. Rehabilitating the native species of an area within a city is possible. We've shown it over and over.

3. *Australian cities do have an urban heritage and identity.*

I am always amazed by the number of people in the United States who ask me whether we have cities in Australia. Perhaps this is one legacy of watching television's fascination with our wildlife. Or maybe it is a sense that we are just a young country. But our cities are quite old compared to many in the world, especially cities in the developing world, which were often small villages one hundred years ago. Melbourne in the 1880s was the third biggest city in the world and was a center of industrial growth that earned it the reputation of being the "Babylon of the South." And we are old enough now to have places such as Fremantle considered for World Heritage designation as one of the most intact nineteenth-century port cities in the world. We have layers of time that can be seen and appreciated, and it is a treat to see Tim's account doing just that, especially regarding Fremantle and Melbourne. He was also able to pick up that each Australian city had to fight for this heritage and has been rebuilding it in recent decades as part of its policies to create sustainable and viable economies. This is not a message often associated with Australia, but it is an important one of interest to any U.S. city contemplating a more sustainable future.

4. *Australian cities do have traditions of regional planning and sustainability planning that work.*

One problem long identified with U.S. cities is that local governments have power over land use and that states cannot intervene or override their decisions. The U.S. founding fathers saw the need for this to ensure that there was a balance of powers and that each place knew best for its area. But although this may have made eminent sense when Jefferson, Madison, and Hamilton were imagining the future, they could never have envisaged cities spreading as far as U.S. cities do today, incorporating sometimes fifty or so local governments and requiring infrastructure for transport, power, water, and sewerage as well as human services that cross all these boundaries. Regional planning is desperately needed in U.S. cities.

Australian cities—especially Perth, Adelaide, and Melbourne—have had a longer history of regional planning. Such planning has had a more checkered history in Brisbane and Sydney. But in the past five years, all Australian cities have rediscovered regional planning with a vengeance. Communities, local governments, businesses, and professional bodies have been crying out for a framework that can enable regional land uses (centers and corridors for population and jobs), regional infrastructure, and regional biodiversity and open space to be clearly assigned. That framework has been provided by the concept of sustainability and the use of a regional plan to embed it. Thus each of these Australian city plans provides a clear statement of how the economic, environmental, and social future of their urban areas is totally synergistic. This is a framework that American cities have not done as extensively or as formally, though a few—including Chicago, New York, Milwaukee, and Portland—are showing now how it can be done, with local government participation. States in Australia have also been more able to use the term *sustainability* in their governance than can be done in the United States, where official attempts to prevent the use of the word in government has made it difficult to use. The WA State Sustainability Strategy remains the most complete state strategy on sustainability, and as U.S. states and cities (especially New York) begin to develop such strategies, I believe it will be of benefit to see the Australian precedent: sustainability strategies are politically successful at framing a future for cities and states.

5. *Australian cities are deeply car dependent but are also now doing something about it.*

The regional plans in Australian cities are all based around new infra-structure plans. In most cases, this has meant a renewed commitment to building rail into and across suburban areas that were developed in the past fifty years on the U.S., or at least the Californian, model. We have re-ceived much encouragement from U.S. cities such as Portland, which led the campaign to build quality transit as the basis of a sustainable future for their city.

The story of Perth's rail revival parallels that of Portland, and like in the United States, a lot more cities are now seeing that the dollars should be going to rail rather than roads. Regional planning and state government financing in Australian cities have seen commitments of around $10 billion in new rail lines in recent years. But in the United States, this is dwarfed by the $110 billion promised since 2000 through ballots in thirty-three states to rebuild transit. These decisions have been popular but always con-tentious, and Tim's stories can only help to show that American cities are not alone in the process of rebuilding based on rail- and transit-oriented vil-lages of denser, mixed land use. Perth's dramatically successful new South-ern Railway, which opened in December 2007 and reached capacity in just a few months, sends a powerful signal as it reaches to car-dependent far-flung outer suburbs that would not normally be considered suitable for rail—in this case, it has worked.

6. *The politics of climate change has arrived.*

Al Gore is one of the greatest heroes in Australia. He was so popular with his film and barnstorming tour that the politics of climate change ar-rived almost single-handedly. Gore was greatly encouraged by the response and mentioned Australia in his Nobel Prize acceptance speech as perhaps the first country to have climate change shape a federal election. Australia's commitment to Kyoto that followed the election put the spotlight firmly on the United States. Now we have to learn a new kind of partnership that can generate global leadership after a decade of sharing global shame as the only two nations to support the climate skeptics. Perhaps there needs to be a three-way alliance among Australia, China, and the United States, because Australia is the nation that provides most of China's resources, China is the nation that produces most consumer goods, and the United States is the nation that consumes the most consumer goods. A sustainability alliance could pledge to demonstrate global leadership in reducing carbon in all three phases of the global economy. Perhaps we could lead the world instead of being the two pariahs. It would make a nice change.

7. Hope is all around.

The benefits of reading this book go well beyond the enjoyment of its individual stories. It is mostly a recognition that although cities may be culturally, economically, and environmentally different, they share the same need to be remade under the global imperatives of sustainability. Most of all, the book is demonstrating that if you scratch the surface of an Australian city, there are people doing heroic work for sustainability. That I have also found in the United States.

Jane Jacobs says that cities have played a critical role in enabling a society to innovate. They do this by travelers finding out about new things discovered in other cities and then bringing these home and adapting them—enabling innovation to spread. This spread of innovations can be traced from city to city by historians. Today we live in a world desperately trying to learn how to become more sustainable, how to use less and live better, how to regenerate the ecology of a city and its bioregion, how to make identity and sense of place mean something in a highly globalized economy, how to make a new economy out of green jobs, and so forth. All these matters require innovations. That travelers like Tim are able to stay long enough and look perceptively enough to see these innovations is a profoundly important exercise—and one that has a long tradition.

There are those who will count the greenhouse gases used by Tim and his family in their travels to point their eco-moralistic fingers. And they have a point—we travelers are indeed a problem when you see how much damage we do. But perhaps the consumption of packaged global tourism experiences is not the same as what Tim and I have been doing. Perhaps there are ideas here that will stick as we try them out in new cities, as we realize that what we have back home may be better. We hope that we may add something to the long sweep of human history created by travelers picking up innovations—this time in green urbanism.

Notes

Chapter 2. Greening and Sustaining Cities

1. I was taking a picture of a CAT bus one day when my five-year-old daughter, Carolena, asked me what was so special about the buses. When I said they were free, she noticed the CAT logo on the side of bus and asked whether that meant all cats could ride them for free! I laughed at the image of cats lining up to board the buses.

2. Future development in the Olympic Park site (which consists of large, old industrial sites) will be held to the same environmental standards and aspirations as the Olympic games. The Town Center will consist of 330,000 square meters of commercial and residential space over the next ten years and will be home to five thousand people, ten thousand employees, a library, child care centers, shops, and restaurants. The long-term development will be heavily office oriented, with about twenty development sites that will be released, with ultimate build-out in about twenty years. Competitive bidding processes are used to select development, with those with the most ecological value receiving greater consideration. Plans must incorporate and respond to a set of Environmentally Sustainable Development (ESD) principles, and there are some specific mandates. All buildings must meet at least 4.5 stars under the Australian Building Greenhouse Rating system and a minimum of 4 stars under the Australian Green Building Council rating system (more on these later in the chapter). Also, they must be willing to connect to the park's water recycling/reclamation system.

Chapter 4. Strengthening Place, Building Community

1. The Perth City Farm's entire operation operates on a shoestring. Rosanne and Thom, the principals, are themselves paid only for part-time work. A handful of others receive some pay but on a part-time basis only, and most who work at the farm are there only temporarily while transitioning to something else or otherwise view it as a short though valuable stop on the way to something else. Rosanne tells of a doctor who is studying the therapeutic and medicinal value of organic gardening. The individual who oversees much of the organic vegetable production on the city farm is working

on a PhD in sustainable agriculture. In some ways, it is remarkable that the farm has held together for what is now an impressive fourteen years on such meager financial help.

2. The organic garlic is a big seller, and the honey produced at the farm is highly sought after as well (and is able to carry a premium price). Soil food (compost generated on-site and given additives) and plants from the farm's nursery also bring in income.

3. Margaret River's new biodiversity strategy builds on linkages between green areas. The council recently tied its plans together into a Sustainability Plan after a series of community-based approaches to its long-term future (see http://www.csiro.au/science/ps2ay.html#intro). Through this process, the town hopes to keep its values and community assets intact despite the pressures for growth from its newfound wealth.

4. Many Australian local authorities have tree protection orders, and local councils commonly regulate tree cutting and vegetation clearance. Ashfield Council, in the Sydney region, for instance, has a tree protection order that requires a permit for pruning or cutting any tree greater than five meters tall. Marrickville Council has adopted a comprehensive "Tree Management Policy" as well as a "Tree Preservation Order." Like the Ashfield order, it mandates a permit for any cutting or pruning of trees taller than five meters or with a trunk diameter of two hundred millimeters or more (Marrickville Council, 2001, n.d.). Some local authorities, such as Gosford, have adopted specific Heritage Local Environment Plans and Development Coastal Plans that protect specific trees or groups of trees (Gosford City Council, 2004).

5. The criteria for significant trees include the following: "historic and/or natural value (i.e. indigenous/cultivated origin; botanic/scientific value; social, cultural and commemorative value; visual and aesthetic value)" (City of Sydney, 2005, p.10).

6. In early 2008, Australian Greenpeace took on the Japanese whaling fleet over its continuing program of "scientific" whaling based on minke whales in Australian waters off Antarctica. They boarded one vessel and delivered an ultimatum to stop, which led to their being imprisoned on the boat and prompting a serious diplomatic incident. Such acts appear to be necessary to make Japan face up to the need to change its cultural reliance on whale meat in its national diet. It will be Australian Greenpeace's legacy that will ensure that this shift occurs.

Chapter 5. Bush Cities: Australia's Urban Ecological Capitals

1. The Downfall Creek Bushland Education Centre has developed and made available to all schools in the Corridor a resource package called "A Living Corridor, A Living Classroom."

2. "'A' reserves are the highest priority reserves and are generally located within residential areas (where it is likely that residents expect a higher level of management because the reserves are under greater pressure from the community), whereas 'B' reserves are located in semi-rural areas of the city" (City of Wanneroo, 2005, pp. 3–4).

References

ABC Radio. 2001. "Ningaloo Reef" broadcast. November 17.

Adelaide City Council. 2004. "Adelaide Building Tune Ups Project, Stage 1 Report." October 15.

———. N.d. "Tindo: The World's First Solar Electric Bus." Fact sheet. http://www.adelaidecitycouncil.com.

Adelaide Film Festival. 2007. "Adelaide's Film Festival to Become Australia's First CO2 Free Film Festival!" Press release, Miranda Brown Publicity.

Apace. 2004. Annual report.

Atticus Informer. 2001. "Interview with Syd Shea." *Atticus Informer* (Perth).

Artforce. 2003. "Painting a Traffic Signal Box." City of Brisbane, Artforce program.

Australian Capital Territory (ACT). 2003. *People, Place and Prosperity: A Policy for Sustainability in the ACT*. Canberra: ACT Office of Sustainability.

———. 2004. *Measuring Our Progress: Canberra's Journey to Sustainability*. Vols. 1 and 2. Canberra: ACT Office of Sustainability.

Australian City Farms and Community Gardens Network. 2007. *Community Harvest* (summer newsletter).

Australian Greenhouse Office. 2007. *Celebrating a Decade of Local Greenhouse Action, Cities for Climate Protection Australia, Reporting 2006*. Canberra.

Australian Koala Foundation (AKF). 2004. *Koala Beach: Koala Plan of Management*. Brisbane: AKF, February.

———. 2005. *Koala Beach Estate: Overall Management Guidelines for the Koala Beach Wildlife and Habitat Management Committee*. Brisbane: AKF, January.

———. N.d. "Koala Bench: A Home amongst the Gum Trees." Brisbane: AKF.

Barron, John. 2007. "Elections? Here's How You Do It, Mate." *Washington Post*, December 9, p. B1.

Bartolomei, Linda, Linda Corkery, Bruce Judd, and Susan Thompson. 2003. *A Bountiful Harvest: Community Gardens and Neighborhood Renewal in Waterloo*. Sydney: UNSW Faculty of the Built Environment.

Beatley, Timothy. 2005. *Native to Nowhere: Sustaining Home and Community in a Global Age*. Washington, DC: Island Press.

Beresford, Quentin, Hugo Bekle, Harry Phillips, and Jane Mulcock. 2001. *The Salinity Crisis: Landscapes, Communities and Politics*. Perth: University of Western Australia.

BioCity. N.d. "Strategic Plan for BioCity, Centre for Urban Habitats." Adelaide: BioCity.

Bland, Lisa, and Andre Brrwa. 2004. "Econotes: Grand Spider Orchid." *Ecoplan News* 51 (Spring).

Blue Mountains City Council. 2004. *Towards a More Sustainable Blue Mountains: A 25 Year Vision for the City*. Katoomba: Blue Mountains.

Bradby, Keith. 2005. "Gondwana Link—Ecological Restoration at the Scale This Country Needs." *Newsletter of the Land for Wildlife Scheme* 8, no. 4, 17–19.

Brisbane City Council. 2004. "Conserving Biodiversity in an Urban Landscape." Brisbane City: Environment and Parks Branch, September.

———. 2007a. *CityShape: The Brisbane Local Growth Management Strategy (LGMS)*. Brisbane: Brisbane City Council, May.

———. 2007b. "Council to Conserve 40% of Bushland as Natural Habitat." Press release. http://newsroom.brisbane.qld.gov.au/home/news_detail.asp?ID=752.

Brown, Andrew, Carolyn Thomson-Dans, and Neville Marchant, eds. *Western Australia's Threatened Flora*. Como: Department of Conservation and Land Management.

Bryson, Bill. 2000. *In a Sunburned Country*. New York: Broadway Books.

Camden Council. 2003. "Natural Aspects Policy." Adopted May 2003.

CERES. 2007. *CERES Community Environment Park 2007 Annual Report*. Brunswick East, Victoria: CERES.

City of Freemantle. 2000. "The City of Fremantle Policy for Respect, Recognition, and Conciliation with Aboriginal People." October.

City of Gosford. 2004. *Sustainability Report 2004*. Gosford, New South Wales: City of Gosford.

City of Melbourne. 1987. *Grids and Greenery: The Character of Inner Melbourne*. Melbourne: City of Melbourne, Urban Design and Architecture Division.

———. 2002. "Procedure for Completing Sustainability Assessments for Council Reports." Triple Bottom Line Toolkit, with International Council for Local Environmental Initiatives.

———. 2003. *Growing Green: An Environmental Sustainability Plan for the City of Melbourne's Open Space and Recreational Facilities*. Melbourne: City of Melbourne, April.

———. 2004a. "Arts Strategy 2004–2007." Melbourne: City Services, Community and Cultural Development Committee, July 6.

———. 2004b. "CH2: Setting a World Standard in Green Building Design." November.

———. 2004c. "City of Melbourne Transforms Laneways with City Art." Press release, September 20.

———. 2004d. "Walking on Air." http://www.melbourne.vic.gov.au/info.cfm?top=75&pa=1519&pg=1698.

———. 2005. "New Study Shows Melbourne's Miracle Comeback." Press release, News and Media Centre, August 19.

———. 2008. "City of Melbourne's six star green building proves cost savings after first year audit report," press release, February 14. www.melbourne.vic.gov.au.

————. N.d. "Queen Victoria Market Solar Energy." http://www.melbourne.vic
.gov.au.

City of Port Phillip. 2002. "Urban Art Strategy." Prepared for the Department of Urban
Design and Architecture by Torque Propriety Limited. June.

————. 2003. "Listening Place." Press release, September 3.

————. 2004. *Streetland: An Easy Guide to Creating Fantastic Street Parties in Your
Neighborhood.* Port Phillip: Port Phillip Community Group.

City of Sydney. 2005. "Register of Significant Trees." Sydney: Council of the City of
Sydney. Adopted December.

————. 2007. "Environmental Management Plan, Final."

————. 2008. "Sustainable Sydney 2030: City of Sydney Strategic Plan," Final Consultation Draft.

————. N.d. "3CBDs Greenhouse Initiative." http://www.3cbds.com.au.

City of Wanneroo. 2004a. "Milestones One and Two of the City's Local Biodiversity
Strategy." Memo file ref. 527/0004BVO1, 01-10.

————. 2004b. "Preparation of a Local Biodiversity Strategy." Memo file ref. 527/
0004V01, 02-06.

————. 2005. "Prioritisation of the City's Natural Areas for Management as Nature
Conservation Areas." Memo file ref. PR/0005VO1, April 26.

Clarke, Peter. 2006. "Backyard Buddies Update." *Ku-ring-gai Council Bushcare News*
50 (Autumn).

Clinton Foundation, 2007. "President Clinton Announces Landmark Program to Reduce Energy Use in Buildings Worldwide," New York: Clinton Foundation.

Commissioner for Environmental Sustainability. 2004a. *Annual Report, 2003–2004.*
Melbourne.

————. 2004b. *Strategic Audit of Victorian Government Agencies' Environmental
Management Systems.* January.

————. 2005. *Strategic, Audit of Victorian Government Agencies' Environmental Management Systems.* January.

————. 2007. *Strategic Audit of Victorian Government Agencies' Environmental Management Systems.* January.

Community and Neighborhood Houses and Centres Association. 2006.
"Community Gardening in SA." Project report. November.

Conservation Commission of Western Australia. 2004. *Forest Management Plan,
2004–2013.* Perth: Conservation Commission of Western Australia.

Cox, Eva. 1995. "Raising Social Capital." In *A Truly Civil Society: The 1995 Boyer Lectures.* Sydney: ABC Books.

Daniels, C. B. and C. Tait. 2005. *Adelaide: Nature of a City.* Adelaide: BioCity.

Department of Infrastructure. 2006. *Meeting Our Transport Challenges—Connecting
Victorian Communities.* Melbourne: State of Victoria.

Department of Planning, New South Wales Government. 2005a. "BASIX Factsheet."
Sydney: Department of Planning, June.

————. 2005b. *City of Cities: A Plan for Sydney's Future.* Sydney: Department of Planning.

————. 2007. *2004–2005 Outcomes: BASIX Ongoing Monitoring Program.* Sydney:
Department of Planning, May.

Downton, Paul. 2005. Letter to the author, June 6.

Drummond, Mark. 2005. "New $1b Iron Ore mine for Pilbara." *West Australian,* July 2.

Dwyer, Alison. 2005. "Building to Reach Our Ambition." *Architecture SA Magazine,* February.

Edwards, Ferne. 2007. "The CERES Urban Orchard Project." http://www.sustainablemelbourne.com (accessed February 29).

Elliott, Anne. 2005. "Letter to Mr. M. Willis, general manager, Blue Mountains City Council." June 5.

Energy Conservation Systems. 2004. "Adelaide Building Tune Ups Project, Stage 1 Report." Prepared for the government of South Australia, Capital City Committee and Adelaide City Council. October 15.

Engwicht, David. 2005. *Mental Speed Bumps: The Smarter Way to Tame Traffic.* Annandale: Envirobook.

Environs Consulting Pty. Ltd. 2002. "Investigating Potential Bush Products in the Great Southern Western Australia: Similar Projects, Key People and Organizations." Prepared for Green Skills Inc., March.

Evans, Melanie. 2002. "The Reconciliation Mural by Melanie Evans: Statement by the Artist." In *Koora Ni Wahdu Balanyo Danaya: The City of Fremantle Policy for Respect, Recognition, and Conciliation with Aboriginal People.* Fremantle: City of Fremantle, October.

Farrelly, Elizabeth. 2005. "Attack of Common Sense Hits Planners." *Sydney Morning Herald,* April 26.

Friends of the Earth. N.d. "Whites Creek Background Paper." Sydney: FoE.

Gallop, Geoff. 2003. "Preface." In *Hope for the Future: The State Sustainability Strategy,* ed. Peter Newman and Michael Rowe. Perth: WA Government.

Gehl, Jan. 2004. *Places for People 2004.* Copenhagen: Gehl Architects.

Girardet, Herbert. 2004. *Creating a Sustainable Adelaide.* Thinker in Residence Report. Adelaide: Department of the Premier and Cabinet, November.

Gold Coast City. 2007. *Gold Coast Local Growth Management Strategy.* Gold Coast City, January.

Gosford City Council. 2004. *Environmental Management Plan.* Gosford: Gosford City Council.

Government of Western Australia. 2000. *Bush Forever.* Vol. 2, *Directory of Bush Forever Sites.* Perth: Government of Western Australia, December.

Green Building Council of Australia (GBCA). N.d. "Case Study: 40 Albert Road." http://www.gbca.org.au.

Greenfleet. 2005. "2 Million Trees Soak Up Vehicle Pollution." Press release, March 30.

Greening Australia. 2003. *Annual Report.* Fremantle: Greening Australia.

———. 2005. *The Greening Australian.* Spring/Summer.

Greening Australia WA Inc. 2004. *2004 Greening Australia (WA) Annual Report.* Fremantle: Greening Australia.

Gruber, Fiona. 2007. "Enter a Green Limelight." *The Australian,* January 2.

Hammond, Philip. 2007. "City of 1 Million Trees." *Courier Mail,* December 27, p. 56.

Hartz-Karp, Janette, and Peter Newman. 2006. "The Participative Route to Sustainability." In *Community Voices: Creating Sustainable Spaces,* ed. Sally Paulin. Crawley: University of Western Australia Press.

Heath, Jim. 1999. "Why Save Orchids under Threat?" *Orchids Australia*, December.

Heath, Tamara. 2003. "Periscopes up for Art in City Lanes." *Moreland Leader*, July 14.

Hodgson, Sean. 2003. "The Artforce Project and Legal Art as a Target-hardening Strategy." Presentation, "Graffiti and Disorder" conference. http://www.aic.gov.au/conferences/2003-graffiti/hodgson.html.

Hoffman, Noel, and Andrew Brown. 1998. *Orchids of South-west Australia*. Nedlands: University of Western Australia Press.

Hopper, Stephen. 2003. "Kari, Marri, Marlock and Mallee." *Splinter: New Directions in Firewood* (August).

Humphries, Robert, Michael Waite, Paul Rogoysky, Peter Huxtable, and Matthew Hess. 2005. "Moving towards Carbon-Neutrality." *Water* 32, no. 4 (June).

Jameson, Glen. 2001. "Timelines Calendars: Entering the Landscape." Presentation, Interpretation Australia National Conference.

Johnson, Murray. N.d.-a. "A Forest Consciousness—Fifty Years of Change in Pemberton." Unpublished paper.

———. N.d.-b. "An Overview of the Firewood Industry and Forest Based Tourism in South Western Australia: A Discussion Paper." Unpublished paper.

Kennedy Associates Architects. N.d. "Clovelly House FAQs." Sydney: Kennedy Associates.

Kenworthy, Jeff, Robert Murray-Leach, and Craig Townsend. 2005. "Sustainable Urban Transport." In *The Natural Advantage of Nations: Business Opportunities, Innovation and Governance in the 21st Century*, ed. Karlson Hargroves and Michael Smith, 371–86. London: Earthscan.

Ku-ring-gai Council. N.d. "Bushcare Volunteer Program," found at: http://www.kmc.nsw.gov.au/www/html/1189-bushcare-volunteer-program.asp.

———. N.d. "Case Study: Kogarah Town Square." http://www.kogarah.nsw.gov.au.

Lambeck, Robert J. 1997. "Focal Species: A Multi-species Umbrella for Nature Conservation." *Conservation Biology* 11, 849–56.

Landry, Charles. 2003. "Rethinking Adelaide: 'Capturing Imagination' Adelaide Thinker in Residence Report." Adelaide, December.

Light, Andrew. "Urban Ecological Citizenship." *Journal of Social Philosophy* 34, no.1 (2003): 44–63.

MacKenzie, Josh. 2002. "Guess Who's Back?" *Blue Mountains Gazette*, November 14.

Manly Council. 2006. *Manly Sustainability Strategy—For Today and Future Generations*. Manly, New South Wales.

Marrickville Council. 2001. "Tree Preservation Order." June.

———. 2003. "RiverLife—Sustainable Water Environments." Prepared in cooperation with Monash University.

———. 2004. *Illawara Road Stormwater Masterplan*. Marrickville: Marrickville Council, October.

———. N.d-a. "Tillman Park Children's Centre: A Fitting Example."

———. N.d-b. "Tree Management Policy."

Marrickville and South Sydney Councils. 2003. *King Street and Enmore Road Heritage and Urban Design*. Development Control Plan no. 34. Marrickville.

McGowan, Chris. 2004. "Adelaide Green City Program—Working towards a Sustainable Community." Speech notes, International Solar Cities Congress, Daegu, Korea, November 14–18.

Melbourne City Council. 2005. *City Plan 2010: Towards a Thriving and Sustainable City*. June.

Men of the Trees. 2006. "11,000 Vehicles Offset through Carbon Neutral Program." Press release, April 28.

Mittermeier, Russell A., Norman Myers, and Cristina Goettsch Meittermeier. 1999. *Hotspots: Earth's Biologically Richest and Most Endangered Terrestrial Ecoregions*. Mexico City: CEMEX and Conservation International.

Mittermeier, Russell A., et al. 2005. *Hotspots Revisited: The Earth's Biologically Richest and Most Endangered Terrestrial Ecoregions*. Washington, DC: Conservation International.

Mobbs, Michael. 2000. *Sustainable House*. Sydney: Choice Publishers.

Moore, Clover. 2007. "Lord Mayor Clover Moore MP's Speech at Earth Hour International Launch." Sydney, December 14.

Mountains to Mangroves Committee. 1998. *Mountains to Mangroves Corridor Strategy Plan*. Prepared by Mary Maher and Associates, Brisbane.

New South Wales Department of Environment and Climate Change. 2006. "New South Wales State of the Environment 2006." Sydney.

New South Wales Department of Planning. 2005a. "NSW Leads the Way for Sustainable Housing," Sydney: New South Wales Government, April 28. http://www.dipnr.nsw.gov.au.

———. 2005b. "Top National Planning Award for BASIX." Press release, http://www.dipnr.nsw.gov.au.

New South Wales Government. 2005. "Green Future for Sydney's New Neighborhoods." Press release, February 8. www.metrostrategy.nsw.gov.au.

Newman, Christy, Peter Newman, and Robert Whitehead. 2006. "Campaign for Sydney: Media Intervention for a Sustainability Agenda." In *Innovation, Education and Communication for Sustainable Development*, ed. Walter Leal Filho. Frankfurt: Peter Lang Scientific.

Newman, Peter, 2002. "Railways and Reurbanisation in Perth." In *Case Studies in Planning Success*, ed. J. Williams and R. Stimson. New York: Elsevier.

———. 2005. "Sustainability in the Wild West." In *The Natural Advantage of Nations: Business Opportunities, Innovation and Governance in the 21st Century*, ed. Karlson Hargroves and Michael H. Smith. London: Earthscan.

———. 2006. "The Environmental Impact of Cities." *Environment and Urbanisation* 18, no. 2, 275–95.

Newman, Peter, and Jeffrey Kenworthy. 1999. *Sustainability and Cities: Overcoming Automobile Dependence*. Washington, DC: Island Press.

Newman, Peter, and Michael Rowe. 2003. *Hope for the Future: The State Sustainability Strategy*. Perth: WA Government.

Newman, P. W. G., E. Stanton-Hicks, and B. Hammond. 2006. "From CSR to Sustainability through Enduring Value." In *Management Models for CSR: A Comprehensive Overview*, ed. Jan Jonker and Marco de Witte. Heidelberg, Germany: Springer Verlag–Management Sciences.

Noranda Bushland Committee. 1999. "Noranda Community Bushland Management Plan."

Paevere, Phillip and Stephen Brown. 2008. "Indoor Environmental Quality and Occupant Productivity in the CH2 Building: Post-Occupancy Summary." Highett, VIC: CSIRO, March.

Passmore, Daryl. 2006. "Green Plan for Brisbane." *Sunday Mail,* August 13, p. 26.

Peatling, Stephanie. 2003. "The Sisters Order Fast Food to Go." http://www.smh .com.au/articles/2003/09/24/1064083060358.html.

Planning SA. 2004. *Hills Face Zone Review.* Adelaide: Planning SA, February.

———. 2006. *Planning Strategy for Metropolitan Adelaide.* Adelaide: Planning SA.

Port Stephens Council. 2002. *Port Stephens Urban Settlement Strategy.* October.

———. 2004. "Progress Report 1 July 2002–31 March 2004: Port Stephens Koala Habitat Restoration Project." March 31.

Port Stephens and Newcastle Councils. N.d. "Nature Watch Diary: Central Coast." Port Stephens, NSW.

Price, Gordon. 2007. "Melbourne." *Price Tags* 93 (April). http://www.sightline.org.

Queensland Centre for Biodiversity. 2005. "Terrestrial Invertebrate Status Review." Brisbane: Queensland Museum, March.

Queensland Government. 2006. *Urban Housing Capacity Template.* Prepared by the University of Queensland, October.

Queensland Government, Minister for Public Works, Housing and Racing. 2005. "2 Million Trees Soak Up Vehicle Pollution." March 30.

Queensland Government, Office of Urban Management. 2005. *South East Queensland Regional Plan.* October.

Queensland Museum. 2005. *Terrestrial Invertebrate Status Review.* Prepared by the Queensland Centre for Biodiversity, Drs. John Stanisic, Chris Burwell, Robert Raven, Geoff Montieth, and Barbara Boehr, South Brisbane.

Raphael, C., L. Sheehy, S. Jennings, and S. Richardson-Newton. N.d. "Role of Environmental Education in Creating Vibrant and Sustainable Communities—Living Smart as a Case Study." http://www.livingsmart.org.au/pdfs/RaphaelFinal%20ICTC.pdf.

Redland Shire Council. 2007. *Redlands Local Growth Management Strategy.* Redland Shire, Queensland: Redland Shire Council, June.

Reid, Alan. N.d. "Timelines Project." *Timeline News.* Melbourne.

Renne, Kara Matina. 2008. "Corporate Social Responsibility and Supply Chains: A Case Study of Indigenous Labeling in Western Australia." ISTP master's thesis, Murdoch University, Perth.

Robins, Juleigh. *Wild Lime: Cooking from the Bushfood Garden.* Sydney: Allen & Unwin, 1996.

Robinson, Chris, and Tim Emmott. N.d. "Growing Broombush: For Fencing Products on Cleared Farmland in Southern WA." Prepared for Greening Australia.

Rose, Michelle. 2003. "Art Pops Up in the City." *Herald Sun,* June 16.

Santor, Frank. 2006. "Next Stage of BASIX to Make NSW More Energy Efficient." Press release, Minister of Planning, June 8.

Schooneveldt, Miranda. 2004. "Bubbles Full of Nothing." *The Age,* June 24.

Schultz, Beth. 2003. "WA's Old Growth Forest Campaign." Nedlands, Western Australia. Unpublished paper.

Smith, A., and M. Penter. 2005. *Living Landscapes: Lessons from the Central Wheatbelt of Western Australia.* Western Australia: Greening Australia.

South Australia. 2007. "News: SA Hosts International Solar Schools Competition." Press release by Hon. Jane Lomax-Smith, MP, July 24. http://www.ministers .sa.gov.au.

South Australia Department for Environment and Heritage. 2005. "Governments Progress on Creating a Sustainable Adelaide," Government of South Australia, February.

South Sydney and Marrickville Councils. 2003. *King Street and Enmore Road Heritage and Urban Design Development Coastal Plan.* August 27.

Subiaco Redevelopment Agency. N.d. "Fact Sheet #5." Subiaco, Western Australia.

Sustainability Street. 2005. "The Street Report." Vol. 1, ed. 1 (January).

United Nations. 2007. "World Urbanization Prospects: The 2007 Revision Population Database." http://esa.un.org.

Urban Ecology Australia Inc (UEA). 1993. *The Halifax EcoCity Project.* Adelaide: UEA.

Vance, Mitzi. 2005. "Wheatbelt Biological Survey Findings Released." *Conservation News* (April), published by Department of Conservation and Land Management.

Veale, Jason, 2006. "Covelly House, East Sydney, New South Wales." In *BDP Environment and Design Guide.* Sydney.

Victoria Department of Infrastructure. 2004a. "Melbourne 2030: Activity Centres, Implementation Plan 4." Melbourne: Victoria Department of Infrastructure.

———. 2004b. "Melbourne 2030: Green Wedges, Implementation Plan 5." Melbourne: Victoria Department of Infrastructure.

———. 2004c. "Melbourne 2030: Urban Growth Boundary, Implementation Plan 1." Melbourne: Victoria Department of Infrastructure.

Victoria Department of Sustainability and Environment. 2005a. *Activity Centre Design Guidelines.* January.

———. 2005b. *Our Environment, Our Future: Victoria's Environmental Sustainability Framework.* April.

VicUrban. 2006. *Melbourne Docklands Ecologically Sustainable Development (ESD) Guide, Melbourne.* Melbourne: VicUrban, May.

Village Voice. 2008. "Brave New World in the Wetlands." epaper. villagevoice.com.

Vox Bandicoot. 2003. *All Hands On for Sustainability: The Sustainability Street Approach, Book One.* Melbourne: Vox Bandicoot.

———. 2005. *The Street Report* 1, no.1 (January).

WA Transport. 1999. *Travel Smart 2010: A 10-year Plan.* Perth: Western Australia Transport Department.

Webb, David, and David Warren. 2005. *Fremantle, beyond the Roundhouse: 50 Fascinating Stories about Australia's Most Diverse Port City.* Fremantle: Langley Books.

Western Australia Department of Education. N.d. "Noranda Primary School—Bush Wardens." Enterprise Education Case Studies.

Western Australia Department of Planning and Infrastructure, 2003. "Report on Dialogue with the City." Perth: DPI.

Western Australia Department of Planning and Infrastructure. 2006. "Travel Smart Ten Years On." Presentation. http://www.dpi.wa.gov.au/travelsmart/15002.asp.

Western Australia Department of the Premier and Cabinet. 2003. "Peer Review Comments on Focus on the Future: The Western Australian State Sustainability Strategy: Consultation Draft, September, 2002 and on the Final Document Hope for the Future, September, 2003." Perth: Department of the Premier and Cabinet.

Western Australia Museum. 2000. *Survey of Invertebrate Diversity.* Perth: Western Australia Museum.

Western Australian Planning Commission. 1998. *Perth's Bushplan*. Perth: Western Australian Planning Commission, November.

———. 2004. *Ningaloo Coast Regional Strategy, Carnarvon to Exmouth*. Perth: Western Australian Planning Commission.

———. 2005. *Proposal to Modify a Component of the Gingin Coast Structure Plan*. Perth: Western Australian Planning Commission.

Western Power. N.d. "Narrogin Bio-energy Plant—Demonstration of Integrated Wood Processing." http://www.westernpower.com.au.

Westing, Pamela. 2002. "The Port Stephens Comprehensive Koala Plan of Management, First Progress Report." Port Stephens Council, November.

Williams, Brian. 2007. "City Facing Bleak Future—Report Highlights Threat from Climate Change." *Courier Mail*, October 18, p. 7.

Wilson, Edward O. 1984. *Biophilia*. Cambridge, MA: Harvard University Press.

———. 1993. "Biophilia and the Conservation Ethic." In *The Biophilia Hypothesis*, ed. Stephen R. Kellert and Edward O. Wilson. Washington, DC: Island Press.

Winton, Tim. 1993. *Land's Edge*. Sydney: Macmillan.

———. 2003a. "A Plea for the Future." Speech at Ningaloo Reef rally, Fremantle, Western Australia, March 9.

———. 2003b. "How the Reef Was Won." *The Bulletin*, August 5, 16–21.

Woodall, Geoff S., and Chris J. Robinson. 2002. "Direct Seeding Acacias of Different Form and Function as Hosts for Sandalwood (*Santalum spicatum*)." *Conservation Science W. Australia* 4(3): 130–34.

World Bank. 2007. *The Little Green Data Book*. Washington, DC: World Bank.

Index

Aboriginal people, 83, 127, 139–47, 173–77, 228–29, 237
Activity centers, 189–91, 196, 198, 201
Adelaide, 17–24, 31, 35, 51–52, 137–38, 156, 194–96, 235
Adelaide Film Festival, 23, 38
Affordability, 205, 206
Agriculture, 69, 109–13
Albada, Duke, 129
Albany Highway, 69
Alcoa, 84, 85, 86
APACE, 181–84, 187
Archer, Mike, 61, 172–73
Architectural heritage, 113–19
Argyle Diamonds, 228–30
Art, 111, 120–21, 125–31, 145
Artforce, 130–31
Arts Strategy, 125
Aussi–WA, 178
Australian Building Greenhouse Rating (ABGR), 22–23, 40, 42
Australian Bush Heritage Fund, 70
Australian Capital Territory, 218
Australian Conservation Foundation (ACF), 45, 170
Australian Greenhouse office, 48–50
Aveda, 83
Avon catchment, 84

Backyard Buddies initiative, 165–66
Bakhtiari, Ali Samsang, 31

Banks, Joseph, 173
Banksia Awards, 31
Bankstown, 38
Banool Avenue, 102–3
Barak, William, 143
Barron, John, 6
BASIX (Building Sustainability Index), 41–42, 205, 234
Bassendean Dunes, 158
Bathers Beach, 126–27
Batman, John, 142–43
Bats, 150, 185
Baulkham Hills, 12, 160, 165
Baverstock, Garry, 62
Bayswater, 179–80
Beach Buddies, 63–64
Beale, Bob, 172–73
Beros, Denis, 87
BioCity, 156
Biodiversity
    Adelaide and, 156
    Brisbane and, 154–55
    education and, 172–76
    Gondwana Link and, 72
    grassroots action and, 164–67
    infrastructure planning and, 154
    Melbourne and, 10, 11
    Perth and, 153–54, 157–64
    South Australia and, 156–57
    Sydney and, 205, 206–7
    threats to, 5–6

urban areas and, 151–52, 158–64
wheatbelt and, 83–86
Biodiversity Guidelines, 161
Biodiversity Production Areas, 191
BioLinkages approach, 169–70
Biophilia, 151, 185, 235
Bioregional Wildlife Corridors, 191
Birrarung Marr Park, 137
Blue gum plantations, 72–73
Blue Mountains area, 7, 12–13, 122–25
"Blueprint for Our Future", 12
Bold Park, 152, 153
Bougher, Neale, 180
Bowman, Martin, 74
Bracks, Steve, 213
Bradby, Keith, 70–71, 73–74
Branding, 12, 123
BREAAM, 40
Brisbane, 15, 118, 129–31, 137, 152–55,
165, 189–93
Brog, Werner, 34–35
Brown, Keith, 178
Brown, Maitland, 139–43
Bryson, Bill, 152
Building Sustainability Index (BASIX),
41–42
Burns Beach, 164
Burr, John Wesley, 142–43
Buses, greening of, 28–31
Bush, defined, 158–60
Bush, George, 6
Bushcare groups, 162, 164–67, 186
Bush food, 73, 176–77
Bush Forever, 158–62
Bushland levy, 16, 153–54, 158
Bushland parks, 151–52
Bush Wardens program, 179
Byrne, Josh, 59
Byron Bay, 124

Calendars, 174
CALM (Conservation and Land Manage-
ment), 77, 79, 81, 89, 160, 180
Campbell, Joan, 126–27
Campbell, Nicole, 54
Campbelltown, 95–96
Canberra, 218
Carbon Credits Bill, 82

Carbon neutrality, 18, 32–34, 38
Carbon Planet, 38
Carbon sequestration, 73, 78–79, 81–82
Cats, 90, 93–95, 157
Central Activities District, 198–99
Central Area Transport (CAT) buses, 31
CERES Sustainability Centre, 112
Certification programs, 200, 202
CH2 office building, 40, 42–44
Chermside Hills Reserves, 152
Chilled beam technology, 47
Christie, Scott, 51
Christie Walk, 51–52
Cities for Climate Protection, 36
City farms, 109–13
City Plan 2010, 10
CityShape, 192
CitySmart, 15
Clarke, Peter, 165–66
Clear Urban Transport for Europe
(CUTE), 29
Climate action plans, 36–37
Climate change, 36–40, 234–35
Clinton Foundation, 37
Close, Robert, 95–96
Cloudlands, 123
Commercials, 23
Community education, 60–61
Community gardens, 109–13
Comprehensive plans, 75–76
Conservation Action Statements, 154
Conservation International (CI), 68
Construction, green, 39–53, 214–15
Contagion hypothesis, 73–74
Coogee Beach, 138, 139, 150, 237
Cook, James, 173
Cooks River, 53–54
Coral Bay, 86–87, 89–90
Council House offices, 40, 42–44
"Cow Up a Tree" (Kelly), 125–26
CSIRO, 79
Cumberland Plain, 205–7

Daniels, Chris, 156
Darling Range, 158, 179
Derkesma, Chris, 12
Dialogue with the City, 208
Distributed water systems, 53

Dobell, William, 125
Docklands, 125, 136, 201–2, 203
Dogs, 90, 93–95
Dreisetl, Herbert, 48
Drought, 4, 42, 57–58
Dryland salinity, 78–83

Earth Hour, 37, 39
EcoHouses, 51–52, 63–64
Ecological corridors, 192
Ecological footprints, 2, 61, 67, 207–8
Ecological social capital, 186–87
Economic incentives
    Adelaide and, 24
    branding and, 123
    bushland levy and, 153–54
    carbon sequestration and, 73
    local governments and, 15–16
    transportation and, 31–34
    tree-planting and, 72–73
    urban biodiversity and, 160–62
Economics, 6, 73, 89, 191
Ecoscapes, 86
Ecotourism, 88–89, 176
Eco-TV project, 23
Education, 60–62, 167, 172–81
Edwards, Ferne, 112
Edwards, Judy, 83
Elections, 6, 8–9
Elliott, Anne, 123–24
Endangered species, 33, 34, 157
Enduring value, 228–30
Energy consumption, 4
Engwicht, David, 36, 104–5
Environmental Sustainability Frame-
    work, 215
Estée Lauder, 83
Eucalyptus, 78–79
Evans, Melanie, 145
Explorers Monument, 139–43

Fairfield Council (Australia), 170–72
Fig trees, 118, 119
Film festivals, 23
Fitzgerald Biosphere Group, 70, 72
Flagship species, 69
Flannery, Tim, 217–18
Floyd, Ted, 169

Flying foxes, 150, 185
Focal species, 12, 84–85
Food, 109–13, 176–77
Food trees, 95–96
Foothills/Ridge Hill Shelf, 158
Forest Heritage Centre, 77
Forests, 74–77, 218
40 Albert Road building, 40, 50–51
Freeman, Tony, 184
Fremantle, 60, 115–17, 120, 126–28,
    131–32, 139–40, 143–47, 182
Fremantle Toy Library, 108–9
Friends of Earth, 167–69
Friends of the Fitzgerald, 70
Friends of the Moore River Estuary,
    225–27
Frost, Stephen, 170
Fungi, 152, 157–58, 180–81, 185, 238

Gallop, Geoff, 227
Gehl, Jan, 133–35, 136
Girardet, Herbert, 18, 216
Global Arc rail, 204
Global Compact, 13–14
Global warming. *See* Climate change
Going Native (Archer and Beale), 61,
    172–73
Gondwana Link project, 69–74
Gore, Al, 2, 6
Gosford, 13, 60, 165, 173–74
Gosford, City of, 16–17
Gould League of Victoria, 173, 178
Grassroots action, 164–67
Gray, Mary, 163–64
Gray–water systems, 58
Greenbank Forest, 154
Green Building Council of Australia
    (GBCA), 40, 44, 50–51
Greenfleet, 32–34
Greenhouse gases, 4, 10, 11, 78–83
Greening Australia, 70, 84, 178–79,
    207
Greenlight initiative, 39
Green wedges, 196–202
Grote Street Business Association, 24
Growth Centers Commission (GCC),
    205
"Grow Us A Home" website, 178–79

Haggerty, Rosanne, 18
Halifax EcoCity Project, 51
Hammond, Brendan, 228–29
Hart, Roz, 181
Hartz–Karp, Janette, 210–11
Hay Street, 138
Heath, Jim, 157–58
Heath, Paul, 123
Heritage, 84, 113–19, 133, 139–47, 161,
    182–83
Heritage Festival, 144–45
Heritage Impact Statements, 113–15
Historic preservation, 118
History, 143–47
Holistic approaches, 236–37
"Hope for the Future", 207, 219–21
Hopper, Steve, 68–69
Hornsby, 165
Hotspots, 68–69, 157
Housing, affordable, 26, 205, 206
Howard, John, 6, 21
Hydrogen fuel cells, 28–31

Iconography, 120–22, 156
Indigenous peoples. See Aboriginal
    people
Infrastructure, 25–26, 154–55, 193. See
    also Transportation
Integrated Wood Processing Plant (IWP),
    79–80
International Council for Local Environ-
    mental Initiatives (ICLEI), 10–11,
    36
Investigative Areas, 189–91
Irwin, Steve, 184

Japan, 89, 143–44
Jetties, 126–27
Johnson, Murray, 75, 76, 77

Kangaroos, 64, 157
Kansai Electric Power Company, 81–82
Karawatha Forest, 152, 154
Karri Forest, 75, 218
Kelly, John, 125–26
Kennedy, Steve, 58
Kings Park, 152
Koala Beach, 90–97, 98

Koala bears, 90–97, 152, 154, 191, 192
Kogarah, 47–50, 61
Kosiosco, 74
Krockenburger, Mike, 45
Ku–ring–gai, 150, 165–66, 169–70
Kyoto Protocol, 2, 6, 81–82

Lambeck, Robert, 84
Landcare program, 166
LandCom, 55
Land for Wildlife program, 166–67
Landry, Charles, 18
Landscaping, sustainability and, 53
Land use, 6, 24–25, 90–92
Lavis, Deb, 23, 24
LEED (Leadership in Energy and
    Environmental Design), 40
Leichhardt, 36–37, 167–69
Lend Lease, 45–46
Libraries, 108–9
LID (low–impact development), 55
Lifestyles, 59–64
Light, Andrew, 165
Light, William, 17
Living Landscape initiative, 84–85, 98
Living Smart partnership, 60, 224
Local Environment Plans, 124, 205
Local government, 9–16, 65. See also
    Regional plans; State sustainability
    plans
Local Growth Management Strategies,
    191–92
Local provenance species, 183–84
Low–impact development, 55

Macquarrie Bank building, 40
MacTiernan, Allanah, 210
Maitland Brown Memorial, 139–43
Mallee alleys, 79
Mallees, 70, 73, 78–82, 235–36. See also
    Solar mallees
Malthouse, Mick, 75
Manley region, 12, 14, 16, 64
Margaret River, 115, 116
Margins, Memories, and Markers,
    127–28
Marketing, 34
Marrickville, 50, 53–54, 107–8

Maud's Landing, 86–88
McDonalds, 124, 127
McGowan, Chris, 22
McPhail, Ian, 213
Meeting Place Community Centre,
    106–7
Melbourne
    green building and, 42–45
    heritage and, 142–43
    public arts and, 125–26, 129
    public space and, 133–37
    regional plan of, 196–202
    renewable energy and, 36, 37, 38
    sustainability as goal in, 10–11,
        13–14
    transportation and, 27
Melbourne 2030, 196–202
Men of the Trees, 34
Mental speed bumps, 36
Metropolitan Open Space System, 194
Minerals industry, 227–30
Mittermeier, Russell, 68, 69
Mobbs, Michael, 52
Model for Urban Stormwater Improve-
    ment Conceptualization (MUSIC),
    54
Monacan nation, 237
Monderman, Hans, 36
Mooney, Nick, 172
Moore, Clover, 39
Moore River Estuary, 225–27, 232
Moort poles, 72, 73
Moreton Bay, 155
MOSS, 194
Mountains Against McDonalds (MAM),
    124
Mountains to Mangroves Corridor,
    155–56
Mount Romance Indigenous Protocol,
    82–83
Multiplex, 40, 58–59, 174
MUSIC, 54

Naragebup, 63
Narrogin, 79–80
National Heritage Trust (NHT), 84, 161,
    182–83
Native Americans, 237–38

Natural resource management zones,
    83–84
Naturewatch Diaries, 174
Negotiated solutions approach, 160
Nepean River, 95
Network City plan, 207–11
Networking, 221–22
Newcastle, 174
Newman, Campbell, 15, 24, 154
Newman, Peter, 202, 225
New South Wales (NSW), 16, 41–42,
    47–50, 90–96, 100–103, 165, 170,
    177
Newtown area, 32, 113–15, 175–76
Ningaloo Reef, 86–90, 97–98, 225
Nongovernmental organizations, 224–25
Noranda Primary School, 179–80, 186
Nurseries, 107–8, 182–83
Nyoongar people, 145–46

O'Clery, Henry, 33–34
Oil Mallee Company, 79, 80–81
Oil mallees, 73, 78–82, 235–36
Olympic Park, 38, 54–55
Oral histories, 146
Orchids, 157–58
Origin Energy, 19
Otteson, Peter, 218

Pedestrians, 131–38
PEM cells, 29
Penguins, 63–64
Penrith, 12
Perth
    biodiversity and, 153–54, 157–64
    bushland parks of, 152, 153, 180–81
    climate change and, 36
    education and, 179–80
    environmental levies in, 16
    Gondwana Link and, 73
    place-strengthening in, 106–7
    regional plan of, 207–11
    Streetlife and, 103
    tortoises and, 174–75
    transportation and, 13, 25–31, 34–35,
        138
    urban agriculture and, 110–11
    water–sensitive urban design and, 55

Perth Biodiversity Project (PBP), 161–62
Peter Levers, 183–84
Phase Change Material tanks, 43–44
Photovoltaic panels, 19–22, 31, 38, 48–50
Pilbara region, 227–28
Piney Lakes, 62–63
Pioneer Park, 145
Place–making, 113–19
Planning. *See* Regional plans; State
    sustainability plans
Plantation forestry, 72–73
Port Phillip, 63, 103–4, 120–21, 125–26,
    127–28
Port Stephens, 92–93, 174, 175
Powerlink Queensland, 154
Price, Gordon, 138
Prisons, 146
Proton Exchange Membrane (PEM)
    cells, 29
Provenance, revegetation and, 184
Public transit, 27–31, 201. *See also* Infra-
    structure; Transportation
Putnam, Robert, 102

Q fleet, 33
Quandongs, 177
Queenscliff Centre, 214–15, 216
Queensland, 6, 33, 189–93
Queen Street Mall, 137–38
Queen Victoria Market, 38
Quenda, 64, 157
Quokkas, 69

Radwich, 60–61
Railroads, 24–27, 193, 204
Rainwater collection tanks, 18, 57–58,
    103
Ramsar, 155
Rann, Mike, 17, 23, 217
Redland Shire, 192
Regional plans
    Adelaide and, 194–96
    lessons learned from, 211–12, 230–32
    Melbourne and, 196–202
    overview of, 188–89
    Perth and, 207–11
    South East Queensland and, 189–93
    Sydney and, 202–7

Register, Richard, 52
Register of Significant Trees, 118
Reid, Alan, 173
Reintegration, 172–73
Renewable energy, 37–40, 78–83
Restoration, 181–84
Retrofitting buildings, 50–53
Revegetation, 72, 73, 92, 182–84
Ribbons of Blue network, 178
Riparian habitat, 170–72
Riverlife, 53–54
Robins, Juleigh, 176–77
Rooftop gardens, 47
Roy Group, 94
Rudd, Kevin, 6, 82

Safe Environmental Planning Policies
    (SEPPs), 90–92
St. Kilda neighborhood, 120–21
Salamander Bay, 93
Salinity, 6, 72–73, 78–83
Salt, Craig, 221–22
Sandalwood plantations, 73, 82–83
Save Our Suburbs (SoS), 202
Schneider, Stephen, 18
Schools, 21, 60–61, 177–81, 186
Scott, Roseanne, 110–11
Seed banks, 182–83, 187
SEQ regional plan, 189–93
Sewer mining, 44
Shea, Syd, 81
Shell Australia, 72
Shiels, Julie, 127–28
Sidewalks, 132
Slow Food, 124
Smith, Michael, 175
Sociability, public spaces and, 131–39
Social capital, 102, 181–84, 186–87
Social Cohesion Project, 103–5
Solar Cities initiative, 21–23
Solar mallees, 19, 21
Solar power, 12, 13, 19, 38, 62–63.
    See also Photovoltaic panels
South Australia, 156–57, 215–18
South East Queensland (SEQ) regional
    plan, 189–93
South West Australia Bioregion, 68–69,
    157

SRT (Sustainable Roundtable), 224
"State of the Environment" (SoE)
    reports, 16–17
State sustainability plans
    Australian Capital Territory and, 218
    lessons learned from, 230–32
    overview of, 212
    South Australia and, 215–18
    Victoria and, 213–15
    Western Australia and, 218–30
STEP program, 31
Stigson, Bjorn, 219
Stirling Range National Park, 69, 72
Stormwater Trust, 167
Strategic plans, 9–11
Streetlife, 103–5
Structure plans, 9–11
Subiaco Redevelopment Authority
    (SRA), 26, 52
Subi–Centro, 26
In a Sunburned Country (Bryson),
    152
Sustainability. See also State sustain-
    ability plans
    activity centers and, 201
    Adelaide and, 194–96
    branding and, 123
    education and, 177–81
    local governments and, 9–16
    regional plans and, 211–12
    Sydney and, 212
    United States and, 231
Sustainability assessments, 10
Sustainability Indicators, 211
Sustainability Practitioners Association
    (SPA), 221–22
Sustainability Street Approach,
    100–103
Sustainable House (Mobbs), 52
Sustainable Melbourne Fund, 10
"Sustainable Penrith", 12
Sustainable Roundtable (SRT), 224
Sustainable Schools Initiative, 177–81
Sustainable Transport Energy Program
    (STEP), 31
Swan BioPlan, 162
Swan Coastal Plain, 157, 158, 160, 179
Swan Regional Seed Bank, 182–83

Sydney
    architectural heritage and, 113–15
    bats of, 150
    community gardening in, 113
    construction in, 45–50
    greening of, 32, 52, 169, 170–72
    McDonalds and, 125
    Olympic Park and, 38
    pedestrians and, 138
    place–strengthening in, 105–9
    public arts and, 131
    regional plan of, 202–7
    renewable energy and, 37, 38, 39
    significant trees of, 118
    sustainability and, 11–13, 53–54, 212
    water supplies and, 55–57, 105–6,
        175–76
–Sydney Morning Herald–, 39, 61
Szencorp, 50–51

Tabart, Deborah, 93
Tamars, 157
TavelSmart, 34–35
Tempe Reserve, 107–8
Terrestrial Invertebrate Status Review
    (TISR), 154–55
Thinker in Residence program, 17–18
Thomas, Rover, 229
Thompson, Phil, 127
Thrombolites, 63
Timeline Project Australia, 173, 174
Tomaree peninsula, 93
"Tommy's Story" (Shiels), 128
Toohey Forest, 152
Toy libraries, 108–9
Trafficable roofs, 47
Traffic signal boxes, 130–31
TramTRACKER, 27
Transformative sustainable infra-
    structure, 25
Transit–oriented developments, 25–26
Transportation
    Adelaide and, 31
    carbon loads and, 32–34
    greening of, 13, 28, 35–36
    land use control and, 24–25
    Melbourne and, 27, 136
    Perth and, 24–27

Sydney and, 204
TavelSmart and, 34–35
Tree Nurturers program, 170
Tree planting, 32–34, 45, 72–73, 84, 157
Trees as icons, 118, 119, 120
Triple bottom line (TBL) reporting, 11
Troy, Paddy, 143, 144
United States, 1–3, 4–5, 230–31
Urban areas
    agriculture and, 109–13
    bushland preservation in, 158–64
    education and, 177–81
    grassroots action and, 164–67
    greening of, 167–72
    nature of, 152–58
    parks of, 151–52
    place and nature and, 172–76
Urban Art Strategy, 127–28
Urban Bushland Strategy, 158, 163–64
Urban Development Institute of Australia (UDIA), 74
Urban Ecology Australia Inc. (UEA), 51
Urbanization, 2, 90
Urban Settlement Strategy, 92

Vale community, 174–75
Vic Health, 127
Victoria, 55–57, 100–103, 104, 177, 201–2, 213–15
Visibility, 143–47
Voting, 6, 8–9

Wanneroo, 161–62
Warundgeri tribe, 142–43
Water Corporation, 222
Waterloo Public Housing Estate, 113
Water Reclamation and Management Schemes (WRAMS), 54

Water–sensitive urban design (WSUD), 54–57
Watershed Center, 105–6, 175–76
Water supplies, 18, 48–59, 205
Waterwise initiative, 58, 65, 222
Western Australia
    biodiversity and, 158
    forests of, 74–77
    Gondwana Link and, 68–74
    Land for Wildlife and, 166–67
    Ningaloo Reef and, 86–90
    offsetting carbon load and, 33–34
    oil mallee and, 78–83
    sustainability and, 88, 178, 218–30
    toy libraries and, 108–9
    wheatbelt biodiversity and, 83–86
Western Australia Forest Alliance (WAFA), 75
Western Power, 79–80, 157–58
Wetlands, 63, 152, 155, 167–69
Whaling, 89–90, 143–44
Wheatbelt, 78–79, 83–86
White, Gilbert, 173
Whitehouse, Simon, 30
Wildflower industry, 72, 73
Wildlife surveys, 173–74
Wilson, E.O., 151, 185
Wind farms, 217
Winton, Tim, 86, 87–88, 127
Wodonga, 104
World Heritage Sites, 122–25, 191, 206
Wyong Shire, 173–74

Yarra River, 133, 137
Yarra Trams, 27

Zebra batteries, 31
Zetland, 55–57